Howdens Ltd.

The first flag and funnel shown were probably the originals, and were reported in use again by 1935, although funnels were plain black in the late 1920s and early 1930s. The second flag and funnel were recorded in 1912. The funnel carrying the Star of David was reportedly used during the Second World War.

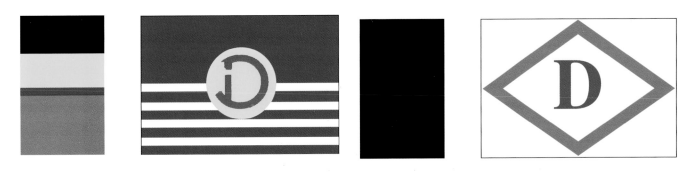

Arthur S. Davidson Ltd.   **Thomas Dunlop and Sons**

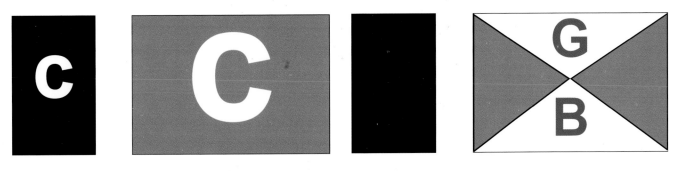

Chellew Navigation Co. Ltd.   **Glover Brothers**

BRITISH SHIPPING FLEETS
Volume 2

Editors: Roy Fenton and John Clarkson

Contributors:
Tony Atkinson, Malcolm Cooper, Bill Harvey, Bill Laxon

Ships in Focus Publications

Published in the UK in 2008 by Ships in Focus Publications,
18 Franklands, Longton
Preston PR4 5PD

Printed by Amadeus press Ltd., Cleckheaton, West Yorkshire
ISBN 978-1-901703-22-1

Cover: *Baltic Eagle*. *[Risto Brzoza, Finland]*
Above: *Baltic Trader* of 1954 in the English Channel. *[FotoFlite/Uwe Detlefsen collection]*

Dunlop's iron ship *Clan Macpherson* at Glasgow. *[John Naylon collection]*

FOREWORD

We are pleased to say that 'British Shipping Fleets', published at the very end of 2000, *was* the start of a series. In the introduction to this book we reserved our position on this issue, explaining that the book had to justify itself in the marketplace. This it has done, and 'British Shipping Fleets Volume 2' is the result. We are only sorry that Bill Laxon, who contributed the history of Glover Brothers, did not live to see its publication.

To new readers we should explain that 'British Shipping Fleets' was devised as a compendium of shipping company histories and fleet lists which cover the spectrum of British shipping, from steam coasters, through tramps, cargo liners, ro-ro and container vessels, to passenger ships. Too large for an article in our journal 'Record', these fleets are perhaps rather small for stand-alone volumes. We have deliberately mixed the companies to include operators of passenger and cargo ships, ocean and coastal tramps. We hope that those whose interest is restricted to one type of ship will find that 'British Shipping Fleets Volume 2' is well worth having, and will appreciate that we have also kept the price to a reasonable level.

Every effort has been made to ensure accuracy and completeness, including checking ships' histories against official registration documents wherever possible, and searching through many private and public collections of photographs. However, we realise it is impossible to say the last word on a company, or to find every surviving photograph. The editors therefore welcome additions and amendments to 'British Shipping Fleets Volume 2', and any substantial information plus photographs of ships not illustrated here will be published in our journal 'Record'.

A follow-up to the first volume of 'British Shipping Fleets' appeared in 'Record' 19, published in March 2002, and to this we can add the following from Capt Maurice Austin. Page 116 of 'British Shipping Fleets' noted that a derivation of the name of the steamer *Isaac Carter* could not be found. Isaac Carter brought the first printing press to Wales in 1718. Both the *Isaac Carter* and the *Baskerville* were built with steam reciprocating engines specifically to manoeuvre in ice where full ahead to full astern movements were often required (this was also useful on the Manchester Ship Canal). The diesel-engined ships could and did run out of starting air which left them stuck. The *Isaac Carter* could be seen often in Glasgow and occasionally in Manchester, the steam ships found the northern water softer and kinder as boiler feed than London's hard water.

We reiterate the belief expressed in 'British Shipping Fleets' that there is no such thing as an uninteresting shipping company and we trust our various authors have succeeded in bringing out the aspects of each fleet's history which made it an individual.

Roy Fenton
Wimbledon

John Clarkson
Longton

April 2008

CONTENTS

NOTES, SOURCES AND ACKNOWLEDGEMENTS

Notes on the fleet lists

Fleet lists are presented in the format used in our journal *Record,* which is shamelessly derived from that developed and refined by the World Ship Society. This format has the merits of being concise, familiar, and flexible enough to accommodate different authors' preferences.

The first line of each entry gives the ship's name with the notation (1) to (4) to indicate that she is the first, second, third or fourth of that name in the fleet. The dates following are those of entering and leaving the fleet, or when management began and finished. Unless otherwise stated on this line, vessels are steam or motor ships with steel hulls.

On the second line is given the ship's official number (O.N.) in the British Register; then her tonnages at acquisition: gross (g), net (n) and in some cases deadweight (d); followed by dimensions: registered length x breadth x depth in feet or, for vessels owned from 1955 onwards, the dimensions are length overall x breadth x draught in feet and in metres for vessels owned from 1974 onwards. For any substantial rebuild, new dimensions are given on a subsequent line.

On the next line is a description of the engine(s) fitted and the name of the engine builder. Steam engines may be single cylinder (1-cyl), two cylinder compounds (C. 2-cyl.), three- or four-cylinder triple-expansion (T. 3-cyl. or T. 4-cyl), or quadruple-expansion four-cylinder (Q. 4-cyl.). For oil engines are given the type (e.g. Sulzer, Burmeister & Wain), the number of cylinders, whether two stroke (2SC) or four stroke (4SC) cycle, single acting (SA) or double acting (DA). Various figures for horsepower are given: nominal (NHP), brake (BHP), indicated (IHP) or shaft (SHP). Nominal horsepower bears least relationship to the engine's actual power, but is often the only figure available. The speed is taken from registration documents or *Lloyd's Register,* and is usually an estimate not a trial figure. Any changes of engine are listed, with dates, on subsequent lines.

Ships' careers and technical details have been derived from or checked against the Closed Registers in Class BT108 and BT110 in the National Archives, Kew whenever these are accessible, to find the exact dates of registration, sales, and renamings, and other figures. Essentially, this applies to ships whose British registry was closed before the end of 1955, as - tragically - later closed registers have not survived to be transferred to the National Archives. For sales, the date given is that on the bill of sale. For ships entering British registry from overseas (for instance, several ships owned by the United Baltic Corporation Ltd.), the date of registration in a British port is given as the best date available for acquisition. This date is inevitably some time after the actual sale, and – rather surprisingly – often after the ship's name has been officially changed.

The port indicated after the title of an owning company is that in which the owners are domiciled. For ships sold to operators using flags of convenience, efforts have been made to indicate the actual owners and the managers (not always the same body). For these vessels, the flag is that of the state in which the ship owning company is domiciled unless otherwise stated.

Although aiming to impose uniformity, the editors have allowed authors to quote additional data in their fleet lists, including port numbers in the Dunlop fleet and detailed British government requisition data in the Chellew and Dunlop fleets.

Photographic sources

We thank all who gave permission for their photographs to be used, and are particularly grateful to the authors themselves, and to Ian J. Farquhar, Nigel Farrell, Fred W. Hawks, Trevor Kidd, John Naylon, Peter Newall, William Schell, and George Scott; to David Whiteside, Jim McFaul and Tony Smith of the World Ship Photo Library, to Peter du Toit of the John H. Marsh Maritime Research Centre; to David Hodge and Bob Todd of the National Maritime Museum; Dr. David Jenkins of the National Waterfront Museum, Swansea; and other museums and institutions listed.

Glover Brothers' penultimate ship, the *Shakespear* (3) of 1926. *[Nigel Farrell collection]*

Flags and funnels
Artwork for the illustrations of flags and funnels was very kindly provided by J.L. Loughran, Custodian of the Ships' Liveries section of the World Ship Society's Members' Questions Section.

General sources and acknowledgements
Sources for fleet list data include *Lloyd's Register*, *Lloyd's Confidential Index*, *Mercantile Navy Lists*, *Lloyd's War Losses*, *Marine News*, *Registers* of William Schell, Rodger Howarth and Tony Starke, and the closed registers in classes BT108 and BT110 in the National Archives. Use of the facilities of the World Ship Society, the Guildhall Library, the National Archives, and Lloyd's Register of Shipping are gratefully acknowledged. Particular thanks also to William Schell, Malcolm Cranfield and John Bartlett for information, Captain John Landels the Yard List Custodian of the World Ship Society, to Heather Fenton for editorial and indexing work, and to Marion Clarkson for accountancy services.

United Baltic Corporation Ltd.
Thanks to Peter Simonsen and Soren Thorsoe for details of Danish ships managed by United Baltic during the Second World War, and to Malcolm Cranfield for the finale to the United Baltic story.

Howdens of Larne
Thanks to Alan Geddes of Belfast for information from local sources, Freddie woods, a former director of John Kelly Ltd., and the late William Darlow for access to company papers.

Thomas Dunlop and Sons
The bulk of the company's history is covered in 'Thomas Dunlop and Sons, Shipowners 1851-1951: A Centenary Review' by G. Rankin Taylor, privately published at Glasgow in 1951. There is also a fair amount of material on the company's sailing ships in 'The Last of the Windjammers' (two volumes) by Basil Lubbock, published originally in 1927-9. Voyage accounts for the late 19th and early 20th century survive in a small collection of company material at the Mitchell Library, Glasgow. Details of war losses are in ADM137 and ADM199 at the National Archives, and closed registers in BT108 and BT110 at the same location. Details of war service are from the government's Service Lists, and 20th century vessel movements are from the Lloyd's Collection at the Guildhall Library. The author is grateful to Sir Thomas Dunlop Bart for a family insight into the company's last years, to Ian Farquhar for material on the 19th century court case involving the *Clan Mackenzie* and to John M. Dunlop for help with family photographs.

Chellew Navigation Co. Ltd.
Thanks to Harold Appleyard, Kevin O'Donoghue, Graham Somner and Bob Langley of the World Ship Society; David Burrell for details of the later history of the company; the Cornwall County Records Office, Truro; Dr P.G. Granger, the National Archives, Kew; Rex Hall, who kindly loaned his original material on Richard Chellew and his steamers; Captain George Hogg, National Maritime Museum, Falmouth; Dr David Jenkins, Curator of the National Waterfront Museum, Swansea for help with details of Frank Shearman's career; Jon Meirion Jones for details of the career of his father, Captain John Alun Jones, and the *Pendeen's* experiences in the River Plate; Charles Loughlin for allowing access to the papers of his late father; the late Bernard May for the photograph of Richard Chellew, who was one of his godfathers; Tony Pawlyn for reading and adding to the text; Roger Penhallurick, Assistant Curator, Royal Institute of Cornwall; Jeffrey Rumble, Trevithick Society Newsletter; Meredith Sampson, National Maritime Museum; Lesley Spurling of Lloyd's Register of Shipping, London; Adrian Symons for proof reading.

Publications referred to were: 'The Royal Cornwall Gazette' 1870-1920; 'The West Briton' 1900-1955; 'Passenger Steamers of the River Fal' by Alan Kittridge; 'Cardiff Shipowners' by David Jenkins; 'Symons Gazetteer of Cornwall' 1884; 'Cornish Place Names' by O.J. Padel; 'Cornish Place Names Elements' by O.J. Padel; 'The Place Names of West Penwith' by P.A.S. Pool.

Chellew's *Cornubia* at Falmouth. *[J. and M. Clarkson collection]*

United Baltic's first three ships: above the *Libau* (later *Baltabor)* and below *St.Thomas (Baltannic)* alongside the *St.Croix (Baltriger).* [Both: Danish Maritime Museum]

UNITED BALTIC CORPORATION LTD.

W. J. Harvey

Following discussions between Andrew Weir and Co. Ltd., London and the Danish East Asiatic Company regarding the inauguration of services to the Baltic States in the aftermath of the First World War and the Russian revolution, it was agreed to test the market by creating a new operating company. Thus, the United Baltic Corporation Ltd. (UBC) was registered in May 1919 with offices at 158 Fenchurch Street, London. The new company was owned equally by both partners and had an issued capital of £2,000,000 in £1 shares. The directors were Hans N. Andersen, Emil R. Gluckstad, John R. Brown, F. L. Harris, and William Weir.

In subsequent months plans and strategy were formulated and by August 1919 advertisements were published detailing the proposed regular sailings for passengers and cargo from East India Docks, London to Danzig and Libau (Liepaja) and to other ports if suitable inducement was forthcoming.

From the outset, in August 1919, only chartered tonnage was employed due to the fragile economy of the area to be served. That tonnage came mainly from the Danish partner's fleet and their subsidiary, the Russian East Asiatic Company. Within a month both Riga and Reval (Tallinn) had been added to the itinerary.

By 1920, sufficient sustainable trade had been built up to justify the purchase of the three vessels that had been on charter, and during June the *Libau*, *St. Thomas* and *St. Croix* were bought and renamed *Baltabor*, *Baltannic* and *Baltriger* respectively.

Expansion of trade and the introduction of refrigerated cargoes led to the 1922 relocation of the London berth to Hay's Wharf. An enthusiastic management were continually looking for new opportunities, so much so that in 1923 Special Holiday

Trips began to be advertised in connection with the regular summer sailings to the Baltic. At about 12 guineas, their 11 to 12-day round trips were to remain popular until the outbreak of the Second World War

All services used the Kiel Canal and branch and agency offices opened on all the regular routes. Warehouses were acquired in Tallinn, Danzig, Warsaw, and other major cities. When Memel (Klaipeda) was added in 1924, the weekly departures (except when interrupted by ice) were on Thursdays to Reval and Riga, and on Fridays to Danzig, Memel and Libau.

After ten years free of major mishap, UBC suffered its first losses in 1929. On 11th January, *Baltara* (1) stranded at the mouth of the River Vistula whilst en route to London and was declared a constructive total loss. Later that year, on 26th December, *Baltabor* stranded en route to Riga. After being ashore nearly three months she was taken to Tallinn for inspection and declared a constructive total loss.

Gdynia and Neufahrwaser (Nowy Port) were added to the itinerary during 1930, despite the recession.

Lord Inverforth and the Kylsant collapse

In the prevailing economic climate not every shipping company was so fortunate in their business, but events were developing that would ultimately affect UBC. The financial problems of the Royal Mail Group were becoming greater by the day and, by 1929, the British Treasury was fearful of an embarrassing collapse of a prestigious British shipping concern. They, together with the Bank of England and the City of London, found it necessary for the first time to intervene to rescue a collapsing, bankrupt business. By the end of 1930 they had formulated a rescue plan, having persuaded

Passengers boarding the *Baltannic*. [*J. and M. Clarkson collection*]

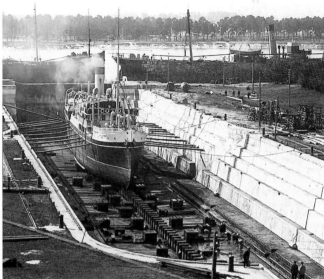

Accidents were infrequent although at times conditions were harsh.
Above left: *Baltannic* (1) with collision damage, place and date unknown, which probably resulted in a visit to the dry dock at Libau (above right). This was one of two dry docks at Libau each 600 feet long and 85 feet wide. *[Kevin J. O'Donoghue collection]*
Right: *Baltannic* (2) stranded on the Sourop Reef 31st May 1927. The salvage vessel alongside is the *Meteor* (353/1877).
[Prof. Theodor F. Siersdorfer collection]

S|s. **BALTANNIC**
London
stranded on Sourop reef 31. May 1927.

Baltonia in icy conditions - the major hazard when trading to the Baltic. *[J. and M.Clarkson]*

Above: *Baltara* (1) after stranding and breaking in two in January 1929. The photograph was taken by R. Machtens of Danzig during extremely hard winter conditions in the Baltic. Below: *Baltabor* (1) after stranding off Nargen Island in December 1929. Salvaged in March 1930 she was sold and broken up at Danzig. *[All: Prof. Theodor F. Siersdorfer collection]*

Lord Kylsant to relinquish control. Under the plan, trustees were appointed to oversee the management of all the Kylsant companies, which had total liabilities in excess of £50,000,000. Their brief was to arrange the best possible terms for salvage on behalf of Royal Mail's creditors.

Sir Walter Runciman MP was appointed deputy chairman of the Royal Mail Steam Packet Company and director of all the principal subsidiary companies, positions he held until November 1931 when he resigned to join the government as President of the Board of Trade. Runciman was a close friend of Richard Durning Holt, of Alfred Holt and Company. Upon hearing of the pending disintegration of the Royal Mail Group, Holt intimated that his Ocean Steam Ship Company Ltd. would be interested in acquiring the assets of Glen Line Ltd. (which had similar trading patterns to Ocean Steam) and/or Elder Dempster Lines. Neither the acquisition of Glen Line nor Elder Dempster were to be easy rides for Holt. After two offers had

been rejected by the Kylsant Trustees, during December 1934 Holt made an offer of £450,000 for Glen Line Ltd. and a further £100,000 for the associated McGregor, Gow and Holland Ltd. However, Andrew Weir - now Lord Inverforth - chairman and founder of Andrew Weir and Co. Ltd. and half owner of UBC, now entered the fray, having watched from the side lines for some time. In January 1935 he submitted a rival bid of £250,000 for Glen Line through UBC. Behind the scenes, Inverforth and Holt had locked horns, and the disagreement was such that Holt approached the Trustees requesting government intervention. Holt complained about receiving verbal threats from Inverforth that the latter would attack Holt's routes if he failed to obtain control of Glen Line for his much lower bid. But in the end Inverforth withdrew his bid for Glen Line on the advice of the government and the Bank of England. On 28th January 1935 Richard Holt submitted a revised offer and eventually succeeded in acquiring Glen Line Ltd.

Undeterred by his unsuccessful clash with Holt, Lord Inverforth continued his search for a suitable acquisition from the Trustees of the Royal Mail Group. His next target was MacAndrews and Co. Ltd. which served the Iberian Peninsula and Mediterranean fruit markets. The main creditor of MacAndrews was the Treasury, which had £175,000 outstanding on Trade Facilities Act (TFA) loans.

However, Inverforth was not alone in wanting MacAndrews. In July 1935, the General Steam Navigation Co. Ltd., London had bid £393,000, and in November 1935 Kaye, Son and Co. Ltd. - a long-time associate of MacAndrews - made a cash offer of £390,950. November also saw Inverforth's formal submission, once again placed through UBC. The bid consisted of £220,000 in cash and a further £175,000 in mortgages as securities for the TFA loans to be repaid over the succeeding 14 years. The Inverforth bid, deemed the most attractive to the Trustees, was successful and MacAndrews and Co. Ltd. became a wholly-owned subsidiary of the United Baltic Corporation Ltd.

Civil war and world war

When *Baltrover* (1) entered service in 1935 nearly 200 passengers could be carried on each voyage to Danzig and Gdynia. Hitherto, the vessels in the fleet catered for a maximum of six or twelve passengers. Expansion continued steadily with the introduction in 1935 of a service from Riga to Newcastle, followed a year later by another between Tallinn and Hull, both catering for the butter trade.

The elation following the acquisition of MacAndrews was short lived, and turned to despair in 1936 when the Spanish trade was plunged into its most difficult period with the outbreak of the Spanish Civil War. Valencia, one of the main ports used, was at the centre of hostilities, having been declared the capital of the new Republic.

Unease in the Baltic States also produced change. Established in 1918, the Baltic States comprised the independent republics of Estonia, Latvia, and Lithuania, territory previously occupied by the Baltic Provinces and parts of various other Russian territories, including Vilnius and

Right: The *Dominica,* with a capacity of almost 200 passengers was bought in 1935 from the Bermuda and West Indies Steamship Co. Ltd. and renamed *Baltrover (1)*. *[Eric Johnson, New Orleans/J. and M. Clarkson collection]*

Below: *Baltrover (1)* in the Thames. *[Newall Dunn collection]*

Kaunas. With a view to survival should hostilities erupt in any of the states, UBC created three subsidiaries to maintain trade and transferred two ships to each. Anglo-Lithuanian Shipping Co. Ltd. was formed in 1937, and Anglo-Latvian Shipping Co. Ltd. and Anglo-Estonian Shipping Co. Ltd. were set up in 1938. All were under the management of UBC, but each had its own house flag which was a variant of the UBC flag.

The second *Baltabor* grounded near Liepaja on 12th February 1939 and remained fast for four months before being refloated and declared a total loss following inspection at Liepaja. This loss was only an aside to what, within a month, was going to shake the company.

With regional tension and the German invasion of Poland leading to the declaration of war, Baltic services were suspended in September 1939, and the ships were placed under the control of the Admiralty or the Ministry of Shipping. Following Germany's invasion of Denmark in 1940, 12 ships owned by the East Asiatic Company, which were at sea at the time of invasion, were transferred to the control of the British Ministry of Shipping and placed under UBC management. This reflected both the association of UBC and East Asiatic and that, with the suspension of Baltic services, all UBC's vessels were under Government control. Only two of the vessels transferred from East Asiatic survived the war, there being a total of 13 losses through enemy action amongst the ships owned and managed by UBC. MacAndrews lost nine. Losses indirectly caused by the war continued into peacetime. On 29th March 1946, *Balteako* struck a submerged wartime wreck in Kiel Bay and sank. The second *Baltara* was more fortunate, going aground on 1st December 1946 and remaining fast for five days before being refloated.

In 1940 the Baltic States were incorporated into the Union of Soviet Socialist Republics (USSR) but in 1941 were occupied by Germany. Recaptured by the USSR in 1944, they remained part of the Soviet Union until 1991.

Above: *Baltavia* (2), formerly the *Chimu*, bought in 1938 soon after her sister ship, the *Cumbal*, which became the *Baltabor* (2). [Roy Fenton collection]

Right: The *Baltabor* (2) sailed for the company for little over a year. She grounded near Liepaja in February 1939 and although refloated in June of that year was declared a constructive total loss. [Kevin J. O'Donoghue collection]

During the Second World War the *Baltannic (2)* and *Baltraffic* served in New Zealand waters. At the same time United Baltic managed a number ships owned by the East Asiatic Company.

Top: *Baltannic* (2) in the floating dock at Wellington, New Zealand on 13th January 1941. *[Wellington Harbour Board, Ref.1000/ Ian J. Farquhar collection]*

Middle: *Erria* of the East Asiatic Company in wartime grey. *[Newall Dunn collection]*

Bottom: The Danish *Kina II* at Liverpool. *[National Maritime Museum G.3920]*

Baltrader (2) was one of the three German 'Hansa A' type ships purchased from the Ministry of Transport in 1947. *[World Ship Society Ltd./Roy Fenton collection]*

Three former German vessels built in 1944 were purchased from the British Government during 1947. Entering service as *Baltrader*, *Baltonia* and *Baltanglia*, they reinstated the names of UBC vessels lost to enemy action. However, these names were to be carried for only a short period. In 1951 UBC moved to new offices at Plantation House, 21 Mincing Lane, London, which they would share with their subsidiary, MacAndrews. To coincide with the move it was decided to amend the fleet naming style by introducing the full word *Baltic* as the prefix instead of '*Balt*'. A new funnel marking was also introduced. Hitherto the funnel had been buff with a black top, similar to that of Bank Line. Henceforth it was to be pale yellow with a black top and bear a black-edged white disc depicting a black foul anchor and the letters UBC.

New ships at last

In 1952 orders were placed for new ice-strengthened vessels, all previous purchases having been second-hand. A large-scale replacement programme was initiated both for UBC and MacAndrews. Orders were for series vessels, constructed in West German shipyards. Limited passenger accommodation was incorporated in some of the vessels, usually to a maximum of four. One later class was produced for both fleets with delivery alternating between owners. Some of the

MacAndrews vessels were additionally provided with tanks in one hold for the carriage of wine. MacAndrews' vessels were constructed to the same ice strengthening standard as their counterparts in the UBC fleet so that if the need arose they could be used safely in the Baltic. To add to confusion, some vessels ordered by UBC were completed for MacAndrews, and vice versa.

The first new buildings were delivered as *Baltic Exporter* and *Baltic Importer* during 1953, and were followed by two further sisters in 1954. By 1962, no less than 13 new vessels had entered the United Baltic fleet. There was to have been another: *Baltic Meteor* was launched as such by Krogerwerft G.m.b.H., Rendsburg in 1955, but was completed for MacAndrews as *Valdivia*. One of the redundant MacAndrews vessels, *Ponzano*, was also transferred in 1960, and renamed *Baltic Spray*.

Palletisation and containerisation

A turning point for the company came in 1969. It was decided to lengthen *Baltic Venture* and introduce side doors to enable palletised cargo to be worked with fork-lift trucks. *Baltic Vanguard* was similarly treated. Containers and unit loads were also becoming more favoured by shippers and UBC decided to test the market. They chartered the West German

Baltic Importer, one of four similar vessels completed in Germany for the company in 1953/54. *[Lerbs, Rendsburg/Uwe Detlefsen collection]*

Top: Baltic Clipper, completed in
October 1954 at Hamburg, was
followed shortly by her sister ship
the *Baltic Comet* from Rendsburg.
[Uwe Detlefsen collection]
Middle: *Baltic Arrow* completed in
1956 and *Baltic Swift* completed in
1957 were slightly larger and also
differed in appearance from the
Baltic Clipper and *Baltic Comet*.
Note how different treatment was
given to the bridge structure,
the aft kingposts and the hull
form forward at the break of the
forecastle. *[Sammlung Mayburg/
Uwe Detlefsen collection]*
Right: Not all UBC ships were
built in classes. The *Baltic Sun*
of 1962 built by Krogerwerft
at Rendsburg was a one off.
*[G.E.P.Brownell/Roy Fenton
collection]*

Top: All United Baltic's new ships had come from Germany until 1965/66 when they took delivery of two ships, the *Baltic Venture* (above) and *Baltic Vanguard,* from builders at Sunderland. *[Newall Dunn collection]*

newbuilding *Elke Kahrs* which was renamed *Baltic Concord* upon completion. Likewise, MacAndrews chartered two container vessels for their Iberian service and sent the one-year-old sisters *Cervantes* and *Churruca* for lengthening and conversion to container carriers.

Baltic Star was lengthened during 1969 to increase the company's conventional cargo capacity. From that point the conventional cargo tonnage was steadily reduced although it was not completely withdrawn for many years. Despite the growth of container traffic, the company did not commit itself to build or purchase a dedicated container ship for the Baltic routes, preferring to charter. MacAndrews, in contrast, committed themselves to containerisation so that by 1973 they were almost fully converted.

In 1973 the Anglo-Finnish Shipping Co. Ltd. was created in partnership with Finland Steamship and *Baltic Jet* placed under its management. Finland Steamship had ordered two ro-ro cargo ships from the Rauma-Repola yard in Finland as *Orion* (yard number 207) and *Sirius* (208) and had taken an option on a third (209). Upon the creation of Anglo-Finnish Shipping Co. Ltd. the

Baltic Viking of 1967 which, along with *Palacio*, made the last United Baltic conventional cargo sailings, is seen here leaving Eastham on the Mersey in June 1969. *[J.and M.Clarkson]*

From 1969 to 1983 United Baltic, rather than commit themselves to building ships to carry containers, chartered several smaller German ships.

The first to be put into service was the *Baltic Concord*, launched by Sietas at Hamburg as the *Elke Kahrs* (499/1969) and renamed whilst fitting out (top). Taken up in 1969 she stayed with them until 1974 after which she reverted to her original name. After being sold in 1984 she became the *Cosmea*, then *Stefanie* and *Beate*.

The second, the *Baltic Unit* (912/1971), again Sietas built and seen right was with United Baltic for only two years from 1971. Completed as the *Heino* the ship was renamed *Baltic Unit* when taken on charter. Afterwards she became the *Scol Venture* and then reverted to *Heino*. A string of names followed - *Eve, Eden, Hacklin White, Eve, Etzel, Bremer Stauer* and then back to *Etzel*. [Uwe Detlefsen]

The *Hans Kroger* (499/1973) was chartered for two periods. In 1973 she was taken for two years and in 1977 for a further year becoming the *Baltic Consort* (bottom) each time and then reverting to her original name. After the second term she was lengthened before reverting to *Hans Kroger*. She later took the names *Brynmore, Bremer Wappen* and *Kilia*. About 1993 she was sold to Moroccan buyers and renamed *Oued Ziz*, then *Kalila*. [Ships in Focus]

A fourth ship, chartered in 1977 for five years was the *Theodor Storm* (999/1977) which was renamed *Baltic Heron*.

third option was transferred to UBC who ordered a further sister (yard number 216). The two UBC vessels were completed as *Baltic Enterprise* and *Baltic Progress*, respectively, for Anglo-Finnish Shipping Co. Ltd. Managed by UBC when delivered, but soon transferred to UBC ownership, they were their first true ro-ro vessels in the fleet, handling conventional containers, freight trailers and wheeled flatbed cargo pallets. Older units made redundant by the new ships were retained by the company and used in the charter market.

Acquiring Stena's folly

In 1975 the Swedish ferry operator Stena Ab took a decision which they were later to regret, and which was also ultimately to affect UBC. Having ordered three ro-ro freight-ferries in Hamburg, Stena ordered three further sisters from Austria. This shipbuilder intended that all three vessels would have the hulls launched without superstructure, which would be built separately and loaded on to a barge. The hull and the barge-borne superstructure would then be towed down river

Above: The *Baltic Enterprise* was launched into ice-filled waters at Rauma, Finland on 6th March 1974. *[Newall Dunn collection]*

Baltic Progress was retained by the company when her sister-ship, *Baltic Enterprise*, was sold to Yugoslavian buyers in 1987. *[Uwe Detlefsen]*

to Galatz, in Romania, where the superstructure would be lifted into position and the ship completed. At least, that was the plan.

In 1976 the first of the trio, *Stena Tender*, launched during the particularly long, hot summer, was due to begin her journey along the River Danube in sections, under tow. It proved to be a trip filled with mishaps and misfortunes. A collapsed road bridge had blocked her intended exit route, delaying her at Vienna for almost a month. Because of the exceptionally hot, dry weather the river levels were lower than anticipated and the ship had to be dragged along the soft bottom by her tugs. Then in October the rains began and continued well into November, by which time the water level was well above normal. When the convoy arrived at Novostad in Yugoslavia, the hull was just able to pass under a bridge, but not so the superstructure. The order was given to anchor upstream and wait for the waters to recede.

It was nearly six months before it could continue downstream. Stena were beginning to despair. The six vessels had all been fixed for charter, as were another 11 larger vessels they had since ordered from Korea. Stena were forced to re-negotiate the deliveries to charterers of the three Austrian sisters, resulting in one charter being cancelled. That left Stena with a surplus vessel which needed work at a time when they had many vessels on order. .

At this juncture UBC entered the story as they were in the market for new ro-ro tonnage and contracted to buy the surplus Stena vessel for £8,000,000 after it had been lengthened and completed. The work was to be undertaken by Werft Nobiskrug, GmbH, Rendsburg, West Germany. This yard had lengthened *Union Melbourne*, one of Stena's Hamburg trio, so they were familiar with the vessel's design and characteristics.

The superstructure was lifted on board and partly welded by the workers who had travelled from Vienna, and who were now living in temporary accommodation built on the vehicle deck. The vessel was not registered, but was towed from the Black Sea to West Germany as a 'steel structure' and at Rendsburg entered dry dock as *Stena Tender* for lengthening and completion. When completed she entered the new weekly Southampton–Bordeaux–Bilbao–Bordeaux–Southampton

service. This service had become necessary when Swedish-Lloyd decided to withdraw their *Patricia*; MacAndrews having a slotting agreement with Swedish Lloyd wherein they took a minimum of 25 slots per sailing.

Integration

Further integration with MacAndrews' fleet saw the *Baltic Vanguard* lengthened and converted into a container ship. Upon completion in 1977 she was renamed *Cortes*. This coincided with *Stena Tender* emerging as *Goya*, both vessels operating on MacAndrews' Iberian services. Coupled with this work, a major investment in the port infrastructure was also undertaken with £1.7 million spent on container handling facilities and equipment at Bilbao, the Spanish terminus for the Liverpool service. In early July 1977 a new weekly container service was also begun between Sheerness, Gibraltar, Cartagena, Cadiz and Lisbon utilising the chartered *Stoller Grund* (998/1972) and *Theodor Storm* (999/1977), the latter being renamed *Baltic Heron*. This replaced the fortnightly conventional cargo sailings by *Palacio* and *Baltic Viking*. Container handling equipment, including a 125-ton crane, was shipped out from the UK to Gibraltar. Also in 1977, *Cervantes* and *Churruca* were transferred from Macandrews to UBC ownership, retaining their names.

Meanwhile, alongside the conversion of *Baltic Vanguard*, UBC took the plunge and purchased *Atlantic Viscount*. She was a sister to the MacAndrews-chartered *Stoller Grund*. Renamed *Baltic Osprey*, not only did she become a dedicated containership, she also heralded another change in naming style: all subsequent UBC vessels would carry bird names as a suffix.

In 1979, *Baltic Eagle*, another large ro-ro and container carrier entered service, operating alongside sistership *Inowroclaw* in a joint service with Polish Ocean Lines. The service converted to container tonnage in 1995 and Euroafrica Shipping Ltd. of Szczecin replaced Polish Ocean Lines in a joint venture with UBC. The remaining conventional units of the Baltic fleet were displaced. Being well suited for service in ice, several were chartered to the Crosbie group in Canada.

The East Asiatic Company, a 50% shareholder in UBC, reappraised their group trading strategy and decided to

The *Goya*, launched as *Stena Tender,* was completed in 1977 after being under construction for over two and a half years. She never carried a 'Baltic' name and was sold to Canadian buyers in 1980. *[Newall Dunn collection]*

In 1977 the *Churruca* along with the *Cervantes* (above) were transferred from MacAndrews to United Baltic ownership. Their stay with the company was brief as both were sold to foreign buyers in 1979. *Cervantes* was on charter to Fred. Olsen when photographed. *[J. and M. Clarkson collection]*

The *Atlantic Viscount* was acquired in 1977, renamed *Baltic Osprey* (above) and ran for the company for eleven years. *[FotoFlite]*

Baltic Eagle entered service in 1979 on the Polanglia weekly service between the UK and Poland. *[Newall Dunn collection]*

The Dutch built *Pacheco* of 1986 on 10th May 1989. *[FotoFlite]*

withdraw from short-sea shipping to concentrate on long-haul and container traffic. Following negotiations, Andrew Weir and Co. Ltd. acquired East Asiatic's 50% share thereby making it a wholly-owned subsidiary from September 1982.

Hard on the heels of gaining full control and faced with much competition on the Baltic routes, Andrew Weir and Co. Ltd. decided to rationalise and consolidate its services. Containers had all but displaced conventional cargo and also took much of the palletised cargo. To that end the ro-ro vessel *Baltic Enterprise* was sold in 1983, leaving her younger sister-ship *Baltic Progress* and the *Baltic Eagle* handling the ro-ro cargo whilst container traffic was covered by *Baltic Osprey*, supplemented by chartered vessels. Then, for almost seven years, nothing changed apart from some fluctuation in cargo quantities. MacAndrews' Iberian services were handled by chartered tonnage alone.

In 1985 two container ships were ordered in Holland for the MacAndrews fleet. Named *Palacio* and *Pacheco*, they carried UBC funnel markings when delivered. However, a review of strategy saw both entering the charter market. Both vessels carried a string of names during numerous charters that usually kept them together until sold in 1992. Even then they remained together.

Meanwhile, Andrew Weir and Co. had acquired Ellermans Line plc, which was also in the Iberian and Mediterranean trades. Vessels of the Ellerman fleet subsequently operated with MacAndrews' names during charters.

A review of UBC's requirements resulted in two new orders in 1988. *Baltic Tern* was ordered to meet needs for carrying containers whilst *Baltic Eider* was to reinforce ro-ro services whilst also carrying containers on deck. However, it was not UBC that placed the orders for the new vessels, but Andrew Weir and Co. Ltd. This was a taste of further changes in the Weir Group. In 1989, Andrew Weir Shipping Ltd. was created to own the vessels previously belonging to or managed by their subsidiary companies Bank Line Ltd., Ellerman Lines plc, MacAndrews and

Baltic Tern on 20th September 1992. *[FotoFlite]*

Co. Ltd., and UBC. At this point, all of the subsidiaries ceased to own ships under their names, and the United Baltic Corporation Ltd. technically ceased to be a shipowner. However, the routes were still operated with vessels carrying *Baltic* names and wearing UBC funnel colours, and the fleet of three ships was, in all but nominal ownership, still part of the fleet created in 1919. But this situation was not to last.

The finale

In 2002 Andrew Weir Shipping re-appraised their operations. As part of a consortium, they had secured a contract to construct and operate a series or ro-ro vessels for charter to the Ministry of Defence. As this operation gained

Baltic Eider, completed in 1989, was ordered by Andrew Weir and Co. Ltd. for United Baltic. Designed to carry ro-ro cargo below decks with containers on deck, she served for only ten years and was then sold to German buyers. *[Uwe Detlefsen]*

momentum, Andrew Weir Shipping decided to dispose of its shipping subsidiaries – Bank Line, United Baltic Corporation and MacAndrews – as going concerns. This turned out to be a complex transaction, involving a number of little-known subsidiaries. It was reported that Bank Line was to pass to the Swire Group, whilst UBC and MacAndrews had been sold to the French group CMA CGM SA. In fact, the reality was more complex.

With effect from 1st January 2003, CMA CGM ('The French Line') acquired from Andrew Weir Shipping the long dormant Anglo-Latvian Shipping Co. Ltd., renamed MacAndrews and Co. Ltd., to operate the short-sea activities of Andrew Weir, effectively what had been the UBC and MacAndrews operations, carried on by *Baltic Tern* and *Pacheco* (ex-*City of Lisbon,* ex *Cervantes,* ex *City of Plymouth*) and chartered tonnage. However, United Baltic Corporation Ltd. remained an Andrew Weir subsidiary, albeit a dormant one, whilst the subsidiary company that passed to MacAndrews/CMA CGM was Polska Zjednoczona Korporacja Baltycka Sp. z o.o ('Polish United Baltic Corporation Ltd.')

Polish United Baltic Corporation Ltd. was established as an agency in Gdynia on 5th November 1930, with three partners, the merchant Marek Myslokowski (52%), Andrew Weir and Company (24%) and a representative of the East Asiatic Company (24%). The agency represented UBC, and acquired a portfolio of contracts with other ship owners. Business was interrupted by the Second World War, but resumed in 1946 and continued until 1972 when the Polish government decided that the state should have a monopoly of shipping agencies, and Polish United Baltic Corporation Ltd. was permitted to represent only UBC. By then, UBC had acquired all the shares in Polish United Baltic Corporation Ltd.

The sale of Andrew Weir's short sea shipping to CMA CGM in 2003 included the *Baltic Tern*, which retained her name under new ownership. The other ship carrying a Baltic name at the time, *Baltic Eider,* was chartered out, and remained under Andrew Weir's management until she was sold and renamed in January 2005. In 2006 the MacAndrews' owned *Baltic Tern* is the last reminder of the United Baltic Corporation, a moderate-sized but significant line which had an unusual joint British-Danish ownership, pioneered services from the UK to part of the Baltic, and owned some distinctive ships.

Running-mate of the *Baltic Tern,* this *Pacheco,* photographed in October 1998 was completed in 1978 as the *City of Plymouth.* [FotoFlite]

FLEET LIST

1. BALTABOR (1) 1920-1930
O.N. 144673 1,320g 788n
215.0 x 34.0 x 20.2 feet
T.3-cyl. by Kobenhavns Flydedok & Skips,
Copenhagen, Denmark; 138 NHP, 759 IHP,
10½ knots.
4.1911: Completed by Kobenhavns
Flydedok & Skips, Copenhagen, Denmark
(Yard No. 88) for the Russian East Asiatic
Co. Ltd. (Baltic Line), Vladivostok, Russia
as LIBAU
3.1919: Transferred to A/S Det
Ostasiatiske Kompagni, Copenhagen,
Denmark.
25.6.1920: Acquired by the United Baltic
Corporation Ltd., London.
17.7.1920: Renamed BALTABOR.
29.7.1920: Registered in London.
26.12.1929: Stranded on Nargen Island
whilst on a voyage from Tallinn to Riga
with cars and general cargo.
28.3.1930: Refloated and taken to Tallinn
but later declared a constructive total loss
and broken up in Danzig.
1.10.1930: Register closed.

2. BALTANNIC (1) 1920-1925
O.N. 145024 1,147g 657n
220.1 x 32.6 x 17.7 feet
T.3-cyl. by Kobenhavns Flydedok & Skips,
Copenhagen, Denmark; 166 NHP.
10.1916: Completed by Kobenhavns
Flydedok & Skips, Copenhagen, Denmark
(Yard No. 127) for A/S Det Ostasiatiske
Kompagni, Denmark, Copenhagen as ST.
THOMAS.
30.6.1920: Acquired by the United Baltic
Corporation Ltd., London and renamed
BALTANNIC.
3.1925: Sold to Partafelagid Skipfelagid
Foroyar, Thorshavn, Faroe Islands and

renamed TJALDUR.
27.6.1947: Wrecked off Mjoanes, Faroe
Islands in approximate position 62.07 north
by 06.35 west whilst on a voyage from
Thorshavn to Klaksvig with general cargo.

3. BALTRIGER 1920-1931
O.N. 145064 1,143g 658n
221.1 x 32.6 x 17.7 feet
T.3-cyl. made in 1916 by Kobenhavns
Flydedok & Skips, Copenhagen,
Denmark; 166 NHP, 1,000 IHP, 13 knots.
3.1917: Completed by Kobenhavns
Flydedok & Skips, Copenhagen,
Denmark (Yard No. 126) for A/S Det
Ostasiatiske Kompagni, Denmark as ST.
CROIX.
30.6.1920: Acquired by the United Baltic
Corporation Ltd., London.
9.10.1920: Renamed BALTRIGER.
18.10.1920: Registered in London.
22.9.1931: Register closed following
sale to Det Stavangerske D/S, Norway,
and renamed RYFYLKE.
5.2.1941: Sunk by gunfire from HM
Submarine SEALION off Stadlandet,

southern Norway whilst on a voyage
from Kirkenes to Bergen.

4. BALTARA (1) 1924-1929
O.N. 124676 2,379g 1,387
300.7 x 38.2 x 22.9 feet
Two Q.4-cyl. by Harland and Wolff Ltd.,
Belfast, driving twin screws; both 241 NHP,
1,195 IHP, 11 knots.
6.5.1909: Launched by Harland and Wolff
Ltd., Belfast (Yard No. 405).
6.7.1909: Registered in the ownership of
the Royal Mail Steam Packet Company,
London as BERBICE.
8.7.1909: Completed.
21.8.1920: Sold to the Admiralty, London.
15.9.1922: Sold to Mitchell, Cotts Ltd.,
London.
29.9.1922: Renamed SUNTEMPLE.
16.1.1924: Acquired by the United Baltic
Corporation Ltd., London.
23.2.1924: Renamed BALTARA.
11.1.1929: Wrecked off the eastern entrance
to the River Vistula whilst on a voyage from
Libau to London with general cargo.
26.1.1929: Register closed.

Opposite top: the Quay at Riga on 13th June 1924 with the *Baltabor,* nearest to the camera, alongside. *[J. and M. Clarkson collection]*

Opposite bottom: *Baltabor.* *[Ambrose Greenway collection]*

Right: *Baltannic.* *[Newall Dunn collection]*

Below: *Baltriger.* *[Newall Dunn collection]*

Bottom: *Baltara.* *[Ambrose Greenway collection]*

Top: *Baltannic* in the Thames on 15th April 1933. *[R.A.Snook/F.W. Hawks collection]*
Above: *Baltannic* on Government service. During the Second World War *Baltannic* was requisitioned to carry refrigerated cargoes from outlying New Zealand ports to the main ports for shipment overseas. *[Ian J. Farquhar collection]*

5. BALTANNIC (2) 1925-1949
O.N. 148640 1, 575g 904n
243.4 x 37.3 x 24.6 feet
T.3-cyl. by Rotterdamsche Droogdok
Maatschappij, Rotterdam, Netherlands; 203
NHP, 1,200 IHP, 13 knots.
1913: Completed by Rotterdamsche
Droogdok Maatschappij, Rotterdam,
Netherlands (Yard No. 40) for Hollandsche
Stoomboot Maatschappij N.V., Amsterdam,
Netherlands as ZAANSTROOM.
1920: Sold to Société Navale Charbonnière,
Antwerp, Belgium and renamed
WESTLAND.
9.7.1925: Registered in the ownership of the
United Baltic Corporation Ltd., London as
BALTANNIC.
1949: Sold to Imperial Chemical Industries

Ltd., London for use as a storage hulk.
4.2.1950: Register closed.
1958: Sold to the British Iron and Steel
Corporation.
7.5.1958: Delivered under tow to the West
of Scotland Shipbreaking Co. Ltd. for
demolition at Troon.

6. BALTRADER (1) 1926-1940
O.N. 148755 1,699g 1,014n
255.4 x 38.2 x 15.4 feet
T.3-cyl. by Akt. Burmeister & Wain,
Copenhagen, Denmark; 165 NHP; 900
IHP, 10 knots.
1919: Completed by Akt. Burmeister &
Wain, Copenhagen, Denmark (Yard No.
266a) for A/S Det Ostasiatiske Kompagni,
Copenhagen, Denmark as BANKA.

15.3.1926: Renamed BALTRADER.
22.4.1926: Registered in the ownership
of the United Baltic Corporation Ltd.,
London.
9.11.1940: Exploded a mine and sank in
position 51.40.07 north by 01.18.02 east
whilst on a voyage from Seville to London
with general cargo, including wine. Two
crew members were lost.
28.2.1941: Register closed.

7. BALTONIA (1) 1926-1936
O.N. 115268 3,839g 2,390n
352.2 x 44.2 x 23.6 feet
T.3-cyl. by Richardsons, Westgarth and
Co. Ltd., Hartlepool; 450 NHP, 2,100
BHP, 12 knots.
4.1902: Completed by Sir Raylton Dixon

and Co. Ltd., Middlesbrough (Yard No. 482).

3.4.1902: Registered in the ownership of the British and African Steam Navigation Co. (1900) Ltd., Liverpool as AKABO.

17.2.1909: Transferred to the British and African Steam Navigation Co. Ltd., Liverpool.

13.12.1926: Acquired by the United Baltic Corporation Ltd., London.

8.2.1927: Renamed BALTONIA.

3.1936: Sold to van Heyghen Frères for £7,700 and demolished at Ghent.

13.3.1936: Register closed.

Top: *Baltrader.* [Roy Fenton collection]
Middle: *Akabo,* later the *Baltonia.* [J. and M. Clarkson collection]
Bottom: *Baltonia.* [J. and M. Clarkson collection]

8. BALTAVIA (1) 1929-1935
O.N. 161302 3,452g 1,801n
344.0 x 43.1 x 20.8 feet
Two T.3-cyl by Stabilimento Tecnico,
Trieste, Italy driving twin screws; 712
NHP, 5,000 IHP.
8.1901: Completed by Stabilimento
Tecnico, Trieste, Italy (Yard No. 334) for
the Chinese Eastern Railway Co. Ltd.,
Vladivostok, Russia as MONGOLIA.
1907: Sold to the Russian East Asiatic
Steam Ship Co. Ltd., Vladivostok.
1913: Sold to the West Australian
Government, Fremantle, Australia, and
renamed WESTERN AUSTRALIA.
1919: Sold to Rederiaktiebloaget
Svenska Lloyd (H. Metcalfe, manager),
Gothenburg, Sweden and renamed
PATRICIA.
5.1929: Acquired by the United Baltic
Corporation Ltd., London.
17.6.1929: Renamed BALTAVIA.
2.1935: Sold to John Cashmore Ltd. and
broken up at Newport, Monmouthshire.
6.6.1935: Register closed.

9. BALTALLIN 1930-1939
O.N. 144615 1,303g 512n
245.2 x 39.2 x 15.0 feet
T.3-cyl. by the Ailsa Shipbuilding Co. Ltd.,
Troon; 292 NHP, 2,100 IHP, 13 knots.
3.2.1920: Launched by the Ailsa
Shipbuilding Co. Ltd., Troon (Yard No.
368).
6.1920: Completed.

Top: *Western Australia* was bought by the West Australian Government for use on the north west coast of the state. Unsuitable for the service she was sent to England in July 1915 to be sold but on arrival was taken over by the Admiralty and converted to a hospital ship. A charter was arranged for the duration of the war. Her Australian officers and crew returned to the Commonwealth and were replaced by British officers and men. A fast ship, she was continuously used on cross channel work running between Southampton and Le Havre and up the Seine to Rouen. On 20th March 1918 she was attacked by a submarine but luckily the torpedo missed. *[Newall Dunn collection]*
Middle: The *Patricia* was purchased in 1929 from Svenska Lloyd and renamed *Baltavia*. *[J. and M. Clarkson collection]*
Bottom: *Baltavia* off Gravesend. *[Newall Dunn collection]*

25.6.1920: Registered in the ownership of the General Steam Navigation Co. Ltd., London as STARLING.

1.4.1930: Acquired by the United Baltic Corporation Ltd., London.

16.4.1930: Renamed BALTALLIN.

26.4.1938: Transferred to the Anglo-Estonian Shipping Co. Ltd. (United Baltic Corporation Ltd., managers), London.

20.9.1941: Torpedoed and sunk by the German submarine U 124 in position 49.07 north by 22.07 west whilst on a voyage from Preston and Oban to Gibraltar with Government stores in convoy OG74. Of the 35 crew and gunners, 18 were lost.

30.1.1942: Register closed.

10. BALTARA (2) 1933-1956

O.N. 142356 3,239g 1,993n

331.2 x 46.7 x 23.2 feet

T.3-cyl. by the Central Marine Engine Works, West Hartlepool; 430 NHP, 2,200 IHP, 11½ knots.

3.1918: Completed by William Gray and Co. Ltd., West Hartlepool (Yard No. 894) for the Shipping Controller, London (F. and W. Ritson, Sunderland, managers) as WAR COUNTRY.

1919: Sold to the French Government, Paris and renamed GLACIÈRE.

1924: Sold to Compagnie Maritime de Transports Frigorifiques, Paris, France.

1932: Sold to S. Behr and Matthew Ltd., London.

4.1933: Acquired by the United Baltic Corporation Ltd., London and renamed BALTARA.

1955: Sold to Afroessa Compania Naviera S.A., Panama (Kyrtatas Brothers, Piraeus, Greece) and renamed NIKFIL under the Costa Rican and later the Panama flag.

3.1960: Sold to the British Iron and Steel Corporation for £27,500 and allocated to Metal Industries Ltd. for demolition.

14.3.1960: Arrived at Rosyth.

18.3.1960: Demolition commenced.

Baltallin completed in 1920 at Troon as the *Starling* for the General Steam Navigation Co. Ltd. and purchased in 1930. *[J. and M. Clarkson collection]*

Above: *Baltara* on 15th June 1935. *[F.W. Hawks collection]*
Below: A post-war view of *Baltara* on 9th August 1952. *[F.W. Hawks collection]*
Comparing views *Baltara* appears to have had her funnel shortened in the intervening years. This was unusual: often funnels were extended to improve draught for the boiler.

Baltraffic photographed off Gravesend on 10th June 1934 by R.A. Snook. *[F.W. Hawks collection]*

11. BALTRAFFIC 1933-1951
O.N. 142597 3,297g 1,994n
331.3 x 46.8 x 23.2 feet
T.3-cyl. by John Dickinson and Sons Ltd., Sunderland; 430 NHP, 2,200 IHP.
7.1918: Completed by John Blumer and Co., Sunderland (Yard No. 247) for the Shipping Controller, London (Morel Ltd., Cardiff, managers) as WAR COPPICE.
1919: Sold to the French Government, Paris and renamed RÉFRIGERANT.
1924: Sold to Compagnie Maritime de Transports Frigorifiques, Paris, France.
4.1933: Acquired by the United Baltic Corporation Ltd., London and renamed BALTRAFFIC.
1951: Sold to Pan-Islamic Steamship Co. Ltd., Karachi, Pakistan and renamed SAFINA-E-TARIQ.
11.1956: Removed from service.
1957: Broken up at Karachi during first quarter.

12. BALTEAKO 1935-1938
O.N. 144503 1,314g 799n
245.2 x 39.2 x 15.0 feet
T.3-cyl. by the Ailsa Shipbuilding Co. Ltd., Troon; 185 NHP, 2,100 IHP, 13 knots.
11.12.1919: Launched by the Ailsa Shipbuilding Co. Ltd., Troon (Yard No. 367).
4.1920: Completed.
10.4.1920: Registered in the ownership of the General Steam Navigation Co. Ltd., London as HERON.

Above: After serving with the British Expeditionary Force as a frozen meat ship in the early part of the Second World War the *Baltraffic* then went out to New Zealand to serve in a similar role to *Baltannic*, remaining there until 1946. *[Ian J. Farquhar collection]*

Above: *Baltraffic* in more familiar waters with Tower Bridge and the Tower of London in the background. *[Roy Fenton collection]*

Balteako, formerly General Steam's *Heron*, bought and renamed in 1935. *[Ships in Focus]*

25.2.1935: Acquired by the United Baltic Corporation Ltd., London.
14.3.1935: Renamed BALTEAKO.
26.4.1938: Transferred to the Anglo-Latvian Shipping Co. Ltd. (United Baltic Corporation Ltd., managers), London.
29.3.1946: Struck an underwater wreck in Kiel Bay and sank north of Fehmarn Island in position 54.30 north by 11.01 east whilst on a voyage from London to Gdynia.
15.6.1946: Register closed.

13. BALTROVER (1) 1935-1946
O.N. 132840 4,916g 3,014n
350.0 x 50.0 x 31.6 feet
T.3-cyl. by Richardsons, Westgarth and Co. Ltd., West Hartlepool; 602 NHP, 3,150 IHP, 12.5 knots.
Passenger capacity: 195.

12.1912: Launched by Irvine's Ship Building and Dry Dock Co. Ltd., West Hartlepool (Yard No. 527).
4.1913: Completed.
18.4.1913: Registered in the ownership of Furness, Withy and Co. Ltd., West Hartlepool as DIGBY.
22.11.1914: Requisitioned by the Admiralty and fitted out in London as an armed merchant cruiser.
21.12.1914: Commissioned as HMS DIGBY in the Tenth Cruiser Squadron.
24.11.1915: Loaned to the French Navy as ARTOIS.
19.7.1917: Returned to the Admiralty as HMS DIGBY.
6.1.1919: Returned to owners.
31.10.1925: Sold to the Bermuda and West Indies Steamship Co. Ltd., Hamilton,

Bermuda and renamed DOMINICA.
21.10.1935: Acquired by the United Baltic Corporation Ltd., London for £21,000.
18.2.1936: Renamed BALTROVER.
1939: Withdrawn from Baltic service and ran for the Ministry of War Transport between Liverpool, Halifax and St. John's until 1944.
1946: Laid up pending disposal in Kames Bay, Kyles of Bute.
13.2.1946: Register closed on sale to Hellenic Mediterranean Lines Co. Ltd., Piraeus, Greece and renamed IONIA.
1965: Sold to the Ionia Shipping Co. S.A., Panama (South East Asia Shipping and Trading Co. Ltd. (George Zee), Hong Kong) and renamed IONIAN.
26.7.1965: Capsized and sank at Djakarta. Wreck later salvaged and demolished locally.

Baltrover, formerly the *Dominica* and the company's second purchase in 1935. *[Ships in Focus]*

14. BALTONIA (2) 1936-1937

O.N. 165333 2,013g 1,019n
303.0 x 42.2 x 17.1 feet
T.3-cyl. by Akers M/V, Oslo, Norway; 320
NHP, 1,675 IHP, 12.5 knots.
1925: Completed by Akers M/V, Oslo,
Norway (Yard No. 406) for A/S Ganger
Rolf (Fred. Olsen, manager), Oslo, Norway
as BUENA VISTA.
8.1936: Acquired by the United Baltic
Corporation Ltd., London.
29.9.1936: Renamed BALTONIA.
29.12.1937: Transferred to the Anglo
Lithuanian Shipping Co. Ltd. (United
Baltic Corporation Ltd., managers),
London.
7.2.1943: Mined and sunk in position 35.58
north by 05.59 west whilst on a voyage
from Seville and Gibraltar to Belfast Lough
whilst carrying a cargo of oranges and
general. Of the 62 crew and gunners, 11
were lost.
3.12.1943: Register closed.

15. BALTANGLIA (1) 1937-1940

O.N. 165459 1,523g 891n
255.6 x 39.4 x 16.5 feet
T.3-cyl. by J. G. Kincaid and Co. Ltd.,
Greenock; 162 NHP, 10 knots.
1921: Completed by the Ardrossan Dry
Dock and Ship Building Co. Ltd., Ardrossan
(Yard No. 319) for Thor Thoresens Linje
A/S (Thor Thoresen, manager), Christiania,
Norway as LAATEFOS.
1923: Sold to Swithun Linje A/S (Sigval
Bergesen, manager), Stavanger, Norway and
renamed LANGFOND.
3.1937: Acquired by the United Baltic
Corporation Ltd., London and renamed
BALTANGLIA.
29.12.1937: Transferred to the Anglo-
Lithuanian Shipping Co. Ltd. (United Baltic
Corporation Ltd., managers), London.
23.1.1940: Torpedoed and sunk by the
German submarine U 19 in the North Sea
position 55.35 north by 01.27 west whilst on
a voyage from Hommelvik to the Tyne and
Rochester with general cargo. The entire
crew was saved.
11.3.1940: Register closed.

Above: *Baltonia* was bought from Norway in 1936. *[Ships in Focus]*

Right: *Langfond* was purchased in 1937. *[J. and M. Clarkson collection]*

Below: *Baltanglia*, of which there seem to be few photographs, served the company for only three years. *[Newall Dunn collection]*

Above: *Baltabor* photographed at Liverpool by Basil Feilden.
Below: As seen by John MacRoberts sailing from Liverpool. *[Both: J. and M. Clarkson collection]*

16. BALTABOR (2) 1937-1939
O.N. 166411 2,592g 1,391n
302.0 x 46.0 x 18.4 feet
Two 6-cyl. 4 SCSA Burmeister & Wain-
type oil engines by A/B Gotaverken,
Gothenburg, Sweden driving twin screws;
629 NHP, 2,600 IHP, 12 knots.
9.1924: Completed by A/B Gotaverken,
Gothenburg, Sweden (Yard No. 376) for
the Panama Mail Steamship Company,
Panama (W.R. Grace and Co., San
Francisco, USA, managers) as CITY OF
SAN FRANCISCO.

1931: Renamed SANTA MONICA.
1936: Renamed CUMBAL.
10.1937: Acquired by the United Baltic
Corporation Ltd., London and renamed
BALTABOR.
26.4.1938: Transferred to the Anglo-
Latvian Shipping Co. Ltd. (United Baltic
Corporation Ltd., managers), London.
12.2.1939: Grounded one and a half miles
west north west of Liepaja whilst on a
voyage from Riga to London with a cargo
of butter and plywood.
21.6.1939: Refloated and taken to Liepaja

but declared a constructive total loss.
1.6.1940: Register closed.

17. BALTAVIA (2) 1938-1957
O.N. 166403 2,592g 1,391n
302.0 x 46.0 x 18.4 feet
Two oil engines 6-cyl. 4SCSA Burmeister
& Wain-type by A/B Gotaverken,
Gothenburg, Sweden driving twin screws;
629 NHP.
10.1924: Completed by A/B Gotaverken,
Gothenburg, Sweden (Yard No. 377) for the
Panama Mail Steamship Company Panama

(W.R. Grace and Co., San Francisco, USA, managers) as CITY OF PANAMA.
1931: Renamed SANTA CATALINA.
1935: Renamed CHIMU.
1938: Acquired by the United Baltic Corporation Ltd., London and renamed BALTAVIA.
1938: Transferred to the Anglo-Estonian Shipping Co. Ltd. (United Baltic Corporation Ltd., managers), London.
1946: Transferred to the United Baltic Corporation Ltd.
1957: Sold to Jebshun Shipping Company (Lam C. Cheong), Hong Kong.
1958: Transferred to Shun Kee Navigation Co. Ltd. (Jebshun Shipping Company), Hong Kong, and renamed SHUN SHING.
18.9.1963: Arrived at Hong Kong to be laid up.
3.6.1964: Breaking up began by Mollers Ltd. at Hong Kong.

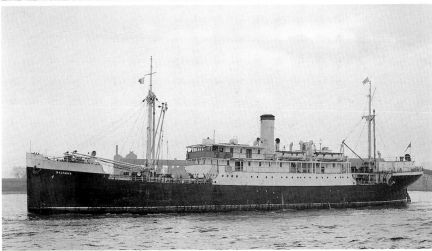

When completed the *City of San Francisco (Baltabor)* and the *City of Panama (Baltavia)* were the first United States passenger ships to be diesel driven and the first built abroad. They had accomodation for 60 passengers in first class and 60 in third.

Top to bottom:
City of Panama. [Newall Dunn collection]
Baltavia passing under the Levensau Bridge on the Kiel Canal in northern Germany. *[Uwe Detlefsen collection]* There appears to have been some variation over the years in the depth of black paint applied to the top of the funnel on *Baltavia* and some of the other ships in the fleet. In this view (left) the cowl is black and the black has been continued down the funnel for a short distance, perhaps to hide soot marks and to maintain a smarter appearance. *[J. and M. Clarkson collection]*
Below left: In this undated view only the cowl is painted black. *[Uwe Detlefsen collection]*
Below: With her new owner's funnel colours after her sale to Hong Kong buyers. *[Ships in Focus]*

18. BALTRADER (2)/BALTIC FIR 1947-1956

O.N. 180643 1,846g 1,440n 990d
289.4 x 44.5 x 15.8 feet
C.4-cyl. by Ottensener Eisenwerk A.G., Hamburg, Germany.

28.2.1945: Launched by Deutsche Werft A.G., Hamburg, Germany (Yard No.450).
29.3.1945: Completed for A.G. für Unten der Eisen en Friedrich Krupp A.G., Bremen, Germany as BETZDORF.
5.1945: Taken as a prize at Kiel, allocated to the Ministry of War Transport, London (T. L. Duff and Co. Ltd., Glasgow, managers) and renamed EMPIRE GAFFER.
21.6.1945: Delivered at Methil.
1946: Owners became the Ministry of Transport, London.
1947: Acquired by the United Baltic Corporation Ltd., London and renamed BALTRADER.
1952: Renamed BALTIC FIR.
1956: Sold to D.D.G. Hansa, Bremen, West Germany and rebuilt by Norddeutscher Lloyd Werftbetrieb, Bremerhaven.
24.6.1956: Re-entered service as ARSTERTURM.
1969: Sold to Universal Shipping and Coastal Trading Private Ltd., Bombay, India and renamed UNIGOOLNAR.
1976: Sold to Sudarsan Liners Ltd., Madras, India and renamed SUDARSAN SHAKTI.
1980: Reported as having been towed from Kuwait to India in a damaged condition.
3.1981: Demolition commenced by City Steel, Mumbai.

19. BALTONIA (3)/BALTIC OAK 1947-1957

O.N. 180674 1,944g 1,410n 965d
287.8 x 44.4 x 15.9 feet
C.4-cyl. by Deutsche Werft A.G., Hamburg, Germany; 1,590 IHP; 11 knots.

1943: Ordered by Schiffbau-Treuhand G.m.b.H., Berlin, Germany.
23.10.1944: Launched by Deutsche Werft A.G., Hamburg, Germany (Yard No. 448).
28.12.1944: Completed for D.D.G. Hansa, Bremen, Germany as FANGTURM.
5.1945: Taken as a prize at Kiel, allocated to the Ministry of War Transport, London (P.D. Hendry and Sons, Glasgow, and later British and Continental Steamship Co. Ltd., managers) and renamed EMPIRE GALLOP.
8.6.1945: Delivered at Methil.
3.1946: Owners became the Ministry of Transport, London.
1947: Acquired by the United Baltic Corporation Ltd., London and renamed BALTONIA.
1953: Renamed BALTIC OAK.
1957: Sold to Bock, Godeffroy and Co. (Deutsche Levante-Linie GmbH, managers), Hamburg, West Germany and renamed PALMYRA.
1960: Management ceased.
27.3.1962: Sank after colliding with the tanker BRITISH MARINER (8,576/1948) off Ushant whilst on a voyage from Hamburg to Istanbul. BRITISH MARINER was declared a constructive total loss and was broken up at Bruges.

Opposite page, top and middle: *Baltic Fir.* [Top: J. and M. Clarkson collection, middle: Ships in Focus]
Bottom: *Baltonia* berthed at Turku, Finland in 1952. [R. Brzoza]

This page, top: *Baltonia* now sailing as the *Baltic Oak.* [Laurence Dunn/World Ship Society Ltd.]
Middle: *Baltic Oak.* [Roy Fenton collection]
Bottom: After her sale to West German buyers the *Baltic Oak* saw a further five years of service as *Palmyra* before being lost in a collision. [FotoFlite/J. and M. Clarkson collection]

Baltanglia. [World Ship Society Ltd./Roy Fenton collection]

20. BALTANGLIA (2)/BALTIC PINE
1947-1954

O.N. 180612 1,923g 935n 931d
279.7 x 44.4 x 15.9 feet
C.4-cyl. by Ottensener Eisenwerk A.G.,
Hamburg, Germany; 1,200 IHP, 10 knots.
29.8.1944: Launched by Deutsche Werft
A.G., Hamburg, Germany (Yard No. 433)
for D.D.G. Hansa, Bremen, Germany as
ADAMSTURM.
5.1945: Taken as a prize at Kiel.
11.7.1945: Delivered to the United
Kingdom.
2.8.1945: Registered in the ownership of
the Ministry of War Transport, London
(Glen and Co. Ltd., Glasgow, managers) as
EMPIRE GANYMEDE.
20.3.1946: Owners became the Ministry of
Transport, London.

10.2.1947: Acquired by the United Baltic
Corporation Ltd., London.
7.3.1947: Renamed BALTANGLIA.
5.1.1953: Renamed BALTIC PINE.
20.5.1954: Register closed on sale to
Hellenic Lines Ltd. (P. G. Callimanopulos,
manager), Piraeus, Greece and renamed
GERMANIA.
26.4.1955: Beached and later abandoned
near Beachy Head after colliding with the
Panamanian steamer MARO (7,588/1919).
30.11.1955: Refloated, but re-beached with
a broken back at Pevensey Bay.
2.1956: Sold to Argo Reederei R. Adler
and Söhne, Bremen, West Germany.
16.2.1956: Towed from Pevensey Bay to
Bremen by the tug VANQUISHER for
repair and reconstruction.
30.6.1956: Re-entered service for

Partenreederei 'Auriga' (Adler and Söhne,
Bremen) as AURIGA.
6.1957: Transferred to Argo Reederei R.
Adler and Söhne, Bremen.
14.1.1965: Arrived at Bremerhaven for
demolition by Eisen und Metall A.G.

21. BALTROVER (2) 1950-1968

O.N. 184272 2,168g 1,021n 3,260d
332.3 x 50.7 x 15.2 feet
C.4-cyl. by Frederikstad M/V A/S,
Frederikstad, Norway; 3,000 IHP, 14 knots.
Two passengers.
21.4.1949: Launched by Frederikstad M/V
A/S, Frederikstad, Norway (Yard No. 325)
for Skibs A/S Vilhelm Torkildsen Rederi,
Bergen, Norway as MARSTENEN.
1950: Acquired by the United Baltic

Baltrover. [Ships in Focus]

36

Corporation Ltd., London and renamed
BALTROVER.
1968: Sold to Marine General
Transporters Corporation, Liberia (Th.A.
Papagelopoulos, Athens, Greece) and
renamed ANGELOS P.
1974: Sold to Arcepey Shipping Co. S.A.,
Panama and renamed ANGEL BELL.
17.2.1976: Caught fire 10 miles off Chah
Bahar, Iran whilst in tow for machinery
repairs in the course of a voyage from
Dubai to Karachi with general cargo.
18.2.1976: Sank in position 25.03 north by
60.07 east.

Baltrover. [Roy Fenton collection]

22. BALTIC EXPORTER 1953-1969

O.N. 185866   1,665g 667n 2,411d
316.6 x 42.3 x 18.3 feet
Two oil engines 10-cyl. 2SCSA by
Maschinenbau Augsburg-Nürnberg A.G.,
Augsburg, West Germany geared to a single
screw shaft; 3,600 BHP, 15½ knots.
Two passengers.
22.11.1952: Launched by Nobiskrug Werft,
Rendsburg, West Germany (Yard No. 563)
for the United Baltic Corporation Ltd.,
London as BALTIC EXPORTER.
3.1953: Completed.
1969: Sold to Nam Fong Shipping Co.
Ltd., Monrovia, Liberia (Ankan Shipping
Co. Ltd., Hong Kong) for £110,000 and
renamed EASTERN DRAGON under the
Somali flag.
1969: Transferred to the Goodwind
Shipping Co. Ltd., Monrovia (Ankan
Shipping Co. Ltd., Hong Kong) and
renamed LUCKY PHOENIX under the
Somali flag.
1969: Transferred to Ankan Shipping Co.
Ltd., Hong Kong and renamed EASTERN
DRAGON under the Somali flag.
1971: Sold to Rosewell Shipping Co. Ltd.
(Rosewell Maritime Co. Ltd.), Hong Kong

Baltrover in the Kiel Canal after repainting.   *[J. and M. Clarkson collection]*

and renamed DAWN OF PEACE under the
Singapore flag.
1972: Sold to Interoceanic Navigation Co.
SA.., Panama (Kings V Shipping Co. Ltd.,
Taiwan) and renamed KING'S OCEAN.
1974: Sold to Edward Shipping and

Mercantile S.A., Manila, Philippines and
renamed PACIFIC QUEEN under the
Panama flag.
30.6.1980: Demolition began by Chi
Young Steel Enterprises Co. at
Kaohsiung.

Baltic Exporter was the first of the four new ships ordered in 1952 to be delivered to the company. *[Uwe Detlefsen collection]*

Top: *Baltic Importer* in the English Channel, 5th October 1959. *[Ships in Focus]*

Middle: *Southern Dragon,* formerly the *Baltic Importer*, looking the worse for wear when photographed in the Straits of Malacca by the late Peter Foxley. *[J. and M. Clarkson collection]*

Bottom: *Baltic Merchant. [Roy Fenton collection]*

Opposite page top: *Baltic Merchant* well turned out under the Italian flag as the *Mari Seconda. [Salvatore Battaglia/Roy Fenton collection]*

Bottom: *Baltic Trader. [Roy Fenton collection]*

23. BALTIC IMPORTER 1953-1969

O.N. 185943 1,683g 715n 2,560d
325.1 x 42.3 x 18.3 feet
1978: 1,683g 674n 2,601d
Two oil engines 10-cyl. 2SCSA by
Maschinenbau Kiel A.G., Kiel, West
Germany geared to a single screw shaft;
3,600 BHP, 15½ knots,
Two passengers.
25.6.1953: Launched by Werft Nobiskrug
G.m.b.H., Rendsburg, West Germany (Yard
No. 564) for the United Baltic Corporation
Ltd., London as BALTIC IMPORTER.
9.1953: Completed.
1969: Sold to the Goodwind Shipping
Co. Ltd., Monrovia, Liberia (Goldwyn
Shipping Co. Ltd., Hong Kong) and
renamed SILVER SWAN under the Somali
flag.
1969: Transferred to Ankan Shipping
Co. Ltd., Hong Kong and renamed
SOUTHERN DRAGON under the Somali
flag.
1973: Sold to Dawn Lines Ltd., Monrovia,
Liberia (United China Shipping Company,
Hong Kong) and renamed EXPERT
MARU under the Panama flag.
1975: Renamed SHINTOKO MARU.
1975: Sold to Glory Star Steamship S.A.,
Panama (Star Line Ltd. (William Wong),
Hong Kong, managers) and renamed
GLORY STAR.
1978: Sold to Wah Po Shipping Co. S.A.,
Panama (Carolina International Enterprises
Ltd., Hong Kong) and renamed WAH PO.
1978: Sold to Gulf Marine Line S.A.,
Panama (Tonbon Shipping Co. Ltd., Hong
Kong) and renamed RITA POINT.
1979: Sold to Well Voy Navigation S.A.,
Panama (Tong Kwong Shipping and
Management Co. Ltd., Tokyo, Japan) and
renamed WELL VOY NO.1
4.1992: Deleted from Lloyd's Register,
continued existence in doubt.

24. BALTIC MERCHANT 1954-1970

O.N. 186028 1,689g 696n 2,560d
325.1 x 42.4 x 18.3 feet
Two oil engines 10-cyl. 2SCSA by
Maschinenbau Kiel A.G., Kiel, West
Germany geared to a single screw shaft;
3,600 BHP, 15½ knots, 2 passengers.
28.11.1953: Launched by Werft Nobiskrug
G.m.b.H., Rendsburg, West Germany (Yard
No. 565) for the United Baltic Corporation
Ltd., London as BALTIC MERCHANT.
3.1954: Completed.
1970: Sold to Seven Seas Shipping Co.
Ltd., Famagusta, Cyprus (Mediterranean
and Overseas Shipping Agency S.p.A.
(Fotis G. Pulides), Genoa, Italy) and
renamed SPAGNA.
1971: Renamed MEDOV SPAGNA.
1973: Sold to Navigazione del Sud
S.p.A., Palermo, Italy and renamed MARI
SECONDA.
1974: Sold to D.P. S.p.A. (Franco De
Paolis), Genoa, Italy and renamed
GIOVANNA D.P.

29.8.1980: Demolition began by Riccardi
Impresa Demolizione at Vado Ligure, Italy.

25. BALTIC TRADER 1954-1971

O.N. 186103 1,698g 696n 2,560d
325.1 x 42.3 x 18.3 feet
Two oil engines 10-cyl. 2SCSA by
Maschinenbau Kiel A.G., Kiel, West
Germany geared to a single screw shaft;
3,600 BHP, 15½ knots. Two passengers .
5.5.1953: Launched by Werft Nobiskrug
G.m.b.H., Rendsburg, West Germany (Yard
No. 566) for the United Baltic Corporation
Ltd., London as BALTIC TRADER.
7.1954: Completed.
1971: Sold to Medov Lines S.p.A.
(Mediterranean and Overseas Shipping
Agency S.p.A. (Fotis G. Pulides)), Genoa,
Italy and renamed MEDOV ITALIA.
1973: Sold to Marittima del Nord SpA,
Genoa, Italy and renamed MONCALVO.
1978: Sold to W.I.P. di Navigazione S.r.l.
(Franco De Paolis), Genoa, Italy and
renamed EMMA D.P.

1979: Transferred to Montenavi S.r.l., Naples Srl (Franco De Paolis, Genoa).
1981: Transferred to W.I.P. di Navigazione S.r.l. (Franco De Paolis), Genoa.
1987: Converted to a cement carrier.
28.10.1990: Laid up at Taranto.
1991: Sold to Sidermar di Navigazione S.p.A., Genoa, Italy.
1992: Sold to Antonio Tricoli Fu Giovanni Bruzia di Navigazione S.r.l. Crotone, Italy.
1.8.1994: Demolition began at Taranto, where she had been laid up since 1990.

26. BALTIC CLIPPER 1954-1965
O.N. 186132 1,198g 465n 1,626d
284.5 x 38.3 x 15.1 feet
Two oil engines 8-cyl. 2SCSA by Motorenwerk Mannheim A.G., Mannheim, West Germany geared to a single screw shaft; 2,000 BHP, 14¾ knots,
Five passengers.
22.6.1954: Launched by Rolandwerft

G.m.b.H., Hamburg, West Germany (Yard No. 851) for the United Baltic Corporation Ltd., London as BALTIC CLIPPER.
10.1954: Completed.
1965: Sold to National Shipping Corporation, Karachi, Pakistan and renamed MAKRAN.
9.12.1971: Bombed and set on fire at Mangla Creek near Chalna during the India-Pakistan war.
31.12.1971: Burnt out, and later demolished.

27. BALTIC COMET 1954-1965
O.N. 186133 1,198g 465n 1,624d
284.5 x 38.3 x 15.1 feet
Two oil engines 8-cyl. 2SCSA by Motorenwerk Mannheim A.G., Mannheim, West Germany geared to a single screw shaft; 2,000 BHP, 14¾ knots.
1976: Two 6-cyl. 4SCSA manufactured in 1974 by Stork-Werkspoor, Zwolle,

Netherlands fluidrive coupled to screw shaft; 1,100 BHP, 11 knots.
Five passengers.
3.7.1954: Launched by Krogerwerft G.m.b.H., Rendsburg, West Germany (Yard No. 1061) for the United Baltic Corporation Ltd., London as BALTIC COMET.
10.1954: Completed.
1965: Sold to National Shipping Corporation, Karachi, Pakistan and renamed PASNI.
1971: Detained at Cochin during the India-Pakistan war.
1973: Sold to the Bangladesh Shipping Corporation, Dacca, Bangladesh and renamed SYLHET.
1977: Sold to Three Star Shipping Lines Ltd., Dacca, Bangladesh and renamed SEAMOON I.
20.12.1978: Arrived at Chittagong for demolition.

Above: *Baltic Clipper* in the Thames in 1956. *[Ships in Focus]*
Below: *Baltic Comet.* *[J. and M. Clarkson collection]*

Baltic Arrow in the Kiel Canal (left) and at Ipswich (above). *[Left: Uwe Detlefsen, above: Roy Fenton collection]*

28. BALTIC ARROW 1956-1978

O.N. 187493 1,385g 519n 1,679d
88.7 x 12.37 x 4.642 metres
Two oil engines 8-cyl. 4SCSA by
Motorenwerk Mannheim A.G., Mannheim,
West Germany; 2,000 BHP, 14½ knots.
Five passengers.
15.8.1956: Launched by Ottensener
Eisenwerk G.m.b.H., Hamburg, West
Germany (Yard No. 501) for the United
Baltic Corporation Ltd., London as
BALTIC ARROW.
12.1956: Completed.
1978: Sold to Colonial Shipping Ltd.,
Georgetown, Cayman Islands (Doric
Shipping Corporation, Miami, Florida) and
renamed DORIC ARROW.
1979: Renamed DELDONA.
1981: Transferred to Lyons Shipping Ltd.,
Georgetown (Doric Shipping Corporation,
Miami, Florida) and renamed YOLI.
1982: Sold to Sea Pacific Line SA, Panama
and renamed SEA PACIFIC.
15-16.12.1983: Sank during the night

while anchored in Chimbote Bay during a
voyage from Callao to Corinto.

29. BALTIC SWIFT 1957-1973

O.N. 187535 1,385g 519n 1,679d
88.7 x 12.37 x 4.642 metres
1973: 1,224g 458n 1,432d
88.7 x 12.37 x 4.630 metres
Two oil engines 8-cyl. 4SCSA by
Motorenwerk Mannheim A.G., Mannheim,
West Germany; 2,000 BHP, 14½ knots.
Five passengers.
26.11.1956: Launched by Ottensener
Eisenwerk G.m.b.H., Hamburg, West
Germany (Yard No. 503) for the United
Baltic Corporation Ltd., London as BALTIC
SWIFT.
3.1957: Completed.
1973: Sold to Reef Shipping Co. Ltd.,
Norfolk Islands and renamed FIJIAN SWIFT.
1976: Sold to Pacific Navigation
Co. Ltd. (Government of the Tonga
Islands), Nukuolofa, Tonga and renamed
HA'AMOTAHA.

1978: Owners became Pacific Navigation of
Tonga Ltd.
23.4.1979: Demolition began by Pacific
Metal Industries Ltd., Auckland, New
Zealand.

30. BALTIC EXPRESS 1957-1972

O.N. 187683 2,941g 1,425n 3,950d
334.3 x 45.6 x 18.1 feet
1980: 1,836g 626n 2,758d
2,926g 1,511n 4,353d
Two oil engines 10-cyl. 2SCSA by
Maschinenbau Augsburg-Nürnberg A.G.,
Augsburg, West Germany geared to a single
screw shaft; 4,180 BHP, 15¾ knots.
Four passengers.
19.9.1957: Launched by Ottensener Eisenwerk
G.m.b.H., Hamburg, West Germany (Yard No.
509) for the United Baltic Corporation Ltd.,
London as BALTIC EXPRESS.
11.1957: Completed.
7.9.1963: Collided with and severely damaged
the West German pilot vessel DITMAR KOEL
(767/1958) near the Elbe No.1 Light Vessel.

Above:: *Baltic Swift* in the Kiel Canal. *[J. and M. Clarkson collection]*

Above: A wintery view of the *Baltic Express* at Helsinki. *[R. Brzoza, Finland]*

Right: *Baltic Express* in a warmer clime. *[Roy Fenton collection]*

Below: *Baltic Jet.* *[World Ship Society Limited]*

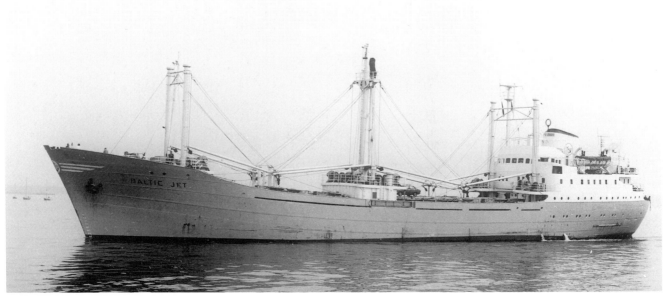

1972: Sold to Marastro Armadora S.A., Panama (Fomentos Armadora S.A., Piraeus, Greece) for £12,000 and renamed MOSKA under the Greek flag.
12.1977: Laid-up with surveys overdue.
5.1980: Surveyed and sold to Seawind Compania Naviera S.A., Panama (Marinestar Shipping Co. Ltd. (F. Zervoudakis, S. Valsamidis and I. Gournaras), Piraeus, Greece and renamed SEAWIND.
4.10.1982: Arrived at Bombay with her engine room flooded. Laid-up at Bombay and subsequently placed under arrest.
27.3.1984: Sold by auction to local shipbreakers.
6.1984: Demolished.

31. BALTIC JET 1959-1979

O.N. 300844 1,481g 590n 1,996d
91.0 x 12.9 x 4.8 metres
Oil engine 7-cyl. 4SCSA by Maschinenbau Augsburg-Nürnberg A.G., Nürnberg, West Germany; 2,520 BHP, 14 knots.
Four passengers.
1958: Ordered from Krogerwerft G.m.b.H., Rendsburg, West Germany (Yard No. 1088) by MacAndrews and Co. Ltd., London.
10.1.1959: Launched for the United Baltic Corporation Ltd. as BALTIC JET.
18.4.1959: Completed.
1973: Managers became Anglo-Finnish Shipping Co. Ltd.
1975: Management ceased.
1979: Sold to Mednari S.a.r.L. (Rima Line Shipping Co. S.a.r.L., managers), Beirut, Lebanon and renamed NAVI STAR.
17.2.1984: Arrived at Mumbai for demolition.
7.1985: Work began by S.S. Jane and Co., Mumbai.

32. BALTIC SPRAY 1960-1963

O.N. 186043 1,305g 589n 1,750d
284.0 x 39.2 x 15.3 feet
1974: 1,989g 1,058n
Fiat-type oil engine 6-cyl. 2SCSA by S.A. Ansaldo, Genoa, Italy; 1,600 BHP.
11.5.1948: Launched.
10.1948: Completed by Furness Shipbuilding Co. Ltd., Haverton Hill-on-Tees (Yard No. 419) for Stockholms Rederi A/B Svea (Eman Hogberg, manager), Stockholm, Sweden as SVENKSUND.
1954: Acquired by MacAndrews and Co. Ltd., London and renamed PONZANO.
6.1960: Transferred to United Baltic Corporation Ltd. and renamed BALTIC SPRAY.
1963: Sold to George N. Iatrou and Others, Piraeus, Greece and renamed MANGANA.
1974: Sold to Prelco Compania Naviera S.A. (Constantinos Haidos), Piraeus, Greece and renamed ELISSAVET.
5.1979: Demolition began by Th. Vitiello-e Papadopoulos and Co., Greece.

33. BALTIC SPRITE 1960-1974

O.N. 301241 960g 422n 1,530d
263.0 x 41.3 x 13.7 feet
Two oil engines 8-cyl. 4SCSA by Maschinenbau Augsburg-Nürnberg A.G., Hamburg, West Germany geared to a single screw shaft.
20.8.1960: Launched by Krogerwerft G.m.b.H., Rendsburg, West Germany (Yard No. 1171).
9.11.1960: Completed for the United Baltic Corporation Ltd., London as BALTIC SPRITE.
1974: Sold to Losinjska Plovidba OOUR Brodarstvo, Rijeka, Jugoslavia and renamed USTRINE.
1991: Sold to Flanonia Shipping Co. Ltd., St. Vincent and the Grenadines (Brodogradaliste Cres Zanatsko Proizvodno I Usluzno Poduzece, Cres, Croatia).

Above: MacAndrews *Ponzano*. Built in England for the Swedish company Svea as the *Svenksund* she spent six years under the Swedish flag. After a further six years with MacAndrews as *Ponzano* she was transferred to United Baltic and renamed *Baltic Spray*, a name she held for only three years.
Below; *Baltic Spray*. Photographed against the sun, she appears to have a much darker hull than usual for United Baltic ships. Other views of her confirm she had the usual light grey paintwork. *[Both: Ships in Focus]*

Above: *Baltic Sprite* in the Thames.
[G.E.P. Brownell]

Left: *Baltic Sprite* at Gibraltar in September 1973. On the 4th September 1973 the *Baltic Sprite* was in collision with the Liberian tanker *Mayfair Loyalty* (12,123/1954) in the Bay of Gibraltar. Putting into Gibraltar she remained there until the 26th September when she sailed for Cadiz, Spain for repairs.
[Ships in Focus]

1994: Transferred to Renzlor Securities Corporation, Panama (Brodogradaliste Cres d.d., Cres, Croatia, managers) (Ferremka Handelsgesellschaft m.b.H., Vienna, Austria).
3.11.1999: Demolition began by Dortel Gemi Sokum Demir Ve Celik San, Aliaga, Turkey.

34. BALTIC STAR 1961-1977
O.N. 302624 1,571g 624n
305.0 x 42.3 x 16.0 feet
1969: 1,769g 786n 2,753d
117.8 x 12.9 x 5.0 metres.
Oil engine 7-cyl. 4SCSA by Maschinenbau Augsburg-Nürnberg A.G., Nürnberg, West Germany; 2,520 BHP.
2.9.1960: Keel laid by Krogerwerft G.m.b.H., Rendsburg, West Germany (Yard No. 1176).
30.1.1961: Launched.
15.5.1961: Completed for the United Baltic Corporation Ltd., London as BALTIC STAR.
1969: Lengthened by Smith's Dock Co. Ltd., Middlesbrough.
3.1977: Sold to Sea Duke S.A., Panama

(Worldwide Shipping Trading S.A. (J. Leontakianakos), Piraeus, Greece, managers) and renamed SKOPELOS SKY under the Greek flag.
1979: Managers became Lesaski Shipping Ltd. (S. Savvas and D. Skiathitis), Piraeus, Greece.
15.12.1979: Wrecked near Portquin, Cornwall in position 50.35.24 north by 04.52.24 west after engines failed in heavy weather whilst on a voyage from Garston to Algiers with a cargo of lubricating oil.

35. BALTIC SUN 1962-1973
O.N. 302995 3,531g 1,819n 4,620d 118.9 x 17.0 x 6.6 metres
Two oil engines 10-cyl. 4SCSA by Maschinenbau Augsburg-Nürnberg A.G., Hamburg, West Germany; 4,780 BHP, 15.5 knots.
Ten passengers.
4.8.1961: Keel laid by Krogerwerft G.m.b.H., Rendsburg, West Germany (Yard No. 1178).
24.2.1962: Launched.
30.6.1962: Completed for the United Baltic Corporation Ltd., London as BALTIC SUN.

1973: Sold to Reefer City (Private) Ltd. (Reefer Lines (Private) Ltd.), Singapore and renamed REEFER CITY.
21.1.1983: Arrived at Kaohsiung for demolition.
3.2.1983: Work began by Chien Yu Steel Industria Co., Kaohsiung.

36. BALTIC VENTURE/MELVILLE VENTURE 1965-1981
O.N. 306224 1,581g 570n 2,999d
280.0 x 46.5 x 18.1 feet
Post 1970: 1,844g 903n 3,391d
97.9 x 14.2 x 5.5 metres.
Oil engine 7-cyl. 4SCSA by Maschinenbau Augsburg-Nürnberg A.G., Nürnberg, West Germany; 2,710 BHP, 14 knots.
One passenger
8.6.1964: Keel laid by William Doxford and Sons (Shipbuilders) Ltd., Sunderland (Yard No. 866).
20.11.1964: Launched.
27.1.1965: Completed for the United Baltic Corporation Ltd., London as BALTIC VENTURE.
8.5.1970: Arrived on the Tyne to be

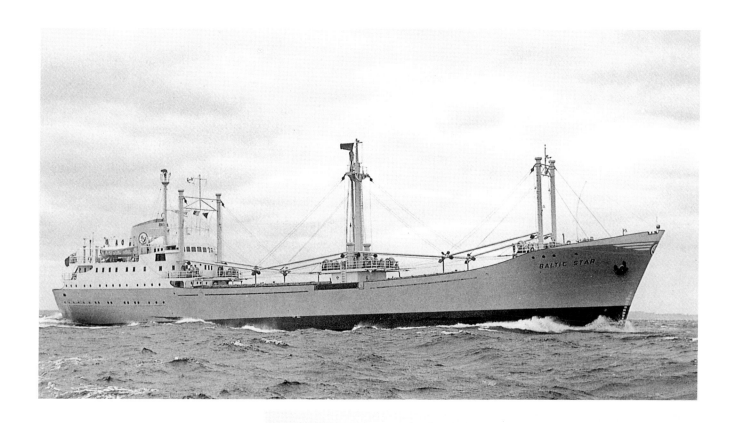

Top: Baltic Star. [Foto-Gaspar/Newall Dunn collection]

Middle: Baltic Star showing additional cargo handling gear fitted during her lengthening in 1969. *[W.J.Harvey/ World Ship Society Ltd.]*

Below: *Baltic Sun. [Ships in Focus]*

lengthened by 41.5 feet by Swan Hunter
Ship Repairers Ltd.
1980: Renamed MELVILLE VENTURE
and transferred to Canadian registry.
1981: Sold to Gulf Maritime (Cypress)
Ltd., Limassol, Cyprus (Gulf Maritime
Ltd. (M. Askari), London) and renamed
GULF VENTURE.
1985: Sold to Progress Shipping Ltd.
(Maldives National Ship Management Ltd.,
managers), Male, Maldives and renamed
PROGRESS LIBERTY.
7.1998: Anchored in Male harbour
following a fire in the engine room whilst
on a voyage to Singapore. Subsequently
drifted ashore on Hululle Island.
14.7.1998: Anchored off Male after being
refloated. Later declared a total loss.
31.10.1998: Arrived at Valinokkam, India
to be broken up by TNSS Steels Private.

Top: *Baltic Venture* in May 1965. *[J. and M. Clarkson collection]*
Middle: After being lengthened in 1970. *[Uwe Detlefsen collection]*
Bottom: The Canadian flag *Melville Venture* under United Baltic management on
14th June 1980. *[René Beauchamp, Montreal]*

37. BALTIC VANGUARD/CORTES/
LADY M.A. CROSBIE 1966-1984

O.N. 308135 1,903/3,005g 869/1,828n
2,675/3,958d
308.1 x 49.4 x 22.9 feet
1976: 3,984g 2,561n 4,826d
118.7 x 15.0 x 6.5 metres
Oil engine 9-cyl. 4SCSA by Maschinenbau
Augsburg-Nürnberg A.G., Nürnberg, West
Germany geared to a controllable-pitch
propeller; 3,620 BHP,14 ¾ knots.
Two passengers
5.7.1965: Keel laid by Doxford and
Sunderland Shipbuilding and Engineering
Co. Ltd., Sunderland (Yard No. 872).
7.1.1966: Launched.
12.5.1966: Completed for the United
Baltic Corporation Ltd., London as

BALTIC VANGUARD.

17.9.1976: Arrived on the Tyne to be lengthened by 80 feet by Middle Dock, South Shields and converted into a container carrier for the Spanish trade.

1977: Renamed CORTES.

1978: Transferred to Canadian registry for charter to Chimo Line (C. A. Crosbie Shipping Co. Ltd., St. John's, Newfoundland, managers) and renamed LADY M.A. CROSBIE.

1984: Sold to Seafame Navigation Ltd. (S. Karydes), Nicosia, Cyprus, and renamed DAUPHINE.

1986: Managers became Chr. M. Sarlis and Co. M.C., later Sarlis Container Services S.A., Piraeus, Greece.

1995: Sold to Loraine Marine Inc., Panama (Seatrans Shipping S.a.r.l., Beirut, Lebanon) and renamed SHERYN M under the flag of St. Vincent and the Grenadines.

1999: Sold to Goldsea Shipping Services S.A. (Albert Ghosn), Beirut and renamed BLUE DOLPHIN under the flag of St. Vincent and the Grenadines.

3.2002: Sold to Jubilee Marine S.A., Majuro, Marshall Islands and renamed JULL II under the Panama flag.

7.2008: Still in existence.

38. BALTIC VIKING/ARCTIC VIKING 1967-1989

O.N. 334541 698/1,599g 432/1,154n 1,265/2,073d

74.5 x 12.6 x 4.1 metres.

Oil engine 8-cyl. 4SCSA by Motorenwerk Mannheim A.G.,

Top: *Baltic Vanguard.* [Turners (Photography) Limited/Newall Dunn collection]
Middle: *Cortes* at Middle Docks, South Shields. [John G. McCulley/Newall Dunn collection]
Bottom: *Lady M.A.Crosbie.* [René Beauchamp, Montreal]

Mannheim, West Germany; 2,200 BHP, 14 knots.

3.1.1967: Keel laid by Krogerwerft G.m.b.H., Rendsburg, West Germany (Yard No.1343).

15.4.1967: Launched.

29.6.1967: Completed for the United Baltic Corporation Ltd., London as BALTIC VIKING.

19.9.1970: Collided with and sank the West German motor vessel THURINGEN (424/1950) whilst transitting the Kiel Canal in fog. The latter was raised on 24.9.1970.

1981: Transferred to Canadian registry for charter to C. A. Crosbie Shipping Ltd., St John's, Newfoundland and renamed ARCTIC VIKING.

1989: Sold to C. A. Crosbie Shipping Ltd., St John's, Newfoundland.

2002: Sold to La Cooperative de Service le Compagnon, Port au Prince, Haiti and renamed LE COMPAGNON under the Panama flag.

2003: Renamed CLARA.

2004: Sold to Caribatlantic Shipping Inc., USA and renamed ARTIC.

6.2005: Sold to Karceo S.A., Panama and renamed ARTICO.

12.2007: Still in existence.

39. BALTIC VALIANT/LADY FRANKLIN 1970-1981

O.N. 338951 2,125g 1,018n 3,627d
103.4 x 15.8 x 5.9 metres.
Oil engine 9-cyl. 4SCSA by Maschinenbau Augsburg-Nürnberg A.G., Nürnberg, West Germany geared to a controllable-pitch propeller; 4,050 BHP. Thwartship thrust propeller forward.

17.1.1969: Keel laid by Krogerwerft G.m.b.H., Rendsburg, West Germany (Yard No. 1368).

5.8.1969: Launched.

18.2.1970: Completed for the United Baltic Corporation Ltd., London as BALTIC VALIANT.

1981: Transferred to Canadian registry

Top: *Baltic Viking.* [Newall Dunn collection]
Middle: *Arctic Viking on 23rd August 1998.* [René Beauchamp]
Bottom: *Baltic Valiant.* [Bengt Sjostrom/Roy Fenton collection]

Right: *Lady Franklin*, formerly the
Baltic Valiant, on 17th September 1997.
Colour would reveal a brilliant red hull.
[René Beauchamp, Montreal]

Bottom: *Baltic Enterprise*. [Newall
Dunn collection]

for charter to C. A. Crosbie Shipping Ltd.,
Montreal and renamed LADY FRANKLIN.
1989: Sold to C. A. Crosbie Shipping Ltd., St
John's, Newfoundland.
11.2003: Sold to Marine Management
Shipbrokerage Chartering Marine
Technology, Dubai, United Arab Republic
and renamed MARIAM III under the Panama
flag.
2004: Renamed MARIAM VI.
1.2005: Transferred to the flag of St. Kitts and
Nevis.
5.2006: Sold to Matco Trading LLC, Sharjah
(Veesham Shipping Inc., Dubai, managers).
24.10.2007: Arrived at Alang to be broken up.
11.2007: Work began.

40. BALTIC ENTERPRISE 1973-1975
Passenger/ro-ro cargo with stern and side
doors.
O.N. 360633 4,668g 1,574n 5,710d
137.5 x 22.4 x 6.6 metres.
1991: 12,110g 3,633n 5,710d.
Two oil engines 9-cyl. 4SCSA by
Stork-Werkspoor Diesel, Amsterdam,
Netherlands geared to twin controllable
pitch propellers; 10,500 BHP, 18 knots;
athwartship thrust propeller forward.
1971: Ordered from Rauma-Repola O/Y,
Rauma, Finland (Yard No. 209 and sister
to Yard Nos 207 and 208) as an option by
Finska Angfartygs Ab, Finland.
18.12.1972: Keel laid for Anglo-Finnish

Shipping Co. Ltd. (United Baltic
Corporation Ltd., managers), London.
6.3.1973: Launched.
20.6.1973: Completed.
1975: Transferred to the United Baltic
Corporation Ltd.
1983: Transferred to Charmian Shipping
Inc., Panama (United Baltic Corporation
Ltd., London) and renamed LIPA.
1987: Sold to Losinjska Plovidba
O.O.U.R. Brodarstvo, Rijeka, Yugoslavia.
1991: Transferred to Steel Hull Ltd.,
Monrovia, Liberia (Losinjska Plovidba
O.O.U.R. Brodarstvo, Rijeka, managers).
1999: Transferred to Croatian registry.
1.2008: Still in existence.

Baltic Enterprise. [Newall Dunn collection]

Baltic Progress. [Above: R Brzoza, below: Uwe Detlefsen collection]

41. BALTIC PROGRESS 1974-1975
Passenger/ro-ro cargo with stern and side doors.
O.N. 360960 4,668g 1,574n 5,710d
137.5 x 22.4 x 6.64 metres.
1994: 3,718g 1,460n 5,615d Length registered as 131.4 metres.
1995: 11,979g 5,480n 5,615d.
Two oil engines 9-cyl. 4SCSA by Stork-Werkspoor Diesel, Amsterdam, Netherlands geared to twin controllable pitch propellers; 10,500 BHP, 18 knots. Thwartship thrust propeller forward.
18.5.1973: Keel laid by Rauma-Repola O/Y, Rauma, Finland (Yard No. 216) for Anglo-Finnish Shipping Co. Ltd. (United Baltic Corporation Ltd., managers), London.
31.8.1973: Launched.
16.1.1974: Completed as BALTIC PROGRESS.
3.2.1974: Delivered.
1975: Transferred to the United Baltic

Corporation Ltd.
1989: Transferred to Andrew Weir Shipping Ltd.
1991: Transferred to Isle of Man registry.
1992: Sold to Clare Business Ltd., Bahamas (R. Strandly, Uitikon-Waldegg, Switzerland) (Goliat Shipping A/S, Oslo, Norway, managers) and renamed TYNE PROGRESS.
1994: Sold to Parkhaven Shipping Co. Ltd., Valetta, Malta (Dodekanisiaki Anonymos Naftiliaki Etairia, Rhodes, Greece) and renamed PARKHAVEN.
1995: Transferred to D.A.N.E. Sea Line (Dodekanisiaki Anonymos Naftiliaki Etairia, Rhodes, Greece) (Manad Navigation Co. Ltd., managers), Panama.
1998: Renamed VEERHAVEN.
1998: Sold to Strofades Dyo Shipping Ltd., Malta (Ionian Bridge Shipmanagement S.A. (Ioannis Georgoulias), Athens, Greece), and renamed STROFADES II.

7.2006: Sold to Southwestern Star Shipping Co. Ltd., La Paz, Mexico (Transportacion Maritima de California S.A. de C.V., Mazatlan, Mexico, managers) and renamed SAN DIEGO under the flag of Antigua and Barbuda.
1.2008: Still in existence.

42. STENA TENDER/GOYA 1976-1980
3,809g 1,614n 6,400d
144.1 x 18.1 x 5.7 metres.
1992: 3,985g 1,858n 3,775d.
1994: 9,085g 2,726n 3,775d.
Two Deutz RSBV12M540 vee-type oil engines 12-cyl. 4SCSA by Klöckner-Humboldt Deutz, Köln, West Germany geared to twin screw shafts with controllable pitch propellers; 11,999 BHP, 18 knots. Two athwartship thrust propellers forward.
12 berthed passengers.
23.4.1975: Keel laid by Osterreichische Schiffswerften A.G., Linz-Korneuburg, Korneuburg, Austria (Yard No. 709).
15.1.1976: Launched for Stena A.B., Sweden as STENA TENDER.
1976: Whilst awaiting completion sold to the United Baltic Corporation Ltd., London, and towed to Werft Nobiskrug G.m.b.H., Rendsburg, West Germany for lengthening and completion.
14.10.1977: Completed as GOYA.
1.1980: Sold to Federal Commerce and Navigation (1974) Ltd., Montreal, Canada.
3.1980: Renamed FEDERAL NOVA.
1980: Sold to Contrast Shipping Line Ltd. (R.B. Kirkconnell and Brother Ltd.) Georgetown, Grand Cayman and renamed CARIBBEAN SKY.
1981: Sold to C.A. Linea Manuare, La Guaira (C.A. Consolidada de Ferrys, Caracas), Venezuela and renamed MANAURE VII.
1982: Sold to Philippine Maritime Inc., Panama.

1982: Sold to Stringham Shipping Corporation, Lone Star Shipping Co. S.A., and Timber Shipping Inc., Monrovia, Liberia (Mare Schiffahrtskontor G.m.b.H. & Co. K.G., Bremen, Germany, managers) and renamed OYSTER BAY under the Panama flag.

1983: Sold to Cenargo Ltd. (Michael Hendry) (Denholm Ship Management Ltd., Glasgow, managers) and renamed VIKING TRADER.

1984: Converted to carry 40 berthed and 36 deck passengers.

1985: Owners became Cenargo Navigation Ltd. (Townsend Car Ferries Ltd., managers), London.

1986: Managers became Thoresen Car Ferries Ltd.

1987: Managers became P&O European Ferries (Portsmouth) Ltd.

1988: Sold to POETS Fleet Management Ltd., London.

1991: Transferred to Pandoro Ltd.

1996: Renamed LEOPARD.

1998: Managers became P&O Ship Management (Irish Sea) Ltd. and renamed EUROPEAN NAVIGATOR.

2003: Sold to Arab Bridge Maritime Co. and Salam International Transport and Trading Co. Ltd., Amman, Jordan and renamed BLACK IRIS.

1.2008: Still in existence.

The *Stena Tender* was completed as the *Goya* (top) in 1977 and then had a succession of names which included *Viking Trader* (middle) and *European Navigator* (bottom). *[Top: David Whiteside collection, middle: FotoFlite, bottom: Trevor Kidd]*

43. CERVANTES 1977-1979
O.N. 334273 1,470g 647n
301.5 x 44.3 x 15.9 feet
1970: 1,593g 735n
323.1 x 44.3 x 15. 9 feet
Oil engine 9-cyl. 4SCSA by Maschinenbau Augsburg-Nürnberg A.G., Augsburg, West Germany; 16 knots.
5.10.1967: Launched by Grangemouth Dockyard Co. Ltd., Grangemouth (Yard No. 539).
2.1968: Completed for Macandrews and Co. Ltd., London as CERVANTES.

1970: Lengthened and converted into a cellular container ship.
1977: Transferred to the United Baltic Corporation Ltd., London.
1979: Sold to Valani Shipping Co., Limassol, Cyprus (N. Adamakis, Piraeus, Greece) and renamed VALANI.

1982: Principal became Christaco Compania Naviera S.A. (T. Halkias, S. Ioannou and V. Atsidis), Piraeus.
5.1985: Sold to Erhardt G.m.b.H., Hamburg, Germany.
1985: Sold to Luisamar S.a.A. di Pomposo Achille (Pietro Lofaro Shipping Agency)

Naples, Italy and renamed MICHELE
PRIMO.
11.8.1976: Laid up at Vigo.
7.1987: Broken up at Vigo by Miguel
Martins Pereira.

44. CHURRUCA 1977-1979

O.N. 336973 1,455g 645n
301.5 x 44.3 x 15.9 feet
1970: 1,577g 728n
323.1 x 44.3 x 15. 9 feet
Oil engine 9-cyl. 4SCSA by Maschinenbau
Augsburg-Nürnberg A.G., Hamburg, West
Germany; 16 knots.
26.8.1968: Launched by Grangemouth
Dockyard Co. Ltd., Grangemouth (Yard
No. 540).
11.1968: Completed for Macandrews and
Co. Ltd., London as CHURRUCA.
1970: Lengthened and converted into a
cellular container ship.
1977: Transferred to the United Baltic
Corporation Ltd., London.
1979: Sold to Lisca Shipping Co. S.A.,
Panama (Alvar Olsson, Varberg, Sweden)
and renamed CONTMAR.
1984: Sold to Contmar Marine S.A.,
Panama City (Erik Thun A/B, Lidkoping,
Sweden).
1995: Sold to Malibu Navigation Ltd.,
Monrovia, Liberia (Naftotrade Shipping
and Commercial S.A. (Nikolaos Varvates),
Piraeus, Greece), renamed UNITY IX
and registered in St. Vincent and the
Grenadines.
11.2003: Sold to SBC Co. Ltd. (Shehadah
Maritime Co. Ltd., managers), Tartous,
Syria.
2.2004: Renamed FAWAZ S.
9.2006: Sold to FWSC Ltd., Marshall
Islands (Raouf Maritime Co., Tartous) and
registered in Batumi, Georgia.
3.2008: Still in existence.

Top: *Cervantes* and her sister *Churruca* were transferred from MacAndrews without
change on name in 1977. *[FotoFlite]*
Middle: *Baltic Osprey*. *[Uwe Detlefsen]*
Bottom: *Baltic Eagle*. *[R. Brzoza, Finland]*

45. BALTIC OSPREY 1977-1988

O.N. 367509 998g 464n 2,225d
88.3(BB) x 13.8 x 4.4 metres
Oil engine 8-cyl. 4SCSA by Motorenwerk
Mannheim A.G., Mannheim, West
Germany; 2,400 BHP. Thwartship thrust
propeller forward.
5.10.1971: Keel laid by Jadewerft
G.m.b.H., Wilhelmshaven, West Germany
(Yard No. 129) for Deidrich Sander, West
Germany as KALKGRUND.
24.6.1972: Launched for Nad Prince
Reederei und Schiffahrtsgesellschaft
m.b.H. K.G., Hamburg, West Germany.
18.10.1972: Completed.
1974: Renamed NAD PRINCE.
1975: Renamed ATLANTIC VISCOUNT.
1977: Acquired by the United Baltic
Corporation Ltd., London and renamed
BALTIC OSPREY.
1988: Sold to Fareast Faith Navigation
S.A., Panama (Wah Tung Shipping Agency
Co. Ltd., Hong Kong) and renamed
FAREAST FAITH.
1991: Sold to the Government of the
People's Republic of China (Guangdong
Province Shantou Special Economic Zone
Joint Shipping Co. Ltd.), Shantou, People's
Republic of China and renamed LONG
TONG.
2.2.1997: Sank following a collision
with the Chinese motor vessel MIN DA
(499/1970) in position 24.08 north by
118.06 east whilst on a voyage from Hong
Kong to Xiamen.

46. BALTIC EAGLE 1979-2002

Ro-ro cargo with twin stern door/ramps.
O.N. 388177 14,738g 4,421n 9,450d
137.1 x 26.0 x 8.2 metres
Two Werkspoor 9TM410-type oil engines
9-cyl. 4SCSA by Stork-Werkspoor Diesel
B.V., Amsterdam, Netherlands; 13,000
BHP, geared to twin controllable-pitch
propellers. Thwartship thrust controllable
pitch propeller forward.
22.12.1978: Keel laid by Rauma-Repola
O/Y, Rauma/Raumo, Finland (Yard No.
258) for the United Baltic Corporation
Ltd., London.
6.4.1979: Launched.
19.10.1979: Completed as BALTIC
EAGLE.
1989: Transferred to Andrew Weir
Shipping Ltd.
1991: Transferred to Isle of Man registry.
2002: Sold to Callaghan Overseas Ltd.,
London (Jay Management Corporation,
Athens, Greece) and renamed OLYMPIC
STAR.
2002: Renamed SEAWHEEL HUMBER.
2005: Renamed BALTIC EAGER.
12.2007: Still in existence.

47. BALTIC TERN 1989-2003

316 TEU container ship with fixed guides.
O.N. 717029 3,896g 1,566n 3,754d 106.6
(BB) x 16.2 x 5.4 metres.
Burmeister & Wain 5L35MC-type oil
engine 5-cyl. 2SCSA by Sang Yong Heavy

Baltic Tern (top). The view of the *Baltic Eider* (above) emphasises the amount of space available on the top deck for the stowage of cargo. *[Upper: Uwe Detlefsen collection, lower: Newall Dunn collection]*

Industries Co. Ltd., Changwon, Korea geared
to a controllable pitch propeller; 3,800 BHP.
Thwartship thrust propeller forward.
24.6.1988: Keel laid by Daedong
Shipbuilding Co. Ltd., Busan, Korea (Yard
No. 325) for the United Baltic Corporation
Ltd., London.
2.9.1988: Launched for Andrew Weir and
Co. Ltd., London
20.10.1989: Completed for Andrew Weir
Shipping Ltd., London as BALTIC TERN.
1991: Transferred to Isle of Man registry.
2003: Sold to CMA CGM (The French
Line), Marseille, France (CMA CGM (UK)
Shipping Ltd., London, managers).
1.2008: Still in existence.

48. BALTIC EIDER 1989-1999

Twin screw ro-ro cargo vessel with stern
door/ramp.
O.N. 717408 20,865g 6,259n 13,866d
157.7 (BB) x 25.3 x 8.5 metres.
Port: Wartsila 9R46 type oil engine 9-cyl.
4SCSA by O/Y Wartsila A/B, Turku/Abo,

Finland geared to a controllable pitch
propeller; 11,073 BHP.
Starboard: Wartsila 6R46 type oil engine
6-cyl. 4SCSA by O/Y Wartsila A/B, Turku/
Abo, Finland geared to a controllable pitch
propeller; 7,382 BHP.
15.12.1988: Keel laid by Hyundai Heavy
Industries Co. Ltd., Ulsan, Korea (Yard
No. 637) for the United Baltic Corporation
Ltd., London.
30.9.1989: Launched for Andrew Weir and
Co. Ltd., London
1.12.1989: Completed for Andrew Weir
Shipping Ltd., London as BALTIC EIDER.
1991: Transferred to Isle of Man registry.
1999: Sold to Harpa Shipping M/V Palau
Ltd. (Harren & Partners G.m.b.H. & Co.
m.s. 'Baltic Eider'), Bremen (Andrew Weir
Shipping Ltd., London, managers).
1.2005: Sold to Morbihannaise et Nantaise
de Navigation, Nantes, France and
renamed MN EIDER under the flag of
French Antarctic Territories.
10.2007: Still in existence.

MANAGED VESSELS

Ships managed by United Baltic Corporation Ltd. on behalf of subsidiaries are included in the main fleet list. In cases of minor discrepancies between British and Danish records (typically of tonnages, horsepower, speeds and casualty numbers), the British figures have been quoted.

M1. PERU 1940-1941
O.N. 167841 6,961g 4,436n 10,325d
425.3 x 55.2 x 27.5 feet
Two 6-cyl. 4SCSA oil engines by
A/S Burmeister & Wain's Maskin- og
Skibsbyggeri, Copenhagen, Denmark
geared to twin screws; 717 NHP, 3,100 IHP,
3,584 BHP, 11.25 knots.
24.11.1915: Keel laid.
24.6.1916: Launched by A/S Burmeister
& Wain's Maskin-og Skibsbyggeri,
Copenhagen, Denmark (Yard No. 306).
22.8.1916: Ran trials and delivered to A/S
Det Østasiatiske Kompagni, Copenhagen,
Denmark as PERU.
11. 4.1940: Arrived at Aden following the
German occupation of Denmark and later
requisitioned by the British Government.
2.5.1940: Registered in the ownership of
the Ministry of Shipping (United Baltic
Corporation Ltd., managers), London.
11.7.1940: Damaged during an air attack at
Portland Harbour.
8.1941: Owners became the Ministry of
War Transport, London.
13.11.1941: Torpedoed and sunk by the
German submarine U 126 in position 01.30
north by 13.20 west whilst on a voyage
from Calcutta and Table Bay to Freetown
and the U.K. with general cargo including
groundnuts and pig iron. The crew of 43
and two gunners were saved.
24.2.1942: Register closed.

M2. CHILE 1940-1942
O.N. 173041 6,956g 4,426n 10,325d
425.3 x 55.2 x 35.4 feet

Peru. [John Marsh collection]

Above: Chile. [John Marsh collection]
Bottom: Siam. [F. W. Hawks/Newall Dunn collection]

Two 6-cyl. 4SCSA oil engines by
A/S Burmeister & Wain's Maskin-og
Skibsbyggeri, Copenhagen, Denmark
geared to twin screws; 6,200 BHP, 11.15
knots.
25. 5.1915: Keel laid.
17.11.1915: Launched by A/S Burmeister
& Wain's Maskin-og Skibsbyggeri,
Copenhagen, Denmark (Yard No. 303).
21.12.1915: Ran trials and delivered to A/S

Det Østasiatiske Kompagni, Copenhagen,
Denmark as CHILE.
4.1940: Arrived at Singapore following the
German occupation of Denmark and later
requisitioned by the British Government.
14.5.1940: Registered in the ownership of
the Ministry of Shipping (United Baltic
Corporation Ltd., managers), London.
8.1941: Owners became the Ministry of
War Transport, London.
7.6.1942: Torpedoed and sunk by the
Italian submarine LEONARDO DA VINCI
in position 04.17 north by 13.48 west whilst
on a voyage from Calcutta and Table Bay
to the Mersey via Freetown with a cargo
of groundnuts, pig iron and cotton seed.
There were five killed amongst the crew of
43 and one gunner.
26.6.1942: Register closed.

M3. SIAM II 1940-1942
O.N. 173043 6,637g 4,223n
410.0 x 55.2 x 27.5 feet
Two 8-cyl. 4SCSA oil engines by
A/S Burmeister & Wain's Maskin-og
Skibsbyggeri, Copenhagen, Denmark
geared to twin screws; 842 NHP, 4,210
BHP, 11.25 knots.
5.8.1912: Keel laid.
5. 2.1913: Launched at the third attempt
by A/S Burmeister & Wain's Maskin-og

Skibsbyggeri, Copenhagen, Denmark (Yard No. 287).

8.4.1913: Ran trials and delivered to A/S Det Østasiatiske Kompagni, Copenhagen, Denmark as SIAM.

16.4.1940: Arrived at Singapore following the German occupation of Denmark and later requisitioned by the British Government.

15.5.1940: Registered in the ownership of the Ministry of Shipping (United Baltic Corporation Ltd., managers), London as SIAM II.

8.1941: Owners became the Ministry of War Transport, London.

30.9.1942: Torpedoed and sunk by the German submarine U 506 in position 03.25 north by 15.46 west whilst on a voyage from Alexandria and Table Bay to Freetown and the UK with general cargo including cotton, grain and copper. The 37 crew and two gunners survived.

16.10.1942: Register closed.

M4. PANAMA 1940-1945
O.N. 172763 6,650g 4,250n

410.0 x 55.2 x 27.5 feet
Two 6-cyl. 4SCSA oil engines by A/S Burmeister & Wain's Maskin-og Skibsbyggeri, Copenhagen, Denmark geared to twin screw shafts; 717 NHP, 3,100 IHP, 3,584 BHP, 11.25 knots.

24.6.1914: Keel laid.

16.1.1915: Launched by A/S Burmeister & Wain's Maskin-og Skibsbyggeri, Copenhagen, Denmark (Yard No. 299).

6.3.1915: Ran trials and delivered to A/S Det Østasiatiske Kompagni, Copenhagen, Denmark as PANAMA.

9.4.1940: At Manila at the time of the German occupation of Denmark and subsequently sailed to Hong Kong where she was requisitioned by the British Government.

22.5.1940: Registered in the ownership of the Ministry of Shipping (United Baltic Corporation Ltd., managers), London.

8.1941: Owners became the Ministry of War Transport, London.

11.4.1945: Capsized and sank in position 44.30 north by 33.30 west while on a voyage from Cardiff to Philadelphia in

ballast. Her crew of 45 were lost.

10.5.1945: Register closed.

M5. KINA II 1940-1946
O.N. 167537 9,823g 6,234n
489.3 x 65.2 x 38.8 feet
8-cyl. 2SCDA oil engine by A/S Burmeister & Wain's Maskin-og Skibsbyggeri, Copenhagen, Denmark; 1,642 NHP, 8,210 BHP, 16 knots.

12. 5.1938: Keel laid.

5.11.1938: Launched by Nakskov Skibsvaerft A/S, Nakskov, Denmark (Yard No. 87).

18.1.1939: Ran trials and delivered to A/S Det Østasiatiske Kompagni, Copenhagen, Denmark as KINA.

9.4.1940: At the time of the German occupation of Denmark on a voyage from Odense to New York when captured by a British destroyer and ordered to Kirkwall, where she arrived the next day and was subsequently requisitioned by the British Government.

27.5.1940: Registered in the ownership of the Ministry of Shipping (United Baltic Corporation Ltd., managers), London as KINA II.

8.1941: Owners became the Ministry of War Transport, London.

4.10.1945: Register closed.

18.10.1945: Redelivered to A/S Det Østasiatiske Kompagni, Copenhagen, Denmark and reverted to KINA.

25.12.1947: Struck a submerged rock and sank during a typhoon in a position 11.58 north by 124.20 east whilst on a voyage from Tabaco to Calbayog in the Philippines with a cargo of copra and 13 passengers. 34 lives were lost.

M6. DANMARK 1941-1942
O.N. 130116 8,391g 5,348n 12,350d
460.1 x 59.7 x 35.6 feet
Two 6-cyl. 4SCSA oil engines by A/S Burmeister & Wain's Maskin-og Skibsbyggeri, Copenhagen, Denmark geared to twin screws; 510 NHP, 4,914 BHP, 12.75 knots.

19.09.1924: Keel laid.

12.09.1925: Launched by A/S Burmeister & Wain's Maskin-og Skibsbyggeri, Copenhagen, Denmark (Yard No. 537).

5.12.1925: Ran trials and delivered to A/S Det Østasiatiske Kompagni, Copenhagen, Denmark as DANMARK.

18.4.1940: Taken as a prize by the British authorities at Colombo following the German occupation of Denmark.

29.5.1940: Registered in the ownership of the Ministry of Shipping (United Baltic Corporation Ltd., managers), London.

8.1941: Owners became the Ministry of War Transport, London.

30.7.1942: Sunk by gunfire from the German submarine U 130 in position 07.00 north by 24.19 west whilst on a voyage from Durban and Table Bay to Trinidad, Halifax and the UK, in ballast. The crew of 47 and two gunners survived.

16.9.1942: Register closed.

Above: *Panama. [John Marsh collection]*
Below: *Kina II. [John Marsh collection]*

M7. AMERIKA 1940-1943

O.N. 167544 10,218g 6,243n
465.4 x 62.2 x 37.2 feet
6-cyl. 2SCDA oil engine by A/S Burmeister
& Wain's Maskin-og Skibsbyggeri,
Copenhagen, Denmark; 1,236 NHP, 6,180
BHP, 15 knots.
56 passengers.
22.12.1928: Keel laid.
21.08.1929: Launched by A/S Burmeister
& Wain's Maskin-og Skibsbyggeri,
Copenhagen, Denmark (Yard No. 559).
21.1.1930: Ran trials and delivered to A/S
Det Østasiatiske Kompagni, Copenhagen,
Denmark as AMERIKA.
9.4.1940: At the time of the German
occupation of Denmark on a voyage from
the USA to Copenhagen via Gothenburg
and proceeded to Liverpool where she was
requisitioned by the British Government.
30.5.1940: Registered in the ownership
of the Ministry of War Transport (United
Baltic Corporation Ltd., managers), London.
8.1941: Owners became the Ministry of
War Transport, London.
22.4.1943: Torpedoed and sunk by the
German submarine U 306 in position
57.30 north by 42.50 west while sailing in
Convoy HX 234 on a voyage from Halifax
to Liverpool with general cargo including
metal, flour, meat and mail. Lost were 42 of
the crew of 72, seven of the 15 gunners, and
37 of the 53 passengers.
12.5.1943: Register closed.

M8. BORINGIA 1940-1942

O.N. 173047 5,821g 3,608n 8,150d
426.5 x 57.2 x 25.5 feet
Two 7-cyl. 4SCSA oil engines by
A/S Burmeister & Wain's Maskin-og

Danmark. [John Marsh collection]

Skibsbyggeri, Copenhagen, Denmark,
geared to twin screw shafts; 827 NHP, 4,140
BHP, 14 knots.
15.6.1929: Keel laid.
31.12.1929: Launched by A/S Burmeister
& Wain's Maskin-og Skibsbyggeri,
Copenhagen, Denmark (Yard No. 560).
12.4.1930: Ran trials and delivered to A/S
Det Østasiatiske Kompagni, Denmark as
BORINGIA.
9.4.1940: At Marseilles at the time of the
German occupation of Denmark.
18.4.1940: Requisitioned by the French
Government, Paris (Compagnie de
Messageries Maritimes, Marseilles, France,
managers).
25.7.1940: Following the fall of France
requisitioned by British authorities at
Singapore.
7.8.1940: Registered in the ownership of
the Ministry of Shipping (United Baltic

Corporation Ltd., managers), London.
8.1941: Owners became the Ministry of War
Transport, London.
2.8.1942: Whilst on a voyage from Cape
Town to the UK collided with the steamer
KALEWA (4,389/1940) which sank.
7.10.1942: Torpedoed and sunk by the
German submarine U 159 in position 35.09
south by 16.32 east whilst on a voyage
from Haifa and Table Bay for the UK via
Hampton Roads with a cargo including
potash and cotton. Lost were 28 of the crew
of 55 and four of the five gunners. Seven
members of the crew were lost when the
steamer CLAN MACTAVISH (7,631/1921)
was torpedoed the next day. The survivors
were finally picked up by steamer
MATHERAN (8,007/1942). The Japanese
submarine I-159 also involved in the attack
reported the BORINGIA as the SELANDIA.
18.11.1942: Register closed.

Amerika at Alexandria, Egypt in 1941. *[National Maritime Museum N.32760]*

Boringia. [Danish Maritime Museum]

M9. ERRIA 1940-1945

O.N. 173049 8,786g 5,582n
440.3 x 62.2 x 33.7 feet
Two 6-cyl. 2SCDA oil engines by
A/S Burmeister & Wain's Maskin-og
Skibsbyggeri, Copenhagen, Denmark
geared to twin screw shafts; 1,283 NHP,
9,300 IHP, 6,160 BHP, 15 knots.
74 passengers.
1.2.1931: Keel laid.
5.9.1931: Launched by Nakskov
Skibsvaerft A/S, Nakskov, Copenhagen
(Yard No. 50).
31.1.1931: Ran trials and delivered to A/S
Det Østasiatiske Kompagni, Copenhagen,
Denmark as ERRIA.
5.1940: Arrived at Vancouver following
the German occupation of Denmark and
requisitioned by the British Authorities.

13.8.1940: Registered in the ownership of
the Ministry of Shipping (United Baltic
Corporation Ltd., managers), London.
21/22.12.1940: Damaged during an air
attack at Liverpool.
8.1941: Owners became the Ministry of
War Transport, London.
6.9.1945: Register closed.
5.4.1946: Redelivered to A/S Det
Østasiatiske Kompagni, Copenhagen,
Denmark.
20.12.1951: Fire broke out in the
accommodation whilst on a voyage from
Portland, Oregon to San Francisco with
passengers and general cargo. The fire
spread rapidly and passengers and crew
abandoned the ship in the lifeboats. Eight
passengers and three crew members lost
their lives.

16.5.1952: Left Portland for Rotterdam in
tow of Dutch tug ZWARTE ZEE (836/1933).
5.7.1952: Arrived at Schiedam and rebuilt as
a cargo ship by Wilton-Fijenoord N.V..
2.1953: Rebuilding completed
16.5.1962: Sold to Okaya and Co. Ltd.,
Tokyo for demolition.
21.5.1962: Arrived at Osaka.
18.6.1962: Work commenced by Sangyo
Shinko K.K. at Izimiohtsu near Osaka.

M10. MALAYA II 1940-1941

O.N. 165982 8,651g 5,515n 13,400d
445.8 x 60.3 x 39.1 feet
Two 6-cyl. 4SCSA oil engines by
A/S Burmeister & Wain's Maskin-og
Skibsbyggeri, Copenhagen, Denmark geared
to twin screw shafts; 987 NHP, 4,934 BHP,
12 knots.
10.1.1920: Keel laid.
5.2.1921: Launched by A/S Burmeister
& Wain's Maskin-og Skibsbyggeri,
Copenhagen, Denmark (Yard No. 316).
14.7.1921: Ran trials and delivered to A/S
Det Østasiatiske Kompagni, Denmark as
MALAYA.
21.12.1930: Run into by the United States
steamer GEORGE WASHINGTON
(23,788/1908) whilst anchored at Chulau
during dense fog whilst on a voyage from
Le Havre to Hamburg with a cargo of soya
beans. Her holds flooded and she was
beached on the north bank of the River Elbe
to prevent sinking.
22.12.1930: Refloated and arrived at
Hamburg.
9.4.1940: At Bahia Blanca at the time of
the German occupation of Denmark and
subsequently requisitioned by the British
Government

The armed *Erria*. [Newall Dunn collection]

7.8.1940: Renamed MALAYA II.
15.8.1940: Registered in the ownership of the Ministry of Shipping (United Baltic Corporation Ltd., managers), London.
8.1941: Owners became the Ministry of War Transport, London.
26.6.1941: Torpedoed and sunk by the German submarine U 564 in position 59.56 north by 30.35 west while sailing in convoy HX 133 on a voyage from Montreal and Halifax to Cardiff with a cargo of metal, wheat and explosives. Of the 45 on board, 39 were lost.
30.10.1941: Register closed.

M11. AFRIKA 1940-1943
O.N. 130117 8597g 5,469n 13,260d
445.8 x 60.3 x 39.1 feet
Two 6-cyl. 4SCSA oil engines by A/S Burmeister & Wain's Maskin-og Skibsbyggeri, Copenhagen, Denmark geared to twin screw shafts; 989 NHP, 4,934 BHP, 12 knots.
12.3.1918: Keel laid.
11.12.1919: Launched by A/S Burmeister & Wain's Maskin-og Skibsbyggeri, Copenhagen, Denmark (Yard No. 314).
27.3.1920: Ran trials and delivered to A/S Det Østasiatiske Kompagni, Copenhagen, Denmark as AFRIKA.
14.4.1940: On a voyage from Aden to Colombo following the German occupation of Denmark captured by the cruiser HMAS HOBART and taken to Colombo where she was requisitioned by the British authorities.
2.12.1940: Registered in the ownership of the Ministry of Shipping (United Baltic Corporation Ltd., managers), London.
8.1941: Owners became the Ministry of War Transport, London.
7.2.1943: Torpedoed and sunk by the German submarine U 402 in position 55.16 north by 26.31 west whilst on a voyage from Halifax to Liverpool in convoy SC 118 with general cargo including 5,000 tons of steel. Lost were 19 of the crew of 49 and four of the nine gunners.
8.3.1943: Register closed.

Bintang. [John Marsh collection]

M12. BINTANG 1940-1942
O.N. 172767 2,779g 1,725n 3,450d
284 8 x 44.2 x 25.4 feet
Two 6-cyl. 4SCSA oil engines by A/S Burmeister & Wain's Maskin-og Skibsbyggeri, Copenhagen, Denmark geared to twin screw shafts; 2,264 BHP, 10.5 knots.
8.1.1920: Keel laid.
19.11.1921: Launched by Nakskov Skibsvaerft A/S, Nakskov, Denmark (Yard No. 4).
28.5.1922: Completed trials and delivered to A/S Det Østasiatiske Kompagni, Copenhagen, Denmark as BINTANG.
9.4.1940: On a voyage from the Panama Canal to Bangkok with 90,000 cases of petrol at the time of the German occupation of Denmark. The crew decided to sail to Hong Kong.
5.1940: Arrived at Hong Kong and later requisitioned by British Authorities. Subsequently registered in the ownership of the Ministry of Shipping (United Baltic Corporation Ltd., managers), London.

8.1941: Owners became the Ministry of War Transport, London.
22.2.1942: Sunk by Axis aircraft in position 31.50 north by 26.10 east whilst on a voyage in convoy from Alexandria to Tobruk with cased petrol. Of the crew of 37, four gunners, a signalman and 12 of the crew were lost.

M13. NANCY 1943
O.N. 175794 1,153g 678n
231.5 x 34.6 x 14.1 feet
M550/4000-type steam turbine by Maskinfabrikken Atlas A/S, Copenhagen, Denmark; 108 NHP, 620 IHP, 9 knots.
1928: C.4-cyl. by Christiansen and Meyer, Harburg, Germany; 108 NHP.
22.4.1921: Launched by Schiffbau-Gesellschaft Unterweser m.b.H., Lehe, Germany (Yard No 180) for A/S Vesterhavet (J. Lauritzen), Copenhagen, Denmark as NANCY.
1921: Completed.
1928: Re-engined by Nakskov Skibsvaerft A/S, Nakskov, Denmark.
8.5.1928: Ran re-acceptance trials.
9.4.1940: Following the German occupation of Denmark captured by Royal Naval vessel and escorted to Kirkwall. Taken over by the Ministry of Shipping.
5.1940: Time-chartered to Transports Maritimes, France, renamed SAINT THOMAS and departed from Kirkwall for Rouen where she was armed.
22.6.1940: Following the collapse of France interned by the Portugese authorities when she called at Lisbon for supplies during a voyage from Brest to Casablanca. Subsequently transferred to Danish registry, renamed NANCY and laid up.
12.3.1943: Sold to Switzerland.
20.7.1943: Sold to A/S Vesterhavet (J. Lauritzen), Denmark.
23.11.1943: Taken over by British authorities.
26.11.1943: Registered in the ownership of the Ministry of War Transport (United

Nancy at Bristol in peacetime. [George Scott collection]

Fort St. Croix photographed by the United States Coast Guard on 1st February 1944. *[Ships in Focus]*

Baltic Corporation Ltd., managers), London.
13.12.1943: Managers became John Kelly Ltd., Belfast.
11.9.1945: Register closed on return to Rederiet 'Ocean' (J. Lauritzen), Copenhagen, Denmark.
8.1.1946: Renamed NANCY LAU.
29.9.1947: Sold to Rederiet Henckel & Schander (Ingolf N. Schander, manager), Veddige, Sweden and renamed HAFSTEN.
12.6.1948: Manager became Hugo Trolle-Henckel.
27.11.1948: Manager became Carl-Otto Pernlov.
11.12.1952: Sold to J.H.T. Schupp, Hamburg, West Germany and renamed JOHANNES SCHUPP.
17.11.1958: Arrived at Hamburg and subsequently sold to Eisen and Metall K.G. Lehr & Co., Hamburg.
29.1.1959: Delivered at Bremerhaven for demolition.

M14. FORT ST. CROIX 1944-1946
O.N. 169769 7,160g 4,245n
424.6 x 57.2 x 34.9 feet

T.3-cyl. by John Inglis Co. Ltd., Toronto, Canada; 229 NHP, 2,500 IHP, 11 knots.
8.12.1943: Completed by Burrard Dry Dock Co. Ltd., Vancouver, British Colombia, Canada (Yard No. 193) for the Government of the Dominion of Canada for bare-boat charter to the UK.
24.2.1944: Registered in the ownership of the Ministry of War Transport (United Baltic Corporation Ltd., managers), London as FORT ST. CROIX.
24.7.1946: Transferred to the Minister of Reconstruction and Supply (Government of Canada) (Park Steamship Co. Ltd., Montreal, managers).
6.11.1946: Sold to the Argonaut Navigation Co. Ltd. (John C. Yemelos, manager), Montreal.
4.3.1947: Renamed ARGOVIC.
13.4.1949: Register closed on sale to Companhia Naviera Coronado S.A., Panama (A. Lusi Ltd., London, managers) and renamed VASSILIS.
1959: Renamed YIOSONAS and transferred to the Greek flag.
1966: Managers became J.C. Carras and Sons

(Shipbrokers) Ltd., London.
22.5.1967: Delivered to Osaka for demolition.
10.8.1967: Breaking up began at Shodo Island by Sanoyasu Shoji K.K.

M15. KAWARTHA PARK 1946-1947
O.N. 175571 7,151g 4,214n
424.7 x 57.2 x 34.9 feet
T.3-cyl. by the Dominion Engineering Works Ltd., Montreal, Canada; 2,500 IHP.
27.6.1944: Completed by Marine Industries Ltd., Sorel, Quebec, Canada (Yard No. 132) for the Government of the Dominion of Canada (Park Steamship Co. Ltd., Montreal, managers) as KAWARTHA PARK.
9.1946: Chartered to the Ministry of Transport (United Baltic Corporation Ltd., managers), London.
1.1947: Sub-chartered to the South American Saint Line Ltd., Cardiff, which assumed management.
1948: Managers became Andrew Crawford and Co. Ltd., Glasgow.
1949: Sold to Kawartha Steamship Co. Ltd. (Counties Ship Management Co. Ltd., managers), London.
1950: Renamed HAVERTON HILL.
1955: Managers became Papachristidis Co. Ltd. and renamed GRAND HERMINE.
1960: Sold to Canuk Lines Ltd. (Papachristidis Shipping Ltd., managers), Montreal, Canada and renamed CANUK TRADER.
1965: Sold to Doreen Steamship Corporation SA, Panama (Quincy Chuang, Hong Kong) (Wheelock, Marden and Co. Ltd., managers, Hong Kong) and renamed ELIZA under the Liberian flag.
1963: Manager became Hong Kong Shipowners and Managers Co. Ltd. (Quincy Chuang), Hong Kong.
1968: Demolished by Fuji, Marden and Co. Ltd., at Hong Kong.

Kawartha Park. [Ships in Focus]

A BALTIC CRUISE IN 1938

For over 50 years, until his death in 1977, Commander Jeffrey Curtis RNR had a keen interest in merchant shipping. A close friend of Laurence Dunn and instigator of the Soviet and Comecom Merchant Ships recognition books, Jeff Curtis was also an excellent photographer. Between 4th and 16th July 1938 he took a cruise on *Baltallinn* from London to Tallinn, the capital of Estonia, and these are a selection of photographs taken during this trip. *[All images courtesy of the Newall Dunn collection]*

An itinerary and a poster (right).
Baltallinn's Captain Bulmer (below left) chatting with his Chief Officer Brown.
Jeff Curtis (5th from the left) with his fellow passengers (below right) including a young boy, Peter Bulmer, who may have been Captain Bulmer's son.

Lifeboat drill on 5th July. Left is Peter Bulmer wearing the Board of Trade standard life jacket.

Relaxing in deck chairs and playing deck games (above left). The arrival of the Kiel Canal pilot at Cuxhaven (left) and keeping cool using the ship's hose (above) on the Kiel Canal whilst the ship was tied up. Note the cars stowed on the hatches.

Kiel Nordhaven (above) with *Glückauf* (1,061/1907) of Kiel, owned by Zerssen und Co. alongside the wharf. Note the large swastika flag. The *Baltallinn* at Tallinn (below left) and passing *Baltanglia* in the Kiel Canal (below right).

At Hull (far left) on the homebound voyage and dropping the Humber Pilot on 15th July (left). Note the Humber Pilot vessel in the background. A tight squeeze (above) berthing at Wilson's Wharf, Southwark on 16th July at the end of the voyage in the Pool of London.

HOWDENS OF LARNE

W. J. Harvey

The port of Larne has played an important role in the commercial life, not only of East Antrim, but also of the region of Northern Ireland as a whole. Through it over the years has flowed a substantial part of the sea passenger and container traffic between Northern Ireland and the mainland. The main traffic nowadays comprises trailers, cars and passengers via P&O services to Cairnryan and Fleetwood. A few years ago Stena deserted Larne in favour of Belfast with the introduction of their new high-speed service. However, the additional mileage involved and the need for road vehicles to negotiate Belfast's rush-hour traffic proved disastrous for shippers, and forced Stena to consider re-activating their conventional Stranraer link, whilst leaving their high-speed service running to Belfast.

For the tourist Larne is the gateway to the famous Antrim Coast Road and the glens of Antrim. For the cargo shipper, it is a port which has changed dramatically over the past 30 or so years.

Larne since the sixties

The container became a common means of transport and Larne rose to the challenge to become a leading lift on-lift off container port. Also around that time the British Railways service to Stranraer saw the introduction of new car ferries. Atlantic Steam Navigation operated ro-ro cargo vessels as well as lift on–lift off container carriers. As cargo handling became more efficient the lift on–lift off services of both Atlantic Steam Navigation and Coast Lines gave way to the large ro-ro freight ferries carrying wheeled trailers which made for quicker turn-round times.

The size of passenger/car ferries also increased as trade grew. Although the political unrest in Northern Ireland saw a decline in tourist passenger traffic, the services held their own and indeed flourished as more road freight was carried in the vacant car deck space. Although the civilian trade had fallen away, the military regularly took deck space for freight and troop movements so the ferry operators were able to show a reasonably balanced account sheet.

Eventually all the normal break-bulk general cargoes were handled by ro-ro ferry and there was no longer a need for dockside cranes in the main port area. However, Larne Lough was home to some privately-owned berths further inland. Magheramorne, owned by the Portland Cement Group, served a cement works and attracted coastal craft of up to around 2,000 tons deadweight. Across Larne Lough opposite the ferry berths are the power station berths that once saw a stream of Kelly colliers providing coal for the station furnaces. After these were converted to oil fuel, a 20,000-ton deadweight tanker every few weeks replaced the colliers. Even that trade has since reduced with the opening of a new power station on the shores of Belfast Lough.

The other berth in which we are interested is Bank Quay (formerly Foster's Quay), home for many years of Howdens Ltd., coal and oil merchants.

Smiley and his nephews

The story of Howdens goes back to around 1830 when one John Smiley of Inver, Larne began what became the prosperous coal and grain merchant business of John Smiley and Sons. It operated from Foster's Quay, although its offices were at Dunluce Street, Larne. Subsequently John Smiley sold the business to three of his nephews, John, Charles and Matthew Howden who restyled the business as Howden Brothers. Two of the brothers had ships registered under their own name (see fleet list).

Other Smiley family members were living in Callowhill, Paisley, Scotland some of whom were involved in other shipping enterprises. Hugh H. Smiley, originally from Larne, had operated sailing vessels but by then was operating several steamers. He was also involved with the Carnlough Lime Company. Both concerns operated vessels with local historical names from the Larne area such as *Olderfleet*, *Dalriada* and *Latharna*. By the turn of the century all three brothers had died and control of the business had passed to William J. R. Harbinson and Charles L. MacKean, both nephews of the Howden brothers and so maintained the family link.

John S. Howden had business interests elsewhere, including investment in the newly-formed Shamrock Shipping Co. Ltd. This Larne-based company was the result of the restructuring of the group of single ship companies controlled by Thomas Jack. John S. Howden was appointed to the board of that new concern, a position he held until his death.

Through their new directorship, Howdens' business thrived and steadily their old vessels were disposed of as a fleet of purpose-built colliers was assembled, not only under direct ownership, but also indirectly through registration under various individual partners.

In 1912 the owner of Larne Harbour, William Chaine (who was also involved with the Shamrock Shipping Co. Ltd.) decided to dispose of the harbour business. At the first meeting of the new harbour company on 31st July 1912 it was agreed that the nominal capital should be £65,000 in £10 shares. Of the shareholders listed, the MacKean family held £11,000; William J. R. Harbinson £3,500 and Charles L. MacKean and William J. R. Harbinson – trading as Howden Brothers – jointly held £10,000, giving a total holding of £24,500. Charles L. MacKean was appointed Chairman, a position held until his death in 1943.

An 11-ship order

At the close of 1914, a bold step was taken when a series of 11 colliers was ordered from A. Jeffrey and Company's shipyard at Alloa. Of varying sizes the vessels (yard numbers 14 to 24) would not only keep the shipyard fully occupied for almost six years but would also more than meet Howden's anticipated requirements for years to come. The directors, it was stated, had decided that part of the order be placed as a form of speculation. With the outbreak of war they possibly foresaw the difficulty in obtaining building space coupled with an opportunity to offer vessels for resale at a premium.

As it happened, the two large sister vessels that had been ordered continually caused pangs of doubt, being almost twice the size of vessels normally owned by Howdens. Therefore, to reduce the risk, it was decided that yard number 17, proposed as *Magheramorne* but not yet commenced, would

Right: *Collin* was sold in 1919, after being raised following a collision. She is seen at Preston in the colours of Monroe Brothers. *[J. and M. Clarkson]*

Below: *Black Rock*, seen in the colours of her original owner, Alfred Rowland, was considered for purchase in 1915, but instead she remained with the company that repaired her, William Thomas of Amlwch, becoming *Eleth*. She foundered in the Irish Sea during February 1951. *[J. and M. Clarkson]*

be cancelled, leaving her sister *Islandmagee* (yard number 20) to be built at a later date, giving time for re-appraisal of the company's requirements. Subsequently, following discussions with the shipyard, Howdens withdrew from the contract and she was offered for resale by the shipyard, being launched as *Crosshands* for her new owners. It is interesting to note that the shipbuilder constructed two vessels originally ordered as *War Cam* and *War Colne* by the Shipping Controller to identical dimensions and machinery to the cancelled Howden vessels. An easy option would be for the shipbuilder to utilise an existing design that fitted their requirements and also, if available, use materials from a cancelled order. One of the *War C* ships may well have been constructed with materials intended for the cancelled *Magheramorne*.

The bold step of ordering so many vessels was fraught with risk. Not only was the war to take its toll, so too did a decline in trade as oil began to reduce coal, albeit on a small

scale at that time. To further reduce financial risk the company was re-organised into a limited liability concern during 1919, whereupon the partners consolidated ownership of the fleet having disposed of their individually-registered vessels.

Losses in war, losses in peace
The war years also played their part in shaping the fleet with accidents and enemy action seeing off several ships. 1915 saw *Kilcoan* sunk by a submarine whilst *Skernahan* was victim of a collision in 1916. During February 1917 *Sallagh* fell victim to a submarine attack. *Collin* was sunk in a collision late in 1918, being subsequently raised and offered for sale early in 1919. At the end of 1918 the fleet stood at one damaged and nine serviceable vessels.

Another vessel that might have ended up in the fleet was the *Black Rock* (362/1891), which had been sunk in collision in the Mersey in August 1913. On 29th September 1913 her registry had been closed, she being declared a constructive total loss. Raised later in 1913, she was sold to William Thomas and Sons, Amlwch, who undertook her repair before offering her for sale. A memorandum of agreement to purchase her for £5,800 was drawn up at Amlwch on 23rd February 1915. This called for a 10% deposit with the balance paid in cash at Amlwch Port within five days of the date of the steamer's readiness for delivery at that port. However, the transaction was not concluded and *Black Rock* was not re-registered until May 1918.

After the war there was a general boom

in shipping followed by a resounding slump. As economy measures *Nellie* was scrapped and *Collin* sold locally during 1919. *Galgorm* and *Cargan* were sold early in 1921 for further trading, leaving six vessels serving the company. A small grab hopper dredger was built locally at the Olderfleet yard, its first construction. Named *Nellie* she was employed in the reclamation of the area around the company berth to enable expansion of the premises. In 1923 with her work completed to a point and the need to recover some of the financial outlay, she passed to the London, Midland and Scottish Railway and, renamed *Rossall*, she moved to Fleetwood but retained her Belfast registry.

Mergers and takeovers

With the slump deepening, other not so well-established local coal merchants, normally in competition, saw the need for mergers in order to survive. Mergers and indeed take-overs became commonplace as the coal strikes and depression bit deeper and deeper into trade. Ireland was almost totally dependent on imports of British mainland coal.

Being a relatively strong and well-established concern, Howdens was approached on numerous occasions and acceded to some of the requests for mergers. John Rainey Ltd., Norman Canning Ltd. and Knox Coal Ltd. were a few that came together with Howdens as a co-operative venture, each company retaining its own identity. The result was a more efficient organisation, utilising the fleet more fully.

During 1933 the company restyled itself again to Howdens Ltd. to reflect both a change of ownership and the differing nature of their business structure. At that time W. Kenneth Harbinson and G. Barry were joined on the board by Arthur S. Davidson, Harry T. Browne and Henry Brennan, the latter pair trading locally on their own account as Browne and Brennan.

Some of the directors had other businesses outside the company. W.K. Harbinson was appointed as manager for the Larne Steamship Co. Ltd. upon its formation in 1934 with the introduction of *Snow Queen*. This fleet was increased by two vessels in 1935 and worked closely with that of Howdens. Indeed, one acquisition was a former Howden vessel *Cargan*. Harry T. Browne and Henry Brennan were also directors of this new concern.

The Second World War saw just as much upheaval and risks as the First, but the fleet suffered much less with *Falavee* being the only loss.

Into the Kelly group

In 1952, with their fleet becoming elderly, it was decided that it would be prudent for Howdens Ltd. to join the Belfast-based group of coal merchanting companies controlled by John Kelly Ltd. In 1953 William K. Harbinson was appointed a director of John Kelly Ltd.

Arthur S. Davidson meanwhile in 1953 purchased two steamers from Arthur Guinness and established a Belfast-based coal business in his own right. In 1958 he scrapped one steamer and purchased a motor ship, and then, within the year, scrapped the second steamer. Control of his business was acquired by the Cawood Group in 1963.

The Larne Steamship Company had reduced their fleet to two vessels pre-war and further reduced it in 1953. One vessel was sold to a company director and the other sold for demolition at the year end, thus winding up the business.

The absorption into the John Kelly Ltd. empire was to provide security for the business that continued to trade under its own name and also allowed Howdens' coal imports to be carried by Kelly vessels, avoiding the need for fleet replacement. *Straide* was sold off leaving *Gracehill*, *Carnduff* and *Finvoy* trading. The latter pair was disposed of in 1955. *Gracehill* carried on until wrecked in early 1957.

Kellys were also rationalising and modernising their fleet in the face of declining coal business as oil became more popular as a fuel. They also had been taken over in 1948 and in 1951 began naming all their vessels with *Bally-* as a prefix. Following the absorption of Howdens' business they placed the newly-acquired small motorship *Ballyedward* on the Larne run, serving both Howdens and the cement works at Magheramorne.

Under Kelly control the business thrived and was steadily modernised along with other members of the group, although Howdens had ceased to be shipowners in 1957 when their black funnel with a dark red band disappeared from the Irish Sea. In 1964. directors of Howdens Ltd. were E. W. P. King, J. S. Kennedy, W. K. Harbinson and J. H.

Browne. Howdens' road transport coal fleet was subsequently repainted into the red Kelly livery although the Howden name and telephone number were displayed in yellow, in contrast to Kelly's white. The oil tanker fleet had a yellow ochre cab and chassis with a white cab front and tank.

As their collier fleet was reduced in the 1980s, Kelly introduced a new concept to group business. They established Kelly's Dragon Line in 1987 to ship containerised coal to Northern Ireland, initially from the South Wales coalfields. A fleet of open-topped 20-foot containers painted in Kelly red was introduced. With the Kelly name and a large white dragon on the side they had a tarpaulin top cover fitted once loaded at the pits. The principle was that they would be transported by rail to the port of embarkation and off-loaded at either Larne or Belfast container terminals. The ship would then return with the empties to the mainland. The loaded units would subsequently be delivered to their destination by articulated tipper trailers. The concept was intended to minimise mechanical handling of the coal and thereby reduce breakages. Coal is graded and sized for different purposes. The more it is handled mechanically the smaller the lumps become, resulting in large quantities of coal slack, which is of less value and not so readily sold. Other savings made were in cargo handling, labour charges and port charges levied on the conventional collier laying on a berth for a longer period.

The ownership of the Kelly Group changed when Ocean Group plc sold their 50% share to their partner, Powell Duffryn. The latter, as proprietor of Stephenson Clarke Shipping Ltd., decided to rename the remaining Kelly vessels. As a result, the *Bally* prefix was swept aside in favour of names of southern English towns, whilst the Kelly funnel was replaced by Stephenson Clarke's black with a silver band. The Kelly title became Kelly Fuels and was subsequently sold to buyers in the Republic of Ireland.

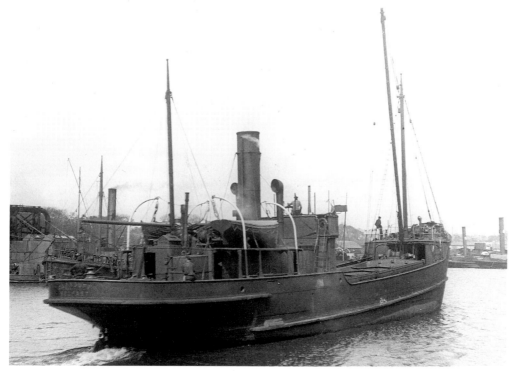

Two of the Howden fleet which survived into the mid 1950s.

Above at anchor in the Mersey is *Gracehill*, destined to be the last of the company's ships when lost on Sanda in March 1957. *[J. and M. Clarkson collection]*

Left is *Carnduff*, arriving at Preston for another coal cargo. With their dark upperworks and funnel which by then was all black, these coal boats were a little drab. *Carnduff* was broken up at Belfast in 1955. *[J. and M. Clarkson]*

JOHN SMILEY AND SON

1. COMET/ANN 1826-1876 Wooden schooner

O.N. 12061 94g
62.0 x 16.5 x 7.1 feet
1826: 36g 43n
63.0 x 17.1 x 6.5 feet
Original steam engine by D. Mc Arthur and Co., Glasgow; 24 HP.
1821: Completed by James Laing, Dumbarton, for Henry Bell and others, Glasgow as the paddle steamer COMET.
25.10.1825: Sank off Gourock following a collision with the paddle steamer AYR with the loss of 70 lives.
1826: Raised, acquired by John Smiley and Son, Larne and converted to a schooner.
1827: Renamed ANN.
1869: Caught fire and burnt when water slaked her cargo of lime in Larne Lough whilst on a voyage to London.
1870: Rebuilt at Larne.
2.1875: Sank in collision with the smack COTTAGER.
Raised and repaired.
1877: Sold to Matthew Howden, Larne.
30.7.1903: Register closed after she foundered off the South Rock Lightship.

MATTHEW HOWDEN

2. ELIZABETH McCLURE 1877-1891 Wooden schooner

O.N. 1705 63g 58n
67.0 x 18.6 x 8.5 feet.
1848: Completed by Andrew Brown, Girvan for Hannah and Co., Girvan as ELIZABETH McCLURE.
1876: Sold to Hugh H. Smiley, Larne.
1877: Sold to Matthew Howden, Larne.
13.10.1891: Wrecked on Hamilton Rock, Lamlash Bay whilst on passage from Irvine to Larne with coal.

3. ANN 1877-1903 Wooden schooner

See 1 above

JOHN S. HOWDEN

4. BLACK DIAMOND 1888-1890 Wooden steamship with iron beams

O.N. 26982 259g 134n
148.2 x 21.6 x 11.6 feet
2-cyl. by V. D. Coates, Belfast; 75 NHP.
10.1864: Launched by the Portland Shipbuilding Company, Troon for Gilmour and Company, Troon as BLACK DIAMOND.
1875: Sold to the Gauchalland Coal Company, Troon.
1879: Sold to Adam Wood, Troon.
1886: Sold to John Milligen, Belfast.
1888: Sold to Woodside and Workman, Belfast.
1888: Acquired by John S. Howden, Larne.
1890: Owners became Howden Brothers, Larne.
28.5.1892: Wrecked on North Gobbin, Islandmagee whilst on a voyage from Ayr to Belfast with a cargo of coal.

5. FERRIC 1899-1903 Iron

O.N. 86545 335g 152n
154.0 x 22.6 x 11.5 feet
C.2-cyl. by McIlwaine, Lewis and Co., Belfast; 330 IHP, 9 knots.
12.1883: Launched by McIlwaine, Lewis and Co. Ltd., Belfast (Yard No. 20) for Hugh J. Scott and Co., Belfast as FERRIC.
11.12.1898: Sunk in collision with the steamer BARON ARDROSSAN (2,823/1892) off Scotstoun House, River Clyde whilst on a voyage from Glasgow to Belfast with a cargo of coal. Her crew of ten were saved. Later salvaged.
6.7.1898: Registered in the ownership of John S. Howden (Howden Brothers, managers), Larne.
8.10.1903: Owners became Charles L. Mackean and William J.R. Harbinson, Larne.
16.1.1905: Wrecked at Black Arch two miles north of Larne whilst on a voyage from Ayr to Larne with a cargo of coal. She was salved but sold for breaking up.
20.3.1905: Register closed.

HOWDEN BROTHERS

6. BLACK DIAMOND 1890-1892
See No. 4 above

7. MONARCH 1900-1917

O.N. 90117 316g 120n
155.0 x 22.7 x 11.3 feet
C. 2-cyl. by McIlwaine, Lewis and Co., Belfast; 60 NHP.
12.1884: Launched by McIlwaine, Lewis and Co., Belfast (Yard No. 23).
6.1.1885: Registered in the ownership of Alexander King, Belfast as MONARCH.
15.8.1900: Acquired by John S. Howden (Howden Brothers, managers), Larne.
8.10.1903: Owners became Charles L. MacKean and William J.R. Harbinson (Howden Brothers, managers), Larne.
15.5.1917: Sold to Alfred E. Bowen, Manchester.
22.5.1919: Sold to James R. Bond, Jersey.
12.6.1919: Foundered ten miles off Ailsa Craig whilst on a voyage from Ayr to Belfast with a cargo of coal.
24.6.1919: Register closed

8. FERRIC 1903-1905 see No. 5.

9. NELLIE (1) 1908-1919 Wooden steamship

O.N. 104460 109g 48n
84.0 x 21.4 x 7.8 feet.
C. 2-cyl. by William Kemp, Glasgow; 30 NHP.
1895: Completed by Robinson and Hill, Belfast for John Robinson senior, Belfast as NELLIE.
21.9.1895: Sold to James Shields, Belfast.
13.9.1907: Sold to Thomas Wilson, Belfast.
16.9.1907: Acquired by W.J.R. Harbinson and Charles L. Mackean, Larne.
14.6.1920: Register closed after she had been broken up in 1919.

10. SKERNAHAN 1915-1916

O.N. 114019 530g 215n
165.0 x 26.7 x 10.6 feet
C.2-cyl. by McKie and Baxter, Govan; 64 NHP, 600 IHP, 9 knots.
1.1902: Launched by R. Williamson and Son, Workington (Yard No. 168).
24.2.1902: Registered in the ownership of the Cape Steam Shipping Co. Ltd. (Dawson Brothers, managers), Glasgow as CAPE YORK.
6.3.1915: Acquired by Charles L. Mackean and William J.R. Harbisson, Larne.
19.4.1915: Renamed SKERNAHAN.
29.1.1916: Sold to the Whitehaven Colliery Co. Ltd. (Henry C. Reynolds, manager), Whitehaven.
11.8.1916: Sunk in collision with the steamer YORKSHIRE (394/1893) seven miles west by south of the Stack, Holyhead whilst on a voyage from Limerick to Whitehaven in Ballast.
23.8.1916: Register closed.

11. CARNDUFF 1910-1955

O.N. 129633 257g 92n
125.2 x 22.6 x 9.5 feet
C. 2-cyl. by Ramage and Ferguson Ltd., Leith; 42 NHP.
7.1910: Completed by Ramage and Ferguson Ltd., Leith (Yard No. 222) for Howden Brothers (W. J. R. Harbinson, manager), Larne as CARNDUFF.
22.8.1921: Owners became Howden Brothers Ltd.
29.6.1933: Owners became Howdens Ltd.
5.11.1955: Arrived at Belfast for breaking up by John Lee.

12. COLLIN 1915-1919

O.N. 136355 284g 100n
120.8 x 22.1 x 9.1 feet.
C. 2-cyl. by A. Jeffrey and Co., Alloa; 87 NHP.
12.1915: Completed by A. Jeffrey and Co., Alloa (Yard No. 14) for Howden Brothers (William J.R. Harbinson, manager), Larne as COLLIN.
16.4.1918: Sunk in collision with the steamer ESPERANTO (217/1908) two miles north of Maughold Head, Ramsey whilst on a voyage from Garston to Belfast with a cargo of coal.
11.12.1918: Raised.
Later sold to D. Smail.
5.1919: Sold to Alexander King, Belfast.
1922: Sold to the Brunswick Shipping Co. (Robert Monroe, manager), Cardiff.
1923: Owners became Monroe Brothers, Cardiff and later Liverpool.
1931: Owners became Monroe Brothers Ltd., Liverpool.
1934: Sold to Alfred S.L. Smith, Bristol.
1936: Owner became Alfred J. Smith, Bristol.
1949: Sold to the Isabel Steamship Co. Ltd., Cardiff for conversion to a sand suction dredger and renamed ISABEL
1964: Sold to the Tay Sand Co. Ltd. (D. Davidson, manager), Dundee.
24.12.1965: Sank alongside the quay at Dundee.
3.1966: Dismantled where she lay by Risdon Beazley Ltd.

Top: *Carnduff* arriving at Preston.
[J. and M. Clarkson]

Above: *Collin,* seen again
at Preston when owned by
Monroe Brothers between
1922 and 1934. *[J. and M.
Clarkson]*

Right: *Collin* at Cardiff after
conversion to the sand suction
dredger *Isabel. [World Ship
Society Ltd.]*

13. GLENO 1915-1916

O.N. 114425 187g 75n
111.7 x 19.0 x 8.5 feet
C. 2-cyl. by C. Houston and Co., Glasgow; 30 NHP, 250 IHP, 10 knots.
1.1902: Completed by the Larne Shipbuilding Co., Larne (Yard No.19) for their own account.
7.5.1902: Registered in the ownership of Anthony H. Poole and Co., Newcastle-upon-Tyne as GLENO.
27.4.1906: Sold to Robert Emmerson (Matthew Worth, manager), Newcastle-upon-Tyne.
26.3.1909: Owner became Matthew Worth, Newcastle-upon-Tyne.
12.1.1915: Owners became Robert Emmerson (G.T. Gillie and Co., managers), Newcastle-upon-Tyne.
13.11.1915: Acquired by Charles L. Mackean and William J.R. Harbisson, Larne.
31.8.1916: Sold to John H. Allen, London.
31.3.1917: Foundered off Godrevy Head whilst on a voyage from Barry to Falmouth with a cargo of flour.
4.5.1917: Register closed.

14. SALLAGH 1916-1917

O.N. 136357 325g 113n
131.7 x 23.1 x 9.6 feet
C. 2-cyl. by A. Jeffrey and Co., Alloa; 50 NHP, 380 IHP, 9 knots.
29.5.1916: Registered in the ownership of Charles L. Mackean (32/64) and William J.R. Harbinson (32/64) trading as Howden Brothers (William J.R. Harbinson, manager), Larne as SALLAGH.
6.1916: Completed by A. Jeffrey and Co., Alloa (Yard No. 15).
10.2.1917: Captured by the German

Above: A slightly faded view of the Larne-built *Gleno* taken by the Goole-based photographer C. Appleyard when she was in Newcastle ownership. *[Roy Fenton collection]*
Below: *Cargan* in the Mersey. *[J. and M. Clarkson]*

submarine UC 65 off Bardsey and sunk by bombs whilst on a voyage from Lydney to Larne with a cargo of coal.
14.2.1917: Register closed.

15. CARGAN 1916-1921

O.N. 136358 274g 99n
120.8 x 22.1 x 9.1 feet
C. 2-cyl. by A. Jeffrey and Co. Ltd., Alloa; 87 NHP.
12.1916: Completed by A. Jeffrey and Co. Ltd., Alloa (Yard No. 16) for Howden Brothers (W.J.R. Harbinson, manager), Larne as CARGAN.
1921: Sold to John Christopher, Waterford.
1926: Sold to K. Williams and Co. Ltd. (John Christopher, manager), Waterford.

1936: Sold to the Larne Steamship Co. Ltd., Larne Harbour.
1938: Sold to the Ramsey Steamship Co. Ltd., Ramsey.
1939: Renamed BEN VOOAR.
24.2.1956: Arrived at Port Glasgow for breaking up by Smith and Houston Ltd.

16. (MAGHERAMORNE)

Proposed: 716g 324n
190.0 x 29.2 x 11.3 feet
T.3-cyl. by A. Jeffrey and Co. Ltd, Alloa; 121 NHP.
1914: Ordered from A. Jeffrey and Co. Ltd, Alloa (Yard No. 17) by Howden Brothers (W. J. R. Harbinson, manager), Larne as MAGHERAMORNE.
1916: Cancelled before work had started.

Top: *Straide.* *[J. and M. Clarkson]*

17. STRAIDE 1917-1954

O.N. 136360 326g 114n
131.7 x 23.1 x 9.6 feet
C. 2-cyl. by A. Jeffrey and Co. Ltd., Alloa;
58 NHP, 400 IHP, 8 knots.
3.1917: Completed by A. Jeffrey and Co.
Ltd., Alloa (Yard No. 19)
27.3.1917: Registered in the ownership
of William J.R. Harbinson and Charles L.
Mackean, Larne as STRAIDE.
22.8.1921: Owners became Howden
Brothers Ltd.
29.6.1933: Owners became Howdens Ltd.
21.11.1953: Sold to John R. Cameron,
Peterhead.

11.12.1954: Arrived at Grays, Essex to be
broken up by T.W. Ward Ltd., Sheffield.
24.3.1955: Register closed.

18. DROMAINE 1917-1945

O.N. 136363 234g 83n
112.9 x 21.1 x 8.9 feet
C. 2-cyl. by A. Jeffrey and Co. Ltd., Alloa;
36 RHP.
6.1917: Completed by A. Jeffrey and Co.
Ltd., Alloa (Yard No.18) for Howden
Brothers (W.J.R. Harbinson, manager),
Larne as DROMAINE.
22.8.1921: Owners became Howden
Brothers Ltd.

29.6.1933: Owners became Howdens Ltd.
1945: Sold to the East Downshire
Steamship Co. Ltd., Dundrum.
1948: Sold to the Cyclades Steamship Co.
Ltd. (Socrates G. Paleocrassas) (Vogt and
Maguire (Chartering) Ltd., managers),
Liverpool and renamed PANTOCRATOR P.
1950: Sold to the Wadsworth Coal and
Lighterage Co. Ltd., Liverpool, converted
into a derrick barge and renamed LADY
KATE.
11.1962: Arrived at Preston to be broken up
by T.W. Ward Ltd., Sheffield.
2.1963: Work began.

Dromaine leaving Preston (left), and laid up in the port as *Pantocrator P* (right). *[Both: J. and M. Clarkson]*

69

19. (ISLANDMAGEE)
O.N. 136148 716g 324n
190.0 x 29.2 x 11.3 feet
T. 3-cyl. by A. Jeffrey and Co. Ltd., Alloa;
105 NHP, 700 IHP, 10 knots.
1917: Laid down by A. Jeffrey and
Co. Ltd., Alloa (Yard No. 20) for
Howden Brothers (W. J. R. Harbinson,
manager), Larne and intended to be
named ISLANDMAGEE but sold before
completion.

31.1.1918: Registered in the ownership
of Cleeves Western Valleys Anthracite
Collieries Ltd. (Venables M. Williams,
manager), Swansea as CROSSHANDS.
2.1918: Completed.
15.10.1925: Sold to John Kelly Ltd.
(William Clint, manager), Belfast.
24.5.1927: Sold to Wilson and Reid Ltd.
(Sir Thomas S. Wilson, manager), Belfast.
4.12.1930: Manager became William Reid.
2.1.1931: Sold by mortgagees in possession

to John S. Monks and Co. Ltd., Liverpool.
20.1.1931: Renamed SEAVILLE.
20.11.1951: Sank following a collision
with the steam hopper MERSEY No.30
(892/1923) near the Q15 buoy in the River
Mersey whilst on a voyage from Douglas to
Liverpool with general cargo. One member
of her crew was lost, the others being
picked up by the pilot cutter JAMES H.
BEAZLEY (459/1921).
28.4.1953: Register closed.

Opposite page: intended to be *Islandmagee*, Jeffrey's yard number 20 became *Crosshands* (top in Kelly colours) and later Monks' *Seaville* (bottom). [NMM P9849 and J. and M. Clarkson]

Right: *Falavee* in Preston Dock. [J. and M. Clarkson]

Bottom: a fine view of *Gracehill* deep laden with coal. [Roy Fenton collection]

20. FALAVEE 1918-1942
O.N. 142476 338g 120n
136.9 x 23.2 x 9.8 feet
C. 2-cyl. by A. Jeffrey and Co. Ltd., Alloa;
75 NHP, 400 IHP, 8.5 knots.
4.1918: Completed by A. Jeffrey and Co.
Ltd., Alloa (Yard No.23).
9.4.1918: Registered in the ownership
of Howden Brothers Ltd. (William J.R.
Harbinson, manager), Larne as FALAVEE.
29.6.1933: Owners became Howdens Ltd.
14.1.1942: Wrecked at the entrance to
Carlingford Lough whilst on a voyage
from Belfast to Newry with a cargo which
included flour.
2.3.1942: Register closed.

21. GALGORM 1918-1921
O.N. 142477 453g 174n
156.5 x 25.2 x 9.8 feet
C. 2-cyl. by A. Jeffrey and Co. Ltd., Alloa;
52 NHP.
7.1918: Completed by A. Jeffrey and Co.
Ltd., Alloa (Yard No.21) for Howden
Brothers (W.J.R. Harbinson, manager),
Larne as GALGORM.
1921: Sold to the Sabah Steamship Co.
Ltd. (Darby and Co., managers), Sandakan,
British North Borneo.
1923: Renamed KALAMANTAN and
managers became Harrison and Crossfield
(Borneo) Ltd.
1934: Broken up locally.

22. GRACEHILL 1918-1957
O.N. 142482 452g 172n
156.5 x 25.2 x 9.8 feet
C. 2-cyl. by the Forth Shipbuilding and
Engineering Co. Ltd., Alloa; 52 NHP.
9.1918: Completed by the Forth
Shipbuilding and Engineering Co. Ltd.,
Alloa (Yard No.21) for Howden Brothers
(W.J.R. Harbinson, manager), Larne as
GRACEHILL.
23.8.1921: Owners became Howden
Brothers Ltd.
29.6.1933: Owners became Howdens Ltd.
8.3.1957: Wrecked on Sanda whilst on
a voyage from Londonderry to Ayr in
ballast.

23. FINVOY 1920-1955

O.N. 142499 374g 132n
145.3 x 23.2 x 9.8 feet
C. 2-cyl. by the Forth Shipbuilding and
Engineering Co. Ltd., Alloa; 75 RHP.
6.1920: Completed by the Forth Shipbuilding
and Engineering Co. Ltd., Alloa (Yard No.24)
for Howden Brothers Ltd. (W.J.R. Harbinson,
manager), Larne as FINVOY.
22.8.1921: Owners became Howden Brothers
Ltd.
29.6.1933: Owners became Howdens Ltd.
1955: Sold to Bremner and Co. (J.R.

Bremner, manager), Stromness.
5.11.1958: Arrived at Irvine to be broken up
by the Ayrshire Dockyard Co. Ltd.

24. NELLIE (2) 1921-1923 Grab hopper dredger.

O.N. 141960 235g 104n
107.0 x 28.0 x 9.2 feet
C.2-cyl. by Campbell and Calderwood Ltd.,
Paisley; 39 NHP.
6.1921: Completed by Olderfleet
Shipbuilding and Engineering Co. Ltd., Larne
(Yard No.1) for Howden Brothers Ltd. (W. J.

R. Harbinson, manager), Larne as NELLIE.
9.1923: Sold to the London, Midland and
Scottish Railway, London and renamed
ROSSALL.
1948: Owners became the British Transport
Commission, London.
1964: Owners became British Transport
Docks Board, London.
1964: Sold to H. G. Pounds, Portsmouth.
1965: Owners became Pounds Shipowners
and Shipbreakers Ltd., Portsmouth.
1976: Sold to Chekoslovac 'Kurzon' and
reported to have been demolished.

Two views of
Finvoy at Preston.
*[Top: Douglas B.
Cochrane/World
Ship Society Ltd.
bottom: J. and M.
Clarkson]*

The dredger *Nellie* as *Rossall*, 7th August 1946. *[World Ship Society Ltd.]*

WM. J. R. HARBINSON AND CHARLES L. MACKEAN, LARNE

1. ROMA 1903-1917
O.N. 116007 158g 49n
95.0 x 18.9 x 8.5 feet
1913: 181g 67n
106.0 x 18.9 x 8.5 feet
C. 2-cyl. by Muir and Houston Ltd., Glasgow; 32 RHP.
1903: Completed by the Larne Shipbuilding Co., Larne (Yard No. 25) for W.J.R. Harbinson and C.L. Mackean, Belfast as ROMA.
1913: Lengthened.
1917: Sold to Henry Renny (Earl J. Leslie, manager), Forfar.
1920: Sold to the Sea Navigation Co. Ltd. (W.J. Stewart and Douglas Cable, managers), London.
1924: Sold to Lowden, Connell and Co., Liverpool.
1924: Sold to the Straits Steamship Co. Ltd. (Alfred Capper, manager), Liverpool.
1938: Sold to Alfred J. Smith, Bristol.
1949: Sold to Bristowe Shippers Ltd. (Arthur Smith, manager), Bristol.
1958: Sold to Renwick, Wilton and Dobson Ltd., Torquay.
10.4.1959: Arrived at Newport, Monmouthshire to be broken up by John Cashmore Ltd.

2. KILCOAN 1905-1915
O.N. 120708 456g 99n
163.2 x 25.1 x 9.7 feet
C. 2-cyl. by Muir and Houston Ltd., Glasgow; 72 NHP, 700 IHP, 10 knots.
17.6.1905: Launched by the Ailsa Shipbuilding Co. Ltd., Troon (Yard No. 138).
8.1905: Completed.
18.8.1905: Registered in the ownership of William J.R. Harbinson and Charles L. Mackean, Larne as KILCOAN.
15.1.1915: Captured by the German submarine U 21 and sunk by bombs in position 53.45 north by 03.46 west, 18 miles north west of the Liverpool Bar Light Vessel whilst on a voyage from Garston to Belfast with a cargo of coal.
30.1.1915: Register closed.

Roma at Preston in later life. *[J. and M. Clarkson]*

Snow Queen on the Mersey. Her name came from a brand of flour sold by her previous owners. *[B. and A. Feilden/J. and M. Clarkson]*

LARNE STEAMSHIP CO. LTD.
W. K. Harbinson, manager,   Larne

1. SNOW QUEEN 1934-1953
O.N. 140819   308g 113n
130.0 x 23.1 x 9.7 feet

C. 2-cyl. by A. Dodman and Co., Kings Lynn; 40 NHP, 9.5 knots.
4.1921: Completed by I.J. Abdela and Mitchell Ltd., Chester (Yard No.414).
6.9.1921: Registered in the ownership of the Moffat Steamship Co. Ltd., Grimsby as MARY NICKERSON.
14.12.1922: Sold to the British Isles Transport Co. Ltd. (William Buckley, manager), London.

9.3.1923: Renamed SNOW QUEEN.
18.9.1934: Sold to Harry Brough, Liverpool (William K. Harbinson, Larne, manager).
19.10.1934: Acquired by the Larne Steamship Co. Ltd., Belfast.
11.1953: Sold for breaking up and allocated to John Lee, Belfast.
12.11.1953: Register closed

Deneside sailing from Preston. *[Douglas B. Cochrane/World Ship Society Ltd.]*

2. DENESIDE 1935-1953
O.N. 132051 329g 130n
133.9 x 23.1 x 9.3 feet
C. 2-cyl. by G.T. Grey, South Shields; 48 NHP.
8.1910: Completed by J.T. Eltringham and Co., South Shields (Yard No. 279) for the Wear Steam Shipping Co. Ltd. (Thomas Rose, manager), Sunderland as DENESIDE.
1917: Owners became the Wear Steam Shipping Co. (1917) Ltd. (Thomas Rose, manager), Sunderland.
1921: Sold to William K. Griffin and Norman S. Race, Cardiff.
1922: Owners became the Deneside Steamship Co. Ltd. (Griffin and Race, managers), Cardiff.
1931: Sold to the Mersey Ports Stevedoring Co. Ltd., Liverpool.
1935: Acquired by the Larne Steamship Co. Ltd., Belfast.

1953: Sold to H.T. Browne and resold to the Tay Sand Co. Ltd. (J. Neilson, manager), Dundee.
18.5.1961: Arrived New Waterway in tow of BLANKENBURG (124/1938) for breaking up by Ijssel N.V. Heuvelman who began work at Krimpen a/d Ijssel on 3.7.1961.

3. CARGAN 1936-1938 See no 15.

In the familiar setting of Preston Dock basin is *Straide,* named after a hill about ten miles from Larne. *[Douglas B. Cochrane/ World Ship Society Ltd.]*

Derivations of Howdens' names

Cargan A village just north north east of Ballymena.

Carnduff The name of a mountain south of Larne near Glynn and also a village to the west of Ballycastle.

Collin Collin Top is a mountain approximately 15 miles north west of Larne. Big Collin is a mountain approximately eight miles south west of Larne.

Dromaine Dromain is a townland half way between Larne and Sallagh Braes.

Falavee Fallowvee is near Garron Head.

Finvoy A village to the south west of Ballymoney.

Galgorm A village just to the south west of Ballymena, near Gracehill.

Glenoe A village approximately five miles south of Larne.

Gracehill A village just to the south west of Ballymena, near Galgorm.

Islandmagee The peninsula of land forming the east side of Larne Lough.

Kilcoan A hamlet near Islandmagee.

Magheramorne A village on the south west side of Larne Lough.

Sallagh Sallagh Braes is an escarpment between Larne and Ballygalley Head.

Skernaghan Skernaghan Point on the east side of Larne Lough.

Straide Straid Hill is approximately ten miles south south west of Larne.

ARTHUR S. DAVIDSON
Belfast

1. CARROWDORE 1953-1958

O.N. 132047 599g 266n
180.2 x 29.1 x 10.4 feet
T.3-cyl. by Aitchison, Blair and Co. Ltd.,
Glasgow; 85 RHP.
27.1.1914: Launched by Scott and Sons,
Bowling (Yard No. 249) for John Kelly
Ltd. (Samuel Kelly, manager), Belfast as
CARROWDORE.
1.1914: Completed.
2.1914: Sold to Arthur Guinness, Son and
Co. Ltd., Dublin.
1953: Acquired by to Arthur S. Davidson
Ltd., Belfast.
1958: Sold via J.B. Vels and Company,
Boom to Van Den Bosch N. V., for
demolition at Boom, Belgium.

2. CLARECASTLE 1953-1959

O.N. 136345 627g 236n
179.9 x 28.6 x 10.8 feet
T.3-cyl. by Aitchison, Blair Ltd, Glasgow;
85 RHP.
7.12.1914: Launched by Scott and Sons,
Bowling (Yard No. 256) for John Kelly
Ltd. (Samuel Kelly, manager), Belfast as
CLARECASTLE.
12.1914: Completed.
10.1915: Sold to Arthur Guinness, Son and
Co. Ltd., Dublin.
1953: Acquired by Arthur S. Davidson Ltd.,
Belfast.
1959: Sold via the British Iron and Steel
Corporation to the Ayrshire Dockyard Co.
Ltd. for demolition at Irvine.

3. MAYFAIR SAPPHIRE 1958-1973

O.N. 181134 1,000g 518n
213.6 x 34.2 x 12.1 feet
Oil engine 2SCSA 6-cyl. by British Polar
Engines Ltd., Glasgow; 97 NHP, 1,320
BHP, 11 knots.

Carrowdore (top) in 1957 and an undated view of her arriving at Preston (middle).
The *Clarecastle* sailing from Preston (bottom). *[J. and M. Clarkson collection]*

76

12.5.1949: Launched by the Grangemouth Dockyard Co. Ltd., Grangemouth (Yard No. 488).
9.1949: Completed for William Robertson (Shipowners) Ltd. (William Robertson, manager), Glasgow as SAPPHIRE
1958: Owners became Gem Line Ltd. (William Robertson Shipowners Ltd., managers), Glasgow.
1958: Acquired by Arthur S. Davidson Ltd., Belfast and renamed MAYFAIR SAPPHIRE.
1959: Owners became A.S. Davidson and Sons Ltd.
1963: Owners acquired by Cawood's Fuels (Northern Ireland) Ltd.
1971: Owners became Cawood's Fuel (Northern Ireland) Ltd., Belfast.
1973: Sold to Comexim Maritime Financial Co. Ltd., Limassol, Cyprus (P.J. Angouras, Piraeus, Greece, manager) and renamed IOULIA K.
1974: Renamed BABI.
1974: Sold to Kappa Shipping Co. Ltd., Limassol, Cyprus (Sissiar Lines S.A. (M.L. Raissis), Piraeus, managers).
23.5.1979: Laid up at Piraeus.
24.6.1983: Breaking up began by Stavros Vamvounakis at Piraeus.
12.10.1983: Work completed.

The *Mayfair Sapphire* as Robertson's *Sapphire*(top) in July 1952. The *Mayfair Sapphire,* deeply-laden, sailing from Preston (middle) and arriving in ballast (bottom). *[J. and M. Clarkson]*

THOMAS DUNLOP AND SONS, GLASGOW
Malcolm Cooper

Beginnings

Thomas Dunlop was born in Old Monkland Parish, Glasgow on 17th April 1831, the son of William Dunlop, a grocer, and Mary Ann Stirling. Very little is known of his early life save that both of his parents had died by time he was 10, but he was clearly a determined and resourceful soul as in 1851, aged only 20, he entered business in his own right as a provision merchant at 231 Cowcaddens on the northern edge of the Glasgow central business district. He married Robina Jack in 1852 and a few years later, having diversified to become a grain merchant, moved his business to a more central location at 249 Argyle Street.

Dunlop's first venture into ship owning came in 1868 when, together with John Neil, a Glasgow biscuit manufacturer, he travelled to London to buy the small wooden barque *Wye* for £2,800. Dunlop and Neil each took equal 32/64th shares in the four-year old vessel, although it seems to have been Dunlop who took responsibility for management. This did not mark a complete turn away from his land-based ventures; indeed he diversified the latter further into flour importing, a trade which was to remain one of the mainstays of the family business for many years.

Thomas Dunlop (1831-1893), the founder of the shipping business and the epitome of a Victorian self-made man. *[The Dunlop Family]*

The *Wye* was sold to owners in the north east of England in 1872, but before she left two further wooden sailing vessels had been acquired. In each case Dunlop and Neil were joined as owners by Andrew Reid, who was Neil's partner in the latter's biscuit business. Both vessels were new, although only the first, the *Marion Neil*, had actually been built to her owner's account. The second, renamed *Andrew Reid* on acquisition, had actually been launched at Southampton as *Lord Palmerston* for another Glasgow owner. As her first appearance on the register was under her new name, it would seem that she was never actually delivered to her original intended owner.

The Clan Line

1874 was to prove the climacteric year for the development of Dunlop's shipping business. In that year he was joined in business by his elder son, also called Thomas, the first step in the creation of a family business dynasty which would become Thomas Dunlop and Sons when the younger Thomas and his only surviving brother Robert (three other brothers died in childhood) were both made partners in 1879. Also in 1874 Dunlop took delivery of two new iron-hulled barques built by two different Wearside shipyards. The second of these to be delivered, the *Robina Dunlop*, was the last ship to be owned by the original Dunlop-Neil-Reid partnership. The first, the *Clan Macleod*, which actually took to the water several months earlier, was a pioneer in two ways. In the first she introduced a new nomenclature to the Dunlop shipping venture. In the second she marked the first step in the independent development of a Dunlop fleet. She and successive sailing vessels carrying Clan names were marketed to a wide range of investors, most of whom held only a few 64th shares. Dunlop and his sons retained only a small shareholding themselves, earning the bulk of their revenues from managing the growing fleet.

The *Clan Macleod* was followed into the fleet during the remainder of the decade by three further new iron barques. Each was slightly larger than its predecessor and each came from a different shipyard. The *Clan Campbell* was delivered in the spring of 1875 by Bartram, Haswell and Co. of Sunderland, the builders of the *Clan Macleod*. The following two vessels came from Clyde builders, *Clan Ferguson* from John Reid and Co. of Port Glasgow in 1876, and *Clan Grant* from D. and W. Henderson of Partick in 1878. By the time the last arrived, two of the ships owned by the original partnership were gone. The *Marion Neil* was sold to London owners in March 1877 and the *Robina Dunlop* was lost in New Zealand waters in August of the same year. Only the *Andrew Reid*, easily the largest of the early vessels, remained in the fleet into the 1880s.

The Clan sailing fleet suffered its first loss in 1881. The *Clan Campbell* was inward bound for Glasgow from Havre in ballast at the end of her fourth voyage when she went ashore on the south east corner of Ailsa Craig in the Clyde estuary. Her loss was the result of misjudgement and an apparent concern to save money. Captain Ewen had negotiated with a tug for a tow up-river while off Corsewall Point, but had only agreed to taking up the

Completed in 1874, the *Robina Dunlop* lasted only just over three years. *[The Dunlop Family]*

tow when he reached the Cloch Lighthouse. He was thus proceeding under sail with the tug in attendance when it was noticed he was taking too much leeway towards Ailsa Craig. Last minute attempts to pass a tow failed and the comedy of errors came to its inevitable conclusion when *Clan Campbell* missed stays while attempting to tack out of danger and drifted onto the rocks. Badly holed, the ship became a total loss although the crew had no difficulty in getting away by boat. Not surprisingly, Captain Ewen was held responsible and lost his certificate for six months.

The loss did not seriously dent fleet expansion as four new sailing vessels, all large full-riggers, were added in the early 1880s. The contract for the first of these vessels, the *Clan Macfarlane*, was signed with Russell and Co. of Port Glasgow on 25th October 1880. Originally, Dunlop and Sons seem to have intended another smallish barque on the model of the 1870s vessels as the contract was only for £11,500 at a rate of £12 per net register ton. The contract, however, was altered before the vessel was laid down and *Clan Macfarlane* was launched on 12th May 1881 as a 1,500-ton fully rigged ship at a total cost of £17,806. She was joined a year and a half later by the *Clan Mackenzie* (below), built by Russell and Co.'s neighbours at Port Glasgow, Robert Duncan and Co.

The *Clan Macfarlane* was to prove a fairly fast ship in service, but the *Clan Mackenzie* was very much the clipper of the Dunlop fleet. At the time of her launch she was described as the heaviest rigged vessel of her size to be built on the Clyde, but in the words of Basil Lubbock, 'for all her big sail plan she worked like a yacht and was as handy as she was speedy.' The *Clan Mackenzie* recorded a whole series of notable passages during her career, once famously sailing away from Thompson's famous emigrant clipper *Thermopylae* and on another occasion sailing from Cardiff to Hong Kong in 90 days. Thom and Cameron's thoroughbred the *Helensburgh*, built by Duncan a year later, was reputedly designed specifically to beat the *Clan Mackenzie*, but when the two did run against each other, on passage from South Wales to San Francisco, the latter registered much the shorter voyage time.

Robert Duncan and Russell and Co. each delivered another full-rigger to Dunlop and Sons in the early 1880s. The former launched the *Clan Robertson* in October 1884 and the latter the *Clan Macpherson* in July 1885. Before either of these ships was even ordered, however, Dunlops engaged in their first experiment with steam. On 29th November 1883 the steamer *Clan Davidson* was launched for the company by Alexander Stephen and Sons, the sixth different builder employed in the decade since the Clan fleet began. At 240 feet and 1,326 tons, she was actually smaller than the contemporary Dunlop sailing vessels and it may be that she was conceived of as something of an experiment. She did not join her sail sisters in the long-distance tramp trades that Dunlops had come to specialize in, spending the entirety of what was to prove a short career in European waters. Surviving voyage records suggest that the *Clan Davidson* did no better than break even in a succession of short tramping voyages. She was still less than two years old when she stranded in the Baltic on 22nd September 1885 and was rendered unsalvageable by a subsequent gale, but her owners must have seen enough promise in her less than glorious career to plan further investments in steam as the first in what was to prove a long series of larger steamers was ordered in 1886.

Clan Mackenzie moored off Gravesend in May 1888. *[John Naylon collection]*

Before moving on to consider what was to prove a very lengthy transition from sail to steam, it is worth looking at the financial performance of the established sailing fleet. The historical literature of the age of sail has concentrated heavily on speed and passage times, with fast vessels getting the lion's share of attention and generally being hailed as the greatest successes. Thus, in the Dunlop fleet, it is the *Clan Mackenzie* that has always received the most column inches, although all of the fully-rigged ships of the 1880s were generally considered to be better than average sailers. It is questionable, however, whether fast passage times necessarily translated into the highest profits, particularly in the closing decades of the sail age when windjammers were being used almost exclusively to carry bulk cargoes on the longest sea routes. This point is born out by a comparison of the voyage results of the *Clan Mackenzie* with those of two of her fleet mates.

The *Clan Mackenzie's* heavy rig and large sail plan resulted in a significantly higher building cost than the similar sized vessels built immediately before and after her. The *Clan Mackenzie* cost £21,360, equivalent to £333.15 per 64th share. The *Clan Macfarlane* in contrast cost £17,806, equivalent to £278.5 per 64th, while the *Clan Robertson* cost £16,550, or £258.12 per 64th. The shareholders in the *Clan Mackenzie* thus required their vessel to earn approximately 20% more than the other vessels to make an equivalent return. As the table below shows, however, the three vessels' voyage earnings over their careers were broadly equivalent. All made a positive return, but it was the shareholders in the more staid *Clan Macfarlane* and *Clan Robertson* that made the best percentage return.

Comparative voyage returns over first 17 voyages – dividends per 64th share

	Clan Macfarlane	Clan Mackenzie	Clan Robertson
Cost	£17,806	£21,360	£16,550
64th share	£278.5	£333.15	£258.12
Voyage number			
1	£60.0.0	£56.5.1	£28.5.9¼
2	£23.12.3¼	£17.9.5½	£25.0.0
3	£20.0.1	£24.0.1	£25.3.10
4	£30.1.1	£25.16.8	£35.2.0
5	£6.9.5	£28.17.4	£47.0.0
6	£8.17.5	£60.5.1	£60.1.0
7	£75.5.4	£20.2.6½	£43.0.0
8	£60.0.6	£20.0.0	£10.0.0
9	£21.1.6	£5.0.0	£16.0.0
10	£10.0.0	£16.0.0	£12.10.0
11	£15.0.0	£23.0.0	£0.0.0
12	£15.0.0	£10.0.0	£20.0.0
13	£10.0.0	£0.0.0	£15.0.0
14	£8.0.0	£22.0.0	£28.0.0
15	£20.0.0	£20.0.0	£25.0.0
16	£20.0.0	£35.0.0	£10.0.0
17	£44.0.0	£22.10.0	£0.0.0
TOTAL	£437.7.7¼	£406.6.6	£400.3.3¼
% Return	157%	122%	155%

One of the relatively few serious accidents to befall the fleet in the age of sail gives a fascinating insight into the tenacity of the Dunlops as business managers. In December 1889 the *Clan Mackenzie* was run down and sunk by the railway steamer *Oregon* while at anchor in the Columbia River. The

Clan Mackenzie was raised and put back into service at a total cost of £12,000, a sum which the vessel's insurers paid out promptly. The vessel was out of service for some six months, and Dunlops took the Oregon Railway Company to court for both the cost of the repairs and demurrage. Both the Oregon and San Francisco district courts decided partially against the British firm, but Dunlop appealed to the Supreme Court in Washington and finally won full damages of £20,000. As a result, the firm was able not only to re-pay its insurers in full, but also to make a significant distribution to the vessel's 64th shareholders. Grateful Lloyd's underwriters presented the company and its managers with inscribed silver plate in recognition of this hard-fought legal success.

The Queens arrive

The second Dunlop steamship was launched from the Linthouse yard of Alexander Stephen and Sons on 12th January 1887. Unlike her predecessor, she was not given a Clan name. Four years after Thomas Dunlop had adopted the Clan nomenclature in 1874 another Glasgow shipowner, Charles Cayzer, had followed suit. Cayzer's Clan Line had grown quickly in size and reputation, and although there were no restrictions at that stage on British vessels carrying the same name, the Dunlops clearly felt that their steam vessels should adopt a new identity. The new vessel was christened *Queen Victoria* and all subsequent powered vessels with one exception were to carry Queen names. There had been a short-lived Queen Line in Glasgow in the 1870s, running a steam service to India, but it had gone into liquidation at the end of that decade. The first of the new ships took the name of Britain's reigning monarch, and subsequent ships were named after other current European monarchs or royal consorts. Dunlop and Sons showed themselves to be aware of royal sensitivities, seeking the permission of the concerned royal house in question to use the name and inviting a royal representative to attend the launch. The Dunlops were not to enjoy a Clyde monopoly on the Queen naming system; indeed another Glasgow shipowner, John Black, actually launched a sailing vessel called *Queen Victoria* within a few months of the Dunlop ship's entry into service. Dunlop sailing ships, of which another was already building, would continue to carry Clan names. Presumably the Dunlops were content that they at least had had one recognizable brand each for Clan-named sailing ships and Queen-named steamers!

The *Queen Victoria* represented a significant step forward over the unfortunate *Clan Davidson*. Fifty feet longer and a thousand tons gross bigger, she was the first steel-hulled vessel in the fleet. She was also fitted with the newly introduced triple-expansion steam engine. The latter innovation was undoubtedly the most important from a Dunlop point of view. While their first steamer had been restricted to European waters, the new generation of vessels would trade worldwide, spending much of their time on the longer distance routes that had only become economical for steam tramps with the arrival of triple expansion.

Stephens' Linthouse yard would produce two further steamers for Dunlop each slightly larger than its predecessor, *Queen Elizabeth* in 1888 and *Queen Margaret* in 1890 (interestingly enough, John Black would use exactly the same names for his next two sailing vessels). The Stephens trio, however, did not mark a complete turn away from sail. In 1887 Russell and Co. delivered the four-masted *Clan Buchanan*. On the previous occasion when this yard had

A painting of the *Queen Elizabeth* (1), the company's third steamer. *[The Dunlop Family]*

heavily involved in constructing sailing ships.

Bartrams delivered the *Queen Adelaide* and *Queen Anne* in 1891, the *Queen Louise* in 1893, the *Queen Olga* in 1894, the *Queen Cristina* and *Queen Eleanor* in 1896 and the *Queen Mary* in 1897. The first two vessels were sisters, as were the second two and the last three, each class marking a step up in size. In the middle of this expansion programme, two new sailing vessels also joined the fleet. The *Clan Graham* and *Clan Galbraith* were both delivered by Russell and Co in the winter of 1893-4. In each case, Dunlop once again gave up a smaller vessel in part payment, the *Clan Grant* in the first case and the *Clan Ferguson* in the second. The *Clan Grant* was actually wrecked in the Pacific after her sale to the shipbuilders but before she could be delivered. Although normally shown as a Dunlop fleet loss, this was not strictly speaking the case, and the insurance paid on her loss was remitted by Dunlop straight to Russell and Company.

Even if counted as a Dunlop vessel, the *Clan Grant* was the company's only sail loss between 1881 and the end of the century. The steam fleet, however, fared much worse. The *Queen Elizabeth* was wrecked off the coast of Japan in March 1891 while carrying coal from that country to Manila. On 23rd April 1895 the *Queen Anne* sailed from Akyab in Burma with a cargo of rice and disappeared. Her loss was almost certainly the result of a serious misjudgement on the part of her captain who ignored local warnings and sailed off into the teeth of a typhoon when even British India ships were staying in harbour. A year later, almost to the day, the *Queen Victoria* was lost on the other side of the Indian Ocean, being wrecked in Algoa Bay while bound for Delagoa Bay from the UK with general cargo. The last loss of the decade was the

delivered a sailing vessel (the *Clan Macpherson* in 1885), they had taken the wooden barque *Andrew Reid* in part payment. On this occasion they engaged in a similar transaction, taking the first and smallest of the company's iron barques, the *Clan Macleod*. Russell would sell this ship on for further trading. She had lengthy careers with two further owners, was hulked in Australian waters, returned to service during the First World War, was hulked again and then lay aground and derelict in a backwater for half a century. Incredibly she would then be re-floated and restored and now sails again as part of Australia's heritage fleet, thus long outliving her builders and her original owners.

At the beginning of the 1890s, Thomas Dunlop was operating a mixed fleet of seven sailing vessels and three steamers. The fleet was to remain mixed for almost another two decades, but it would become progressively more dominated by steam. Although two new sailing vessels would be added in the early 1890s, these would replace smaller vessels, and the number of sailing vessels was to remain constant at seven into the early years of the 20th century. The steam fleet, however, was to grow progressively, matching the sailing fleet in numbers by the turn of the century and then beginning to outstrip it.

Investment in new steam tonnage was to come in two distinct phases, one in the 1890s and one in the 1900s, each involving a different builder, neither of them Clyde-based. In the first phase, Dunlop took delivery of no fewer than seven new steam tramps from Bartram, Haswell and Co between 1891 and 1897. Bartrams, of course, had built the first two Clan sailing ships back in 1874-5, and it might well be that the two firms had maintained at least a slight business relationship ever since. It is still surprising that Dunlop should have turned so decisively away from the numerous Clyde shipyards on their doorstep. It might simply have been that they could not find the berths when they needed them as some of the bigger Clyde builders of tramp tonnage were still

The iron four-masted barque *Clan Buchanan* of 1887, laid up on the west coast of the USA with her royal yards sent down. *[Monterey Maritime Museum]*

The last two sailing vessels to be delivered to the company, the *Clan Graham* (top) and the *Clan Galbraith* (above). The *Clan Graham* was photographed off Cape Flattery, at the entrance to the Columbia River, by the well known tugmaster-photographer H. H. Morrison. *[Top: John Naylon collection, above: Monterey Maritime Museum]*

The two sons of Thomas Dunlop. Sir Thomas Dunlop (1855-1938) started his business training at the age of 16 and became a partner in 1879 (left). He was created baronet in 1916. Robert Jack Dunlop (1857-1938) took a major role in the management of the fleet and served on the Merchant Shipping Advisory Council of the Board of Trade from 1923 to 1932 (right). *[Both: The Dunlop Family]*

Queen Cristina which was blown on to a reef off Australia by a hurricane on 23rd December 1899 while on passage from Shanghai to Newcastle, New South Wales in ballast. It is striking that all four steam losses were in distant waters. This was a reflection of the trades in which the fleet was deployed. While many British tramp owners concentrated on the Black Sea and Atlantic grain trades, Dunlop's Queens traded worldwide, often making long multi-staged voyages well away from UK ports.

The company founder did not live to see either the completion of the 1890s expansion programme or the late decade marine losses. Thomas Dunlop died in Glasgow on 30th January 1893 at the age of 61 having built his business up from the humblest of beginnings to a good-sized shipowning and grain/ flour trading enterprise. His two sons, Thomas and Robert Jack, had already been partners in the firm for more than a decade, and with both going on to achieve some eminence in their chosen fields, the family succession and the firm's prospects were reasonably assured.

Up until the end of the 1890s, the Dunlop fleet was run on the traditional 64th share system, with individual shareholders taking 64th shares in individual vessels, each of which was run as a separate entity under the general management of Thomas Dunlop and Sons. One of the problems with this system was that an individual share in a steam vessel was a relatively expensive asset, and although single 64th shares could be and were owned on a joint basis, there were likely to be problems in accessing the full range of potential investors. Consolidating the fleet into one company could solve this problem, and give the added benefit of offering shareholders a return based on the entire performance of the fleet, insulating them from the risk of a poor voyage result by an individual vessel. Dunlop went down this route in March 1899, consolidating ownership of the entire steam fleet in the Dunlop Steamship Co. Ltd. The sailing vessels were left outside this arrangement and continued to be run as separate enterprises on the 64th principle until December 1906 when the remaining vessels were combined in a new and separate company, the Merito Shipping Co. Ltd. The latter company was to have a somewhat truncated operating existence, as all the sailing ships would be sold by 1911, and thereafter it operated as a single-ship company for the one steamer registered in its name until 1918. After that the company was kept in existence simply as an investment vehicle, holding some shares in other Dunlop shipping ventures.

Sail versus steam

At the turn of the century, Thomas Dunlop and Sons was managing a fleet of seven sailing vessels and six steamships. The last sailing ship had joined the fleet in early 1894 and investment in steam tonnage had been far heavier, but the fleet had remained broadly balanced because of the loss of four steamers, all of them relatively new, in the 1890s. The first decade of the 20th century was to see a fresh wave of investment in steam tonnage, but before considering this it is worth pausing to look at the comparative performance of the sail and steam fleets. The Dunlop shipping venture was relatively unusual in that it continued to operate sail and steam fleets in tandem for well over two decades. The first steamer joined the fleet in 1883, while the last sailing ship was not sold until 1911. This was not just a matter of the company continuing to run old sail tonnage until it reached the end of its economic life. From the mid-1880s to the early 1890s, Dunlop was ordering both new steamers and new sailing vessels. Between 1883 when the first steamer (*Clan Davidson*) joined the fleet and the beginning of 1894 when the last sailing ship (*Clan Galbraith*) was launched, the company added five new sailing ships and seven new steamers.

As we have already seen, the sailing ships ordered in the early 1880s earned a perfectly healthy financial return. These vessels, however, were ordered before steam had made an impact on the business. A more relevant case is the four-masted *Clan Buchanan*, which joined the fleet in 1887 at the same time as the first of the Queen-named triple-expansion steamers. It is not quite possible to analyse the *Clan Buchanan*'s full business life under Dunlop colours as her surviving voyage accounts end in 1906 when she was transferred to the Merito Shipping Co. Ltd., but a combination of the figures that do exist and an estimate for her final trading voyages and sale does give a reasonably good picture. The ship had returned its 64th shareholders' original investment by the end of its seventh voyage, less than halfway through what might originally have been expected to be its normal economic life. By the end of its 14th voyage, it had returned an additional 52%, with this figure going up to 84% when the estimated revenues for her sale are added.

It is noteworthy that the *Clan Buchanan* earned her greatest returns on voyages 2 to 4 in the late 1880s and early 1890s. These results, and similar ones from older members of the sailing fleet, were probably what persuaded the Dunlops to order their last two sailing ships in the early 1890s. It needs also to be remembered here that sail tonnage was significantly less expensive than steam. The *Clan Graham* and *Clan Galbraith* cost just under £16,900 each, and in both cases the call on 64th shareholders was reduced by the residual value of their shareholdings in *Clan Grant* and *Clan Ferguson* respectively, which were taken by the builder in part payment for the new vessels. In contrast, the *Queen Louise* and the *Queen Olga*, the first of which entered the fleet immediately before the sail pair and the second immediately after, cost just under twice as much - £32,290 in the first case and £31,248 in the second. Not only did this mean that an individual 64th shareholding cost approximately £500 instead of half that, but it also meant that the steamers had to earn twice as much as the sailing vessels to provide the same percentage return on investment. As the huge expansion of the British steam tramping fleet in the late 19th century makes clear, there was no shortage of investors with the desire and the means to buy 64th shares at £500 per share. Investment in sail, however, offered a significantly cheaper means of entry, and one which both recent and contemporary experience suggested could provide a respectable and perhaps even equal rate of return.

Further analysis of voyage results suggests that voyage returns were more or less in balance between the sail and steam fleets through the late 1880s and most of the 1890s, but that the sailing fleet began to slip further and further behind thereafter. The steam fleet was able to reach a similar rate of profitability to the sail fleet because it was able to compensate for its higher capital costs by undertaking more voyages. The table below shows a fairly typical example of this. The *Queen Adelaide* managed a total of 13 voyages between her delivery in 1891 and her transfer to the Dunlop Steamship Co. Ltd. in 1899. In that eight-year period she earned a total return almost equivalent to her construction cost. As an added bonus, a significant salvage award had presented shareholders with a windfall gain equivalent to more than 50% of their original investment.

Clan Buchanan – financial performance, 1887-1908	
Cost	£18,057
64th share	£282.3.0
Voyage	
1	£30.12.3
2	£63.0.3
3	£78.5.9
4	£67.3.9
5	£15.0.0
6	£20.10.0
7	£21.0.0
8	£15.0.0
9	£6.5.0
10	£12.10.0
11	£40.0.0
12	£45.0.0
13	£4.0.0
14	£10.0.0
SUB-TOTAL	£428.7.0
% return (1887-1906)	152%
Estimated result, 1907-8 plus sale	£91.13.0
ESTIMATED TOTAL	£520.0.0
Estimated total return	184%

Queen Adelaide – financial performance, 1891-1899	
Cost	£32,727
64th share	£511.7.6
Voyage	
1	£35.0.0
2	£25.0.0
3	£15.0.0
4	£23.10.0
5	£25.0.0
6	£50.0.0
7	£30.0.0
8	£35.0.0
9	£35.0.0
10	£40.0.0
11	£55.0.0
12	£95.0.0
13	£45.10.0
TOTAL	£509.10.0
% return (1891-1899)	100%
Salvage award per 64th share	£312.0.5

The last additions to the sail fleet earned respectable returns in their early years but thereafter suffered as a result of the general erosion of business remaining for the world's sail fleet and the consequent squeezing of sail freight rates. While the earlier members of the sail fleet had all covered the initial cost of their construction at the mid-way stage in their lives, the last two vessels fell well short of this, and like the other surviving members of the sailing fleet spent the final years of their time under Dunlop colours struggling with long port lay-ups and longer unprofitable voyages. The contrast in business performance with the steam fleet can be illustrated by considering the fortunes of the last new member of the Dunlop sail fleet, the *Clan Galbraith*, alongside those of the steamer *Queen Olga* which joined the fleet in the same year. After five years, the *Queen Olga* had completed eight voyages earning a total return equivalent to 79% of her capital cost. The *Clan Galbraith* took ten years to complete nine voyages, by which time she had only earned a total return equivalent to 75% of her capital cost. To put it another way, the steamer was earning roughly four times as much as the sailing vessel per annum; even taking account of her far higher capital cost, she was earning double the annual percentage return on investment.

Clan Galbraith
Voyage 1 (1894-5)
Glasgow – Sydney – Newcastle N.S.W. – San Francisco – Dublin
64th return = £20.0.0
Voyage 2 (1895-6)
Swansea – San Francisco – Hull
64th return = £22.0.0
Voyage 3 (1896-7)
Swansea – San Francisco – Limerick
64th return = £0.0.0
Voyage 4 (1897-8)
Liverpool – San Francisco – Havre
64th return = £15.0.0
Voyage 5 (1898-1900)
Greenhithe – San Diego – Vancouver – Delagoa Bay – Newcastle N.S.W. – San Francisco – Hull
64th return = £71.0.0
Voyage 6 (1900-01)
Tyne – Santa Rosalia – Tacoma – Antwerp
64th return = £37.0.0
Voyage 7 (1902-03)
Cardiff – Algoa Bay – Portland, Oregon – Cardiff
64th return = £25.0.0
Voyage 8 (1903-04)
Cardiff – San Francisco – Melbourne – Belfast
64th return = £0.0.0
Voyage 9 (1904-05)
Hamburg – Santa Rosalia – Puget Sound – Dunkirk and Antwerp
64th return = £7.10.0
Total capital cost = £16,876
64th share = £263.13.9
64th return after 10 years = £197.10.0 (75%)

Queen Olga
Voyage 1 (1894-5)
Sunderland – Cardiff – Aden – Muscat – Calcutta – Hamburg
64th return = £33.0.0

Voyage 2 (1895)
Cardiff – Port Said – Batoum – Java – New York
64th return = £32.0.0
Voyage 3 (1895-6)
Philadelphia – Hiogo – Shanghai – Amoy – Hong Kong – Singapore – New York
64th return = £43.0.0
Voyage 4 (1896-7)
New York – Kobe – San Francisco – Bombay – Liverpool – Dunkirk
64th return = £68.0.0
Voyage 5 (1897-8)
Cardiff – Aden – Calcutta – Singapore – Java – New York
64th return = £50.0.0
Voyage 6 (1898)
New York – Singapore – Hong Kong – Shanghai – Japan – Singapore – Java – New York – Avonmouth
64th return = £90.0.0
Voyage 7 (1898-9)
Cardiff – Aden – Karachi – Hull
64th return = £25.0.0
Voyage 8 (1899)
Cardiff – Aden – Shaleip – Calcutta – Rangoon – Java – New York
64th return = £44.0.0
Total capital cost = £31,248
64th share = £488.5.1
64th return after 5 years = £385.7.2 (79%)

A final footnote on the closing years of the Dunlop experience of sail can be provided by looking at one of their 20th century sailing voyages in more detail. The *Clan Robertson* started her 17th voyage on 5th August 1903 when she sailed from Antwerp for Tacoma with a cargo of cement and iron. She arrived at Tacoma on 2nd January 1904 just a few days short of five months later earning a freight of £1,731. She spent just over three months at Tacoma before sailing on 9th April 1904 for Sydney, New South Wales with a cargo of timber. She arrived at Sydney on 4th June, earning a freight of £1,756. On 27th July she coasted to Newcastle, New South Wales and on 18th August sailed from that port for Junin on the west coast of South America with a cargo of coal. She arrived there in November earning a freight of £1,439 and on the last day of the month coasted to Iquique. She sailed from Iquique for Dunkirk with a cargo of nitrate two days after Christmas. She arrived at Antwerp on 23rd April 1905, earning a freight of £2,323. On 14th May 1905 she left Dunkirk in tow for London, where she arrived the next day to load cargo for her next voyage. Total freight revenues had come to £7,249, but total voyage costs were £7,332. On top of this, Dunlop charged a management fee of £217, bringing the total loss to £300. In total, the voyage had taken one year and nine months – it had earned shareholders nothing.

Pre-war expansion
After a four-year gap following the delivery of the last Bartram-built steam tramp in 1897, the Dunlop fleet began a new phase of expansion and fleet renewal in 1901. The company continued to avoid Clyde builders, turning from the Wear to the Tyne, and ordering two 4,260-ton 360-foot vessels from the Northumberland Shipbuilding Co. Ltd. The *Queen Cristina* (2) entered service at the beginning of July and the *Queen Alexandra* later the same month. In the following year, the

company disposed of the oldest member of both its sail and its steam fleet. The *Clan Macfarlane* had enjoyed a fairly successful and blameless 21-year career and Dunlop were able to take advantage of short-term strength in the second-hand market for sailing vessels to get a price of £6,800 from Swedish buyers. The *Queen Margaret* was only 12 years old, but she was significantly smaller than the new vessels joining the fleet and Dunlop may not have thought her economical enough to justify the costs of passing survey.

A series of further new steam ships were ordered from the Northumberland yard throughout the remainder of the decade. The *Queen Helena* appeared in 1904, the *Queen Amelie* in 1905 and the *Queen Elizabeth* (2) in 1907, all of them sisters of the 1901 pair. The new *Queen Elizabeth*, unlike all the other steamers in the fleet, was registered in the name of the Merito Shipping Co. Ltd., which otherwise owned only sail tonnage. Another, slightly larger pair, the *Queen Eugenie* and *Queen Maud*, joined the fleet in 1909. In contrast to the 1890s, the effect of new investment was not largely cancelled out by marine losses. There were only two Dunlop casualties in the first decade of the 20th century, only one of them in the steam fleet. *Queen Cristina* appears to have been a jinxed name for the company. The first vessel of this name had been lost in 1899 when only three years old. The second did only slightly better, going aground in the fog near Crescent City, California in October 1907 when only six years old. After this Dunlops appears to have decided that the Regent Queen of Spain was indeed bad luck for them as they did not use the name again.

Dunlop began to dispose of their remaining sail tonnage in 1907 when the *Clan Mackenzie* and *Clan Robertson* were sold to the same Norwegian owner. The *Clan Buchanan* was sold in the following year, also to a Norwegian. The *Clan Macpherson*, actually slightly older and smaller than the *Clan Buchanan*, would undoubtedly have followed had she not become the last and most tragic of Dunlop's relatively short list of sailing ships losses. On what was probably intended to be the penultimate leg of her last voyage, she sailed from Newcastle, New South Wales for Valparaiso with a cargo of coal on 24th June 1909. The intention was almost certainly to load a cargo of nitrate for Europe in one of the Chilean ports and bring her home for sale. In the event, she never arrived at Valparaiso and no trace of her crew of 25 was ever discovered. There were a number of sailing ship losses on this route due to spontaneous combustion of New South Wales coal, but the formal inquiry into the disappearance rejected this possibility, deciding instead that the vessel had most probably failed to weather a gale.

There was one further disposal from the steam fleet in 1908, the 17-year old *Queen Adelaide* being sold to another Glasgow owner. Thus on New Year's Day 1910, the Dunlop fleet stood at two sailing vessels and ten steamers. The size of the fleet in vessel numbers had actually fallen by one from the situation a decade before (when there had been seven sailing vessels and six steamers), but its aggregate carrying and earning capacity was far higher.

The turn of the decade brought another phase of fleet renewal and replacement. The four vessels delivered in 1893-4, the last two sailing ships, the *Clan Graham* and *Clan Galbraith*, and two of the Bartram steam tramps, the *Queen Louise* and *Queen Olga*, were all sold in 1910-11. The two Clans went to Norwegian owners and the two Queens to Greeks (one of them after a short stay with a London owner). On the credit side, the company took delivery of three new steamers in 1911-12, all of them just under 5,000 tons and just over 400 feet. One, the *Queen Louise* (2), came from Northumberland Shipbuilding, the other two, *Queen Adelaide* (2) and *Queen Margaret* (2), came from Robert Duncan and Co. of Port Glasgow. The latter pair were the first steamers ordered from Clyde builders since the first *Queen Margaret* of 1890, and were, with the sale of the last two Clans, the only Clyde-built ships in the fleet.

Completed in 1896 the *Queen Eleanor* (1) was sold to Italian buyers in 1913 and renamed *Luigi*. She was lost in 1918. *[J. and M. Clarkson collection]*

To war

Dunlop maintained its apparent policy of selling vessels in middle rather than old age, almost certainly driven by survey considerations, by making one further clear out of tonnage before the First World War. In 1913 no fewer than three ships were sold, the last two survivors of the Bartram building programme of the 1890s, the *Queen Eleanor* and *Queen Mary*, both of which went to the same Genoese owners, and the first ship of the Northumberland building programme of the following decade, the *Queen Alexandra*, which was sold to a London company. Thus when war broke out in August 1914, the Dunlop fleet consisted of eight steamers, all built in the previous 10 years.

Vessel positions at the commencement of hostilities are shown below. It was entirely typical of the Dunlop tramping business in the pre-war years that none of the vessels were anywhere near European waters or a UK port. Three ships were in the Indian Ocean, one in the North Pacific, two on the west coast of South America, and two on passage (in opposite directions) around South America. The first of them would not return to British waters until *Queen Eugenie* arrived at Cardiff from Karachi and Marseilles on 20th September, and *Queen Louise* arrived at Swansea from the west coast of North America two days later.

Fleet dispositions, August 1914		
Vessel	**built**	
Queen Helena	1904	On passage from Norfolk, Virginia (departed 16/6) for Nanaimo, B.C. (arrived 7/9).
Queen Amelie	1905	In port at Saleef (arrived 18/7), to sail for Calcutta (mid-August).
Queen Elizabeth	1907	In port at Karachi (arrived early August), to sail for Rangoon (28/8).
Queen Eugenie	1909	On passage from Karachi (departed 30/7) for Marseilles (arrived 29/8).
Queen Maud	1909	In port at Guayamas (arrived late July), to sail for Astoria (arrived 18/8).
Queen Adelaide	1911	In port at Vladivostock, to sail from Nicolaievsk for Muroran and Astoria (30/8).
Queen Louise	1912	On passage from Vancouver and San Francisco (departed 30/6) for Swansea (arrived 22/9).
Queen Margaret	1912	In port at Valparaiso (arrived 23/7), to sail for San Francisco (26/8).

Two further vessels would join the fleet early in the course of the war. The first was actually the company's only second-hand acquisition since the early days of the wooden sailing fleet. The *Elfland*, acquired from Fred Drughorn of Newcastle in December 1914, was in fact only eight months old and a product of the same Tyneside shipyard which had built six of her new fleet-mates. She was renamed *Queen Alexandra* (2). Near the end of 1915 she was joined by the newly-built *Queen Mary* (2), a product of Russell and Co. of Port Glasgow. The latter was not only the largest ship the company had yet owned but, in terms of gross tonnage, was to retain that distinction until after the Second World War.

Largely because it was spread all over the world, the Dunlop fleet came only gradually under government control. The *Queen Eugenie* was the first vessel requisitioned on 29th April 1915, but she only served a week as an Expeditionary Force transport before returning to commercial service. Two further vessels, the *Queen Louise* and the *Queen Adelaide*, came under government control in May 1915. The former served throughout the Gallipoli campaign, returned to commercial service in June 1916 and then was requisitioned again in November of the same year. The latter stayed in government service until her loss in 1917. Most of the fleet was occupied on government business by the winter of 1916-17. The exceptions were the *Queen Eugenie*, which did not serve again after her brief 1915 requisition, the *Queen Elizabeth*, which was not taken over until July 1918, and the new *Queen Mary*, which never came under government control. The vessels that did serve were deployed on a range of different services. The deployments of the *Queen Alexandra*, summarised in the table below, were fairly typical.

Queen Alexandra – government service, 1915-19			
Service	**Dates**	**Service**	**Dates**
Collier (C.782)	21/10/1915 to 22/1/1916	Collier	1/7/1917 to 24/1/1918
Collier (Uganda Railway)	23/1/1916 to 30/8/1916	Wheat	25/1/1918 to 17/5/1918
Collier (colonial service)	31/8/1916 to 12/11/1916	Com. Branch (ore)	18/5/1918 to 27/6/1918
Wheat (Australia)	13/11/1916 to 11/3/1917	Collier	28/6/1918 to 15/8/1918
Wheat (Gulf)	12/3/1917 to 18/5/1917	Wheat (US: 2 voyages)	16/8/1918 to 17/2/1919
Collier	19/5/1917 to 18/6/1917	Collier	18/2/1919 to 26/3/1919
Wheat (States)	19/6/1917 to 30/6/1917	Wheat (Canada)	27/3/1919 to -6/6/1919

The peak of the German submarine offensive against Allied shipping came in 1917, and Dunlop's war losses all occurred in that year. In fact, the company lost four ships in just under six months, all in European waters or in the North Atlantic approaches to European ports. The most tragic loss was the first, the *Queen Eugenie*, which was sunk by *UC 67* in the Mediterranean on 25th March. The vessel was torpedoed in the night and appears to have gone down quickly taking the master and 34 members of the crew with her. An empty lifeboat was seen the next day, but there was no definite news of her loss until a letter was received from an apprentice in a German prisoner-of-war camp. He and a gunner had been picked up by the submarine – they were the only survivors.

The second loss, less than a month later, was the newest vessel in the fleet. The *Queen Mary* was still less than two years old when she was sunk on 16th April in the Western Approaches by *U 60*, taking nine men down with her. Still on commercial service, she was in bound from New York for Havre with general cargo when struck by a torpedo in the engine room north west of Fastnet. One engineer and three Chinese firemen were killed in the explosion, but the ship remained afloat for some time, allowing a distress message to be sent before she was abandoned. Another five Chinese crewmen drowned when a boat capsized before the remaining survivors were picked up by a naval vessel and landed in Ireland. An idea of the extent to which wartime inflation was impacting on the cost and value of ships can be gained by looking at the payments made to Dunlop under the War Risks Insurance Scheme for their first two losses. For the *Queen Eugenie*, built in 1909, Dunlop received £48,268. For the slightly larger *Queen Mary*, built in 1915 when wartime price rises were already beginning to bite, they received £116,965.

On 18th June the *Queen Adelaide* was sunk by *U 70* with the loss of three men off St. Kilda when inbound under escort from the St Lawrence for the east coast of Scotland. She was also struck in the engine room, but on this occasion the ship went down in only six minutes. The only casualties, however, were two engineers and a fireman killed in the explosion, and the rest of the crew was picked up by the escort. Like the *Queen Mary*, the *Queen Adelaide* was not armed. Even at this fairly late stage in the war, there were not enough guns available to give all merchant ships a defensive armament, and many ships on trans-Atlantic service still had none.

Finally, on 17th September, the *Queen Amelie* fell victim to a rare attack by U-boats working together, being shelled and then torpedoed by *U 95* and *UB 62* off the Shetlands. The vessel was employed on the munitions service to North Russia and was returning to Britain with a partial cargo of flax. She was armed with a 4.7-inch gun, and when one submarine appeared on the starboard beam, her fire was sufficient to drive the enemy under. The U-boat re-emerged astern, to be quickly followed to the surface by a second to starboard. The *Queen Amelie* fought her assailants for two hours until her ammunition ran out. By this time the vessel had been hit or near-missed about 30 times, and the master decided to abandon ship. The burning freighter was first torpedoed by one of the submarines and then shelled until she sank. Amazingly enough considering the length of the engagement, none of the 39-strong crew were injured and all were rescued safely the same day.

The German submarine menace also accounted for a number of former Dunlop ships sailing under other colours. The most unfortunate were the former Clan sailing vessels, five of which were still earning a decent living under Norwegian colours when war broke out. Four of these were lost in exactly the same six-month period as their steam successors and one, the *Clan Galbraith*, still sailing under her original name, was sunk by the same U-boat that would later account for the *Queen Adelaide*.

The depleted Dunlop fleet had one lucky escape on 20th January 1918 when the *Queen Margaret* was mined near the Nab Light Vessel just after leaving Portsmouth for Boulogne. The explosion flooded number 1 hold, but the damage was localised enough for the ship to remain afloat and be brought into Southampton on the same day for repair. Later in the same year another member of the fleet profited from a rare opportunity to take revenge against the German submarine service. Early in the morning of 9th May the *Queen Alexandra* was proceeding up the Channel under escort when she sighted a submarine on the surface close under her bows. The U-boat was rammed at full speed under port helm and disappeared. The *Queen Alexandra* proceeded on her way, but her escort, the patrol boat *P.33*, dropped a buoy on the site, and when the latter returned at daybreak she found a large track of thick oil and acid stretching eastward from the scene of the action. The wreck was subsequently found by the French Navy and discovered to be that of *UB 78*, which had gone down with all hands.

Reconstruction and depression

Despite its losses, the Dunlop fleet ended the war in reasonably robust shape with six relatively modern steamers. Only the 14-year old *Queen Helena*, which was damaged in a post-war mining incident in December 1918, might normally have been scheduled for replacement, but times were anything but normal. The disruption to normal shipping business caused by the war lasted into 1920, and with port congestion adding to what was really an artificial tonnage shortage, freight rates and ship prices (both new and second-hand) experienced a sharp but short-lived boom. Some established ship-owners would fatally damage their businesses by seeking to replace war losses while prices were so high, and a number of new entrants to the sector would see their businesses flower and perish in little over a year. Thomas Dunlop and Sons, however, took the opposite course, selling its old fleet in its entirety, and with the exception of a brief experiment in an entirely new shipping trade, staying out of the business until conditions and prices returned to normal.

The *Queen Helena*, *Queen Elizabeth*, *Queen Maud* and *Queen Alexandra* were all sold in 1919 to British owners at or near the peak of the market, in some cases before the vessels concerned had actually been released from Government requisition. The *Queen Margaret* and *Queen Louise* would remain in the Dunlop Steamship Co. Ltd. until 1922. In that

Sir Thomas Dunlop, seated bottom right with Lady Margaret and guests aboard the *Harbinger* in the early 1920s. A keen yachtsman, his yawl *Harbinger* is shown to the right. *[Both: The Dunlop Family]*

Two of the four ships disposed of in 1919: *Queen Elizabeth* (2) in a graving dock at Barry (above) and the *Queen Maud* (1) (below). Both had a number of further owners before being lost, the former by fire in 1937 and the latter wrecked in 1932. *[Above J. and M. Clarkson collection; below: Nigel Farrell collection]*

year the company itself would be wound up with the *Queen Margaret* also being sold to another British venture and the *Queen Louise* entering a new venture under a different guise.

Only a few tramp owners were engaged in the tanker business in the immediate aftermath of the First World War. The war itself, however, had produced a considerable expansion in the oil industry and there was a significant enough shortage of specialist tonnage for even old sail tonnage to be bought up for conversion into powered tankers. With industry conditions

making economic planning in their traditional business a near impossibility, the Dunlops appear to have decided that the time was ripe for an experiment in the tanker business. To this end, they used some of the proceeds from the sale of the old fleet to buy the war standard *Waziristan* from Common Brothers and convert her to a tanker. Renamed *Coylet* she was placed in a newly floated single-ship company and re-entered service in the spring of 1921. In the same year the last remaining member of the original fleet, the *Queen Louise*, was also converted. She kept her original name but was also transferred to a new single ship company, the Cadogan Steamship Co. Ltd. The latter company was registered on 14th June 1922 with a capital of £46,000. It was an English rather than a Scottish company, with its office in London, and management was actually transferred to R.S. Dalgleish Ltd. with whom the Dunlops had a business relationship and in which one of Sir Thomas Dunlop's sons served as a partner. The Dunlops themselves were significant shareholders and would take over management within two years.

The tanker ventures were not destined to last long. The *Coylet* was abandoned on fire off Florida on 8th February 1922 and was subsequently sunk as a hazard to shipping by a US coastguard cutter. On 23rd January 1924 the *Queen Louise* grounded in Holyhead Bay, damaging herself severely enough to be declared a constructive total loss after re-floating and sold for scrap. Whether the ships were not earning a promising enough return, or the losses simply discouraged the Dunlops from risking more in a business in which they were not yet properly established, is not clear. One way or the other, the family turned its back on the tanker business and re-entered traditional tramping.

The new Dunlop steam tramp fleet was launched in 1924 with the purchase of three war standards. All were acquired at a fraction of the price at which they had originally been sold by the government to their first private owners. The *Sierra Blanca*, renamed *Queen Eleanor* (2), came from Belgian owners, and the *Bembridge*, renamed *Queen Olga* (2), from the London-based Temperley Steamship Co. Ltd. The most interesting case was the *Evangelos*, which was renamed *Queen Maud* (2). She was one of a group of nine Far East-built standards bought on credit while still on the stocks by the Greek ship owner E.E. Ambatielos. Ambatielos intended to sail the vessels to Europe and sell them at a profit, but completion was delayed and second-hand prices collapsed and the deal fell apart. The vessels were re-possessed and after a court decided that Ambatielos had no case for damages due to late delivery, were sold at the much reduced prices then prevalent in the market.

The *Queen Olga* was registered in the name of the Cadogan Steamship Co. Ltd. which was returned to Dunlop management. The *Queen Eleanor* and *Queen Maud* were placed in an entirely new company, the Queen Line Ltd., registered on 23rd January 1924 with a called up capital of £70,987. The family business of Thomas Dunlop and Sons which was behind both ventures was still headed by the sons of its founder, both now senior statesmen in the Glasgow business

The *Sierra Blanca* was the first of three ships purchased in 1924. She was renamed *Queen Eleanor* (2) and is seen leaving Lyttelton, New Zealand. *[Ian J. Farquhar collection]*

Sir Thomas (left) at the wheel of his steam yacht *Ariana*. The *Ariana* (above), was built by Ramage and Ferguson at Leith in 1902, was bought by Sir Thomas in about 1924 and sold following his death in 1938. *[Both: The Dunlop Family]*

community. Thomas had been Lord Provost of Glasgow from 1914 to 1917, had been created a baronet in 1916 and GBE a year later. Robert, who was more actively involved in the ship management side of the business, was director of the Glasgow Chamber of Commerce, representing it on the Clyde Navigation Trust, and would become President of the Chamber of Shipping of the United Kingdom in 1934, having served on its council for over 30 years.

The *Queen Maud* of 1919 was bought from Greek owners in 1924 and after 11 years service was sold to other Greek owners. *[J. and M. Clarkson collection]*

The Dunlops would trade through more than a decade with the trio of war standards. It was a significantly smaller fleet than the one operated before the First World War, but direct family investment in the ships was significantly higher than it had been in the earlier period and there was significantly less public capital which could be attracted into shares in shipping companies than had been the case when the fleet was 10-12 strong. Although the war had produced significant changes in the structure of world seaborne trade, and significantly weakened the British merchant marine's dominance of it, the inter-war Dunlop tramps were engaged in trades very similar to those of their pre-war brethren. A series of snapshots of the fleet at six-month intervals through 1928 and 1929 demonstrates that it was still very much a world-wide tramping business.

Fleet dispositions, 1928-1929	
1st January 1928	
Queen Eleanor	On passage from Port Pirie (dep 24/12) to Port Natal (arr 17/1)
Queen Maud	On passage from west coast South America to New York (arr 10/1)
Queen Olga	On passage from Houston (dep 11/12) to British Columbia (arr 6/1)
1st July 1928	
Queen Eleanor	On passage from Port Pirie (dep 21/6) to Port Natal (arr 18/7)
Queen Maud	In port at Tocopilla (arr 29/6 from Buenos Aires, dep 7/7 for Pisagua)
Queen Olga	On passage from Liverpool (dep 1/6) via Capetown for Sydney NSW (arr 20/7)
1st January 1929	
Queen Eleanor	Arr New York from Buenos Aires (dep 12/1 for Montevideo)
Queen Maud	On passage from New York (dep 21/12) to Montevideo (arr 13/1)
Queen Olga	On passage from Tandjong Priok (dep 28/12) to Brisbane (arr 28/1)
1st July 1929	
Queen Eleanor	In port at New York (arr 30/6 from west coast South America, dep 11/7 for Montevideo)
Queen Maud	Arr New York from west coast South America (dep 5/7 for WC South America)
Queen Olga	In port at South Shields (arr 23/6 from Hull, dep 9/7 for Dutch East Indies)

The onset of the Great Depression in 1929 had a severe impact on all shipping companies. The small Dunlop fleet traded reasonably well through the early part of the slump, but thereafter was forced into long-term lay-up along with much of the rest of the British merchant marine. The *Queen Eleanor* was laid up on the Clyde between March and October 1931. She then traded until November 1932 when she laid up again, this time at Blyth. She stayed there until late August 1934 before returning to service. The *Queen Maud* kept sailing until August 1932 after which she was laid up on the Clyde until February 1934. The *Queen Olga* was laid up at Barry from December 1930, leaving there in April 1931, but only to lay up on the Clyde, where she remained until the following April. After one North Atlantic voyage she laid up at Blyth from June to December 1932, but thereafter managed reasonably consistent employment through the period when both her sisters were laid up.

A new fleet and a new war

The entire fleet was trading again by the beginning of 1935. By this time, however, the vessels were approaching an age where replacement would normally make good business sense, provided new tonnage could be found at attractive prices. The company was fortunate that its decision to renew its fleet coincided with the introduction of the so-called Scrap and Build scheme by the British government which offered loans to cover the cost of building new ships in British yards with the proviso that two tons of old tonnage be scrapped for every new ton built. Dunlop became one of the biggest users of the scheme, ordering four new Doxford Economy-type shelter-deck motor ships through it, financed by Treasury loans totalling £359,450 deferred for two years and then re-payable over 12 at an interest rate of 3%. In addition, one of the partners in the firm, Robert J. Dunlop junior, ordered a fifth on behalf of the Lomond Shipping Co. Ltd., a new company he set up and subsequently managed himself.

In common with most of the other owners involved in the scheme, Dunlop did not scrap the vessels already in its fleet to meet the terms of the loan. Second-hand prices were beginning to rise, and the three standards could command far better prices from other owners than from shipbreakers. Instead, they entered the second-hand market themselves, buying a motley fleet of old vessels which was then sold on for scrap at a small loss. The most distinguished member of this collection was the former Glen Line steamer *Pembrokeshire*, but it also included a US-built war standard, a Doxford turret ship and several small North Sea/ Baltic traders built in the 1880s.

Scrap and Build tonnage (including that utilized to build the *Dunkeld*)			
Name	Tons	Built	Previous names
Agii Victores	1,639	1895	*Siciliano, Capelbay, Cairnloch*
Aimilios	3,638	1898	*Nicolaos Zafirakis, Cambrian King, Ullapool*
Bomarsund	4.337	1907	*Cooee, Neumunster*
Comte De Flandre	3,621	1907	*Akropolis, Alpine Range, Kintail*
Comtesse De Flandre	3,174	1907	*Bankdale*
Dania	2,247	1888	*Dannebrog, Paul Pagh, Theodoros, North Flint*
Hedwig	1,827	1892	*Hedwig Fischer, Mary, Praga, Hedwig Fischer, Pollux, Byzanz, Godrevy*
Hillcroft	2,268	1912	*Sheba*
Marie Schroder	742	1889	*Hammerburg, Stella Maris, Beta, Sirius*
Nordsee	1,293	1890	*Klaipeda, Hochsee, Johannes Tiemann, Balmore*
Pembrokeshire	7,805	1915	
Roi Leopold	3,174	1906	*Karnak*
Stork	2,029	1904	
Tiber	1,343	1899	
Virgo	3,835	1906	*Gwynmead, Elgin*
Wytheville	6,098	1919	

Doxfords of Sunderland only built one of the new vessels. The remaining three Queens and the sister ordered for Lomond Shipping were built to the Doxford design by Barclay, Curle at Whiteinch on the Clyde. As these vessels entered service, the war standards were sold for further trading. The *Queen Maud* (2), the only one of the trio whose name would be re-used for a new building, was the first to go, sold to Greek owners in May 1936. The *Queen Olga* was sold at the end of the same year to British owners, but the *Queen Eleanor* was retained until early 1938 before going to a London broker who quickly sold her on to Italian owners. By this time all the new vessels were in service. Barclay Curle delivered *Queen Adelaide* (3) in September 1936. She was followed by *Queen Victoria* (2) from the same builder and *Queen Maud* (3) from Doxfords, both in November. Barclay, Curle also delivered the *Queen Anne* (2) in January 1937 and finally the *Dunkeld* for the Lomond Shipping Co. Ltd. in May of the same year. The *Queen Anne* was registered in the name of the Cadogan Steamship Co. Ltd.; the other three Queens went to the Queen Line Ltd. The vessels were all effectively sister ships, although the *Queen Maud* differed in having a compact central superstructure while the other four all had a split superstructure with number 3 hold between the bridge and the funnel.

The completion of the fleet renewal coincided with the passing of the old generation of managers. Sir Thomas Dunlop and Robert Jack Dunlop both died in 1938 aged 83 and 81 respectively. The business by this time was being run by the third generation, Thomas, who now became the second Baronet, and his brother Robert Jack Dunlop. They were joined as partners in 1938 by the first representative of the fourth generation, Thomas Dunlop junior, son of the second Sir Thomas. With four modern motor ships and a fifth in an associated company, the Dunlop tramp fleet could claim to be one of the most up-to-date in Britain. Unfortunately, war was on its way again, and the latest generation of Queens would be exposed to the threat of another U-boat offensive after only three years of earning peacetime profits.

Dunlop would lose three of their four Queen motor ships during the war, all sunk by submarines while sailing in African waters. The first to go was the *Queen Maud*. Outward bound from Cardiff with coal and government stores for Freetown and thence around Africa to Alexandria, she did not make the first port, being torpedoed and sunk 200 miles from her destination by *U 38* on 5th May 1941. The ship had sailed from the UK in convoy but was sailing on her own following its dispersal when she was struck on the port side by two torpedoes in quick succession, the first just abaft the bridge and the second aft in number 5 hold. The ship was sinking by the stern, but

The first of the new fleet, what appears to be an almost new *Queen Adelaide* (3) with topmasts lowered approaching the entrance to the Manchester Ship Canal at Eastham. *[B. and A. Feilden/J. and M. Clarkson collection]*

Sir Thomas Dunlop, the second baronet (top left), was born in 1881. He joined the company in 1904, was made a partner in 1911, and died in 1963 after a long and active life.

Peter Mitchell Dunlop (middle) served an apprenticeship with the shipbrokers Howard Houlder Partners. He became a partner in the Dunlop family firm in 1911 but retired from the business in 1919 to take up farming.

Thomas Dunlop junior (top right) was born in 1912 and was a partner from 1938. He served as a major in the Royal Signals Corps during the Second World War and became the third baronet on his father's death.

Sir Thomas Dunlop, the first baronet (right), with his grand-daughter, Dorothy Frances Dunlop, and Thomas Dunlop, Sir Thomas's eldest son and father of Dorothy, at the launch of the *Queen Victoria* on 15th September 1936. Dorothy was then 14 years of age and had been fascinated by ships from childhood. One can see how thrilled she was to be launching their latest ship. *[All: The Dunlop Family]*

Queen Victoria (2) at Cape Town whilst on charter to, and in the colours of, Westralian Farmers. *[Ian J. Farquhar collection]*

Dunkeld was owned by the Lomond Shipping Co. Ltd., a single-ship company set up by Robert J. Dunlop in 1937. *[Ian J. Farquhar]*

the U-boat commander appears to have been a man in a hurry, as he put another torpedo into the engine room, causing the ship to break in two and the superstructure to collapse on the jolly boat which was just getting away. Despite this, only one man was lost in the sinking, and the vessel's master, Captain R.J. McDonald, who had commanded the *Queen Eleanor* (2) through the Great Depression, survived the war to command other vessels in the post-war fleet.

The next loss was altogether more tragic. The *Queen Victoria* sailed from Table Bay for Aden with government stores and a crew of 48 on 21st June 1942 and simply disappeared. No distress signal was heard or wreckage found. It was determined later that she had been torpedoed and sunk on 28th June in the Mozambique Channel by the Japanese submarine *I-10*.

The third and final loss was the *Queen Anne*, torpedoed and sunk by *U 509* off Cape Town on 10th February 1943 on a round Africa to the Middle East voyage very similar to the ones which had claimed her two sisters. She was less than a day out of Cape Town in a convoy of six ships under the escort of two armed trawlers when hit on the starboard side in numbers 2 and 3 holds (a combined hold without an intervening bulkhead). The vessel swung around after the explosion and was thus hit on the port side by a second torpedo arriving only seven minutes after the first. This caused the vessel to break in two, with both halves sinking in only three minutes, washing some of the crew into the water. Despite this, only five lives were lost in the sinking. These included Captain C.H. Radford, who had been relieving the usual master Captain C.R. Williamson for the voyage in question. Both Radford and Williamson were also veterans of the inter-war fleet, having commanded the *Queen Olga* (2) and the *Queen Maud* (2) respectively. Sadly, Williamson's escape was to prove only a temporary one as he was to be lost in the only government-owned vessel to be sunk under Dunlop management during the war.

In 1940 following the German conquest of Denmark Dunlop had been assigned the management of two small Danish motor ships, the *Bornholm* and the *Gudrun Maersk*. These vessels sailed safely throughout the war, although Dunlop passed over the management of the latter to another firm

mid-way through the conflict. In 1943-44, the company was assigned the management of two Canadian-built war standards, the *Fort Missanabie* and the *Fort Aspin*, followed up in 1945 by the British-built *Empire Freetown*. The *Fort Missanabie* was the vessel lost. She had already had a near escape when the hull cracked in heavy weather while on a Russian convoy in the winter of 1943-4. The crack had been re-welded and a four-foot plate welded and riveted over it and around the entire shell of the ship. Transferred to the Mediterranean, she was on her way in convoy from Taranto to Augusta in ballast on 19th May 1944 when she was hit by a torpedo from *U 453*. The explosion took place under number 2 hold, but the ship broke in two across number 3 hatch in exactly the same place as the previous crack had appeared. The forepart sank immediately, taking Captain Williamson and 11 others down with it. The after part was taken in tow but sank before it could be brought to port. The *Fort Missanabie* was actually the last ship to be sunk by a U-boat in the Mediterranean. *U 453* did not survive long to celebrate her success, being depth-charged to the surface and sunk by gunfire from British destroyers two days after her successful attack.

Post-war reprise

When hostilities ended in 1945, Thomas Dunlop and Sons owned just one ship, the *Queen Adelaide*. All three of her Queen sisters had been torpedoed, and her fourth sister, the *Dunkeld*, had left Dunlop control in 1943 when the Lomond Shipping Co. Ltd. sold her to J.A. Billmeir. From the start, the company took a cautious approach to re-building its business. As a result of the huge standard shipbuilding schemes sponsored by the Allied governments, there was no shortage of modern tonnage potentially available for purchase. Economic prospects were uncertain, however, and many traditional trades were either completely disrupted or threatened by political upheaval and rising nationalism in many different areas of the globe. In contrast to the buying frenzy that had brought so many companies to ruin after the First World War, there was no general rush to re-build fleets through purchases of now surplus state-owned tonnage.

Queen Anne in New Zealand waters. Bought as the *Kelmscott* in 1949 and renamed *Queen Anne* (3) she had served the company for only five years when she was sold to Polish Ocean Lines. *[George Scott collection]*

Dunlop took its first tentative step towards reconstruction in April 1947 when it bought the Liberty *Samaye*. The vessel was renamed *Queen Victoria* (3) and registered in the joint ownership of the Queen Line Ltd. and the Cadogan Steamship Co. Ltd., the latter of which had been without any vessels since the loss of the *Queen Anne* (2) in 1943. The experiment was not to prove a successful one. The Liberty proved expensive to run compared to the Doxford economy ships that had made up the fleet over the previous decade, and also appeared to have some built-in defects requiring almost continuous expenditure. She was sold in January 1949 after only 18 months in the fleet to T. and J. Harrison, who appear to have cured her of her expensive and unreliable ways.

The *Queen Victoria* was replaced almost immediately in the fleet by another war-built oil-burning steam ship. Built by Readhead of South Shields in 1943, the *Kelmscott* had served six years on the newsprint run from Newfoundland to the UK. She was renamed *Queen Anne* (3) and was again placed in the joint ownership of the Queen Line Ltd and the Cadogan Steamship Co. Ltd.

In 1951, the company entered what was to prove its last exercise in fleet renewal. The two shipowning companies were still cash rich as a result of relative under-investment since the end of the war, and with second-hand values appearing to be on the ascendant, the decision was taken to increase their shipping exposure. In July the *Argos Hill*, built in 1942 as the *Empire Torrent*, was purchased from Counties Ship Management. Another oil-burning steamer, she was renamed *Queen Maud* (4) and again placed in joint company ownership. Later the same year, an opportunity was taken to dispose of the 15-year old *Queen Adelaide* and replace her with a similar motor ship half her age. The new acquisition, the *Stanpark* (ex-*Jersey Hart*), was renamed *Queen Eleanor* (3) and became the sole property of the Queen Line Ltd.

1951 marked the 100th anniversary of Thomas Dunlop and Sons, and to mark the event the company commissioned a

company history. This slim, privately printed volume came out before the *Queen Eleanor* joined the fleet. It spoke modestly but confidently of a bright future, encapsulated in its report were details of the company's first planned new building in a decade and a half, a ship booked for delivery by Swan Hunter in 1954. In the event, however, the new order was never confirmed, and the *Queen Eleanor* turned out to be the last ship the company was to own. 1954 was marked not by the delivery of a new ship but by the sale of two of the existing fleet, the *Queen Anne* to Polish Ocean Lines and the *Queen Maud* to a Panama-flagged concern run by London Greeks. The *Queen Eleanor* herself soldiered on until 1956, when she too was sold, bringing to an end 88 years of Dunlop ship ownership.

The apparently sudden departure of Dunlop from the shipping business was the end product of a series of factors that had been at work since the end of the war. The war-built standards with which the company had been forced to replace its losses to the enemy had been constructed to the austere standards of the conflict and required both significant maintenance and heavy investment to meet surveys. These additional costs were all the harder to meet in market conditions in which the two largest world trading blocks, the USA and the USSR, restricted a significant amount of business to ships flying their own flags. In addition, as small limited companies like those in the Dunlop group built up their financial resources to build new ships designed for modern conditions, they came under attack from asset strippers seeking to exploit the widening gap between a firm's net financial worth and its value as a going shipping concern. The final blow was the ongoing increase in the replacement cost of ships. Even by the early 1950s, the cost of one new tramp steamer was in excess of the total cost of the four Queen motor ships ordered through Scrap and Build 15 years before – a difference only partially compensated for by general inflation. Survival in the ocean tramping trades simply required a different business model than that on which Thomas Dunlop and Sons had flourished for so long.

FLEET LIST

All are steel-hulled steam or motor ships unless otherwise stated. Engine dimensions are given in brackets following the name of the builder. Port numbers are given after registration details.

1. WYE 1868-1872 Wood barque

O.N. 44529 349g 332n
116.2 x 26.8 x 17.0 feet
7.3.1863: Launched by J. Blumer, Sunderland for Robert Gayner, Sunderland as WYE.
9.3.1863: Registered at Sunderland (34/1863) in the ownership of Robert H. Gayner as WYE.
1.1864: Sold to Alexander Adamson, London.
4.2.1864: Re-registered at London (52/1864).
11.1868: Sold to Thomas Dunlop (32/64 shares) and John Neil (32/64 shares), Glasgow for £2,800.
10.12.1868: Re-registered at Glasgow (143/1868) in the ownership of Thomas Dunlop and John Neil.
12.8.1872: Sold to Francis Stafford and Co., Blyth for £2,000.
23.4.1873: Re-registered at North Shields (21/1873).
1879: Broken up.
4.12.1879: Register closed.

2. MARION NEIL 1871-1877 Wood barque

O.N. 63840 399g 379n
130.3 x 28.1 x 17.3 feet
7.1871: Completed by Reay and Nisbet, Sunderland for Thomas Dunlop (24/64), John Neil (24/64) and Andrew Reid (16/64), Glasgow as MARION NEIL at a cost of £4,275
14.8.1871: Registered at Glasgow (64/1871) in the ownership of Thomas Dunlop, John Neil and Andrew Reid.
3.1877: Sold to James Hardie, London.
3.4.1877: Re-registered at London (43/1877) in the ownership of James Hardie.
5.9.1885: Wrecked at East London.
21.10.1885: Register closed.

3. ANDREW REID 1872-1885 Wood barque

O.N. 67983 829g 790n
177.0 x 32.0 x 21.0 feet
3.1870: Launched by Bartlett, Southampton for Richardson, Glasgow as LORD PALMERSTON but not registered.
1872: Sold to Thomas Dunlop, John Neil and Andrew Reid, Glasgow for £7,500 and renamed ANDREW REID.
24.7.1872: Registered at Glasgow (60/1872) in the ownership of Thomas Dunlop (16/64), John Neil (16/64), Andrew Reid (16/64), Thomas Thomas (8/64) and Charles Ferguson (8/64).
23.3.1885: Taken by Russell and Co., Port Glasgow in part payment for CLAN MACPHERSON (sale price £4,000).
3.1886: Sold by public auction at Rio de Janeiro and converted into a coal hulk.
30.4.1886: Register closed.

4. ROBINA DUNLOP 1874-1877 Iron barque

O.N. 68101 512g 493n
142.9 x 29.7 x 17.5 feet
4.1874: Launched by John Crown, Sunderland for Thomas Dunlop, John Neil and Andrew Reid, Glasgow as ROBINA DUNLOP.
12.5.1874: Registered at Glasgow (55/1874) in the ownership of John Neil.
13.8.1877: Lost in Cook Straits, New Zealand.
13.10.1877: Register closed.

5. CLAN MACLEOD 1874-1887 Iron barque

O.N. 68086 671g 646n
179.5 x 31.3 x 17.5 feet
18.2.1874: Launched by Bartram, Haswell and Co., Sunderland (Yard No.75) for Thomas Dunlop and Sons, Glasgow as CLAN MACLEOD.
30.3.1874: Registered at Glasgow (32/1874) in the ownership of Thomas Dunlop.
1887: Taken by Russell and Co., Port Glasgow in part payment for CLAN BUCHANAN.
1888: Sold to Sir Roderick W. Cameron, Glasgow.
15.8.1900: Sold to J.J. Craig, Auckland, New Zealand.
17.8.1900: Glasgow register closed; transferred to Auckland (4/1901).
14.12.1905: Renamed JAMES CRAIG.
19.6.1911: Sold to British New Guinea Development Co. Ltd., Sydney, New South Wales and converted into a storage hulk at Port Moresby.
19.8.1918: Sold to Henry Jones and Co. Ltd., Hobart, re-rigged and returned to service.

1921: Laid up at Recherche Bay.
11.1925: Sold to Catamaran Coal Mining Company and hulked, drifted ashore in 1932 and abandoned.
1972: Refloated and towed to Hobart for temporary repairs in the following year.
1981: Towed to Sydney for full restoration.
2001: Returned to service as part of the Australian Heritage Fleet.

6. CLAN CAMPBELL 1875-1881 Iron barque

O.N. 71713 749g 729n
185.0 x 31.5 x 18.3 feet
10.3.1875: Launched by Bartram, Haswell and Co., Sunderland (Yard No.80) for Thomas Dunlop and Sons, Glasgow as CLAN CAMPBELL.
10.4.1875: Registered in Glasgow (32/1875) in the ownership of Thomas Dunlop.
18.1.1881: Wrecked on the south east corner of Ailsa Craig having delayed taking a tow from the tug COMMODORE until too late, and three last-minute attempts to pass a hawser having failed, whilst on a voyage from Le Havre to Glasgow. All saved.
4.3.1881: Register closed

7. CLAN FERGUSON 1876-1893 Iron barque

O.N. 73869 823g 799n
199.2 x 31.6 x 19.3 feet
21.9.1876: Launched by John Reid and Co., Port Glasgow (Yard No.5s) for Thomas Dunlop and Sons, Glasgow as CLAN FERGUSON.
27.10.1876: Registered at Glasgow (89/1876) in the ownership of Thomas Dunlop.

Clan Macleod after being sold out of the fleet in 1887. [World Ship Society Ltd.]

6.11.1893: Sold to William Todd Lithgow (Russell and Co.), Port Glasgow for £4,850 to help finance building of CLAN GALBRAITH.

13.9.1895: Frederick Wilhelm Dalstrom, Hamburg, Germany empowered to sell vessel for not less than £3,250 at Hamburg.

9.1895: Sold to Schlubach & Co., Hamburg; re-sold to J.V. Peral, Honduras and renamed JUANA PERAL.

19.9.1895: Register closed.

1898: Transferred to Peruvian registry at Callao.

1909: Sold to Pablo Arana, Callao.

1912: Renamed CLAUDINA.

1930: Hulked.

8. CLAN GRANT 1878-1893 Iron barque

O.N. 78591 1,055g 1,005n

211.0 x 34.1 x 21.0 feet

20.3.1878: Launched by D. and W. Henderson and Co., Glasgow (Yard No.184) for Thomas Dunlop and Sons, Glasgow as CLAN GRANT.

11.4.1878: Registered at Glasgow (27/1878) in the ownership of Thomas Dunlop.

13.10.1893: Sold to William Todd Lithgow (Russell and Co.), Port Glasgow for £6,000 to help finance building of CLAN GRAHAM.

27.11.1893: Struck on reef north of North Watcher Island in South China Sea whilst on a voyage from Amoy to New York with a cargo of tea while still under Dunlop control.

2.12.1893: Foundered.

5.2.1894: Register closed.

9. CLAN MACFARLANE 1881-1902 Iron ship

O.N. 84317 1,588g 1,484n

249.1 x 38.3 x 22.8 feet

12.5.1881: Launched by Russell and Co., Greenock (Yard No.35) for Thomas Dunlop and Sons, Glasgow as CLAN MACFARLANE.

3.6.1881: Registered at Glasgow (49/1881) in the ownership of Thomas Dunlop.

11.8.1902: Sold to Rederi A/B Standard (Ernst Roberg, manager), Gothenburg, Sweden for £6,800.

15.8.1902: Register closed.

10.1910: Sold to Laiva Oy Sampo (V.A. Makela, manager), Viborg, Finland.

23.8.1913: Arrived at Auckland under tow in a dismasted condition and sold as a hulk.

27.3.1934: Foundered in a typhoon at Noumea.

10. CLAN MACKENZIE 1882-1907 Iron ship

O.N. 86731 1,684g 1,597n

259.5 x 38.2 x 23.1 feet

30.11.1882: Launched by R. Duncan and Co., Port Glasgow (Yard No.185) for Thomas Dunlop and Sons, Glasgow as CLAN MACKENZIE at a cost of £21,360.

27.12.1882: Registered at Glasgow (172/1882) in the ownership of Thomas Dunlop.

Two views of the early iron barque *Clan Ferguson* after she had left the fleet, that below showing her loading guano as the Peruvian *Claudina*. [Above: Monteray Maritime Museum; below: John Naylon collection]

Clan Macfarlane. [World Ship Society Ltd.]

27.11.1906: Transferred to the Merito Shipping Co. Ltd. (Thomas Dunlop and Sons, managers), Glasgow.
1907: Sold to Rederi Majorka (K. Bruusgaard, manager), Drammen, Norway for £4,500 and renamed MAJORKA.
6.11.1907: British register closed.
14.8.1917: Mined and sunk in a field laid by the German submarine U 71 west north west of Cape Wrath in position 58.30 north by 05.20 west whilst on a voyage from London to Stornoway in ballast.

11. CLAN DAVIDSON 1883-1885 Iron steam ship
O.N. 87724 1,326g 854n
240.6 x 34.1 x 17.3 feet
C.2-cyl. by Alexander Stephen and Sons, Glasgow (28, 52 x 36 inches); 140 NHP.
29.11.1883: Launched by Alexander Stephen and Sons, Glasgow (Yard No.281) for Thomas Dunlop and Sons, Glasgow as CLAN DAVIDSON.
7.12.1883: Registered at Glasgow (135/1883) in the ownership of Thomas Dunlop.
22.9.1885: Stranded on Sorgrund, Bothnia (outside Holmon) whilst on a voyage from Uleaborg to London with a cargo of wood, subsequently rendered unsalvageable by a gale.
27.10.1885: Register closed.

12. CLAN ROBERTSON 1884-1907 Iron ship
O.N. 89962 1,703g 1,625n
259.5 x 38.3 x 23.3 feet
4.10.1884: Launched by R. Duncan and Co., Port Glasgow (Yard No.212) for Thomas Dunlop and Sons, Glasgow as

Clan Mackenzie, the fastest but by no means the most profitable member of Dunlop's sail fleet. *[World Ship Society Ltd.]*

CLAN ROBERTSON at a cost of £16,500.
25.10.1884: Registered at Glasgow (88/1884) in the ownership of Thomas Dunlop.
1907: Sold to Rederi A/S Maletta (K. Bruusgaard, manager), Drammen, Norway and renamed MALETTA.
7.5.1907: Register closed.
1923: Broken up.

13. CLAN MACPHERSON 1885-1909 Iron
O.N. 90066 1,680g 1,601n
260.5 x 38.2 x 23.2 feet
16.7.1885: Completed by Russell and Co., Port Glasgow (Yard No.128) for Thomas Dunlop and Sons, Glasgow as CLAN MACPHERSON at a cost of £16,000.
15.8.1885: Registered at Glasgow (80/1885) in the ownership of Thomas Dunlop.

5.12.1906: Transferred to the Merito Shipping Co. Ltd. (Thomas Dunlop and Sons, managers), Glasgow.
24.6.1909: Left Newcastle, New South Wales for Valparaiso with a cargo of coal and disappeared. Insured value £8,000.
1.12.1909: Posted missing at Lloyd's.
14.12.1909: Register closed.

14. QUEEN VICTORIA (1) 1887-1896
O.N. 93344 2,312g 1,506n
290.0 x 39.0 x 22.5 feet
T.3-cyl. by Alexander Stephen and Sons, Linthouse (20, 33, 51 x 42 inches); 240 NHP.
12.1.1887: Launched by Alexander Stephen and Sons, Linthouse (Yard No.299) for Thomas Dunlop and Sons, Glasgow as QUEEN VICTORIA at a cost of £26,500.
24.1.1887: Registered at Glasgow (3/1887) in the ownership of Thomas Dunlop.

Clan Robertson. [John Naylon collection]

22.4.1896: Wrecked at Algoa Bay whilst on a voyage from Glasgow and Birkenhead to Delagoa Bay with general cargo.
21.9.1896: Register closed.

15. CLAN BUCHANAN 1887-1908 Iron four-masted barque
O.N. 93374 2,140g 2,072n
283.5 x 40.5 x 24.5 feet
24.3.1887: Launched by Russell and Co., Port Glasgow (Yard No.162) for Thomas Dunlop and Sons, Glasgow as CLAN BUCHANAN at a cost of £17,800.
21.4.1887: Registered at Glasgow (40/1887) in the ownership of Thomas Dunlop.
5.12.1906: Transferred to the Merito Shipping Co. Ltd. (Thomas Dunlop and Sons, managers), Glasgow.
7.11.1908: Sold to Skibs A/S Valerie (Thomas Berg, manager), Stavanger, Norway and renamed VALERIE.
10.11.1908: British register closed.
22.4.1917: Captured and sunk with gunfire by the German submarine UC 21 in the Bay of Biscay 30 miles west of Cordonan Light whilst on a voyage from Bordeaux to St Thomas in ballast.

16. QUEEN ELIZABETH (1) 1888-1891
O.N. 96011 2,507g 1,628n
300.0 x 40.1 x 23.1 feet
T.3-cyl. by Alexander Stephen and Son, Linthouse (21, 33, 54 x 42 inches); 250 NHP.
23.10.1888: Launched by Alexander Stephen and Sons, Linthouse (Yard No.314) for Thomas Dunlop and Sons, Glasgow as QUEEN ELIZABETH at a cost of £28,500.
30.10.1888: Registered at Glasgow (101/1888) in the ownership of Thomas Dunlop.
20.3.1891: Stranded at Ikishima whilst on a voyage from Japan to Manila with a cargo of coal.
13.5.1891: Register closed.

17. QUEEN MARGARET (1) 1890-1902
O.N. 97656 2,678g 1,732n
310.0 x 41.0 x 23.5 feet
T.3-cyl. by Alexander Stephen and Sons, Linthouse (23, 37, 59 x 42 inches); 300 NHP.
18.6.1890: Launched by Alexander Stephen and Sons, Glasgow (Yard No.326) for Thomas Dunlop and Sons, Glasgow as QUEEN MARGARET at a cost of £35,000.
27.6.1890: Registered at Glasgow (72/1890) in the ownership of Thomas, Thomas junior and Robert Jack Dunlop.
23.5.1899: Transferred to the Dunlop Steamship Co. Ltd. (Thomas Dunlop and Sons, managers), Glasgow.
5.1902: Sold to L. Possehl and Co., Lübeck, Germany and renamed LUBECK.
6.5.1902: British register closed.
1912: Sold to F. Chiama and A. Danove, Genoa, Italy and renamed LELA.
13.11.1916: Captured and sunk with gunfire by the German submarine U 50 in the Bay of Biscay in position 47.08 north by 09.16 west whilst on a voyage from the UK to Italy with a cargo of coal.

Clan Macpherson in blustery weather with the watch aloft on the fore yard. After a 24-year career she went missing in the Pacific during 1909. *[J. and M Clarkson collection]*

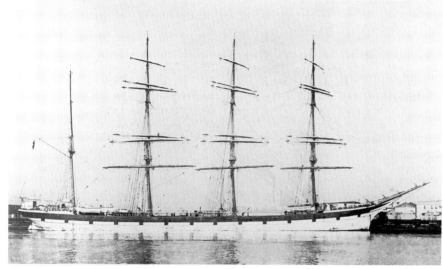

Clan Buchanan, Dunlop's first four-master (above), and below under the Norwegian flag as *Valerie*. *[Top: Monteray Maritime Museum; below: John Naylon collection]*

98

Queen Margaret (1), probably on trials. *[Glasgow University Archives, DC101/0516]*

18. QUEEN ADELAIDE (1) 1891-1908
O.N. 98642 2,832g 1,825n
310.0 x 41.1 x 23.6 feet
T.3-cyl. by John Dickinson, Sunderland
(23.5, 38, 62 x 42 inches); 310 NHP, 1,150
IHP, 10½ knots.
9.5.1891: Launched by Bartram and Sons,
Sunderland (Yard No.147) for Thomas
Dunlop and Sons, Glasgow as QUEEN
ADELAIDE.
19.6.1891: Registered at Glasgow (59/1891)
in the ownership of Thomas, Thomas junior
and Robert Jack Dunlop.
21.6.1891: Trial trip.
30.3.1899: Transferred to the Dunlop
Steamship Co. Ltd. (Thomas Dunlop and
Sons, managers), Glasgow.
1.8.1908: Sold to John James Ferguson,
Glasgow.
18.3.1909: Transferred to Allied Co. Ltd.
(J.J. Ferguson, manager), Glasgow.
3.4.1909: Beached in a sinking condition
and became a total loss at Cape Blanco,
Morocco after striking submerged wreckage
whilst on a delivery voyage from South
Africa to shipbreakers at Genoa with a
cargo of scrap iron.
28.5.1909: Register closed.

19. QUEEN ANNE (1) 1891-1895
O.N. 98644 2,784g 1,810n
309.7 x 41.1 x 19.7 feet
T.3-cyl. by John Dickinson, Sunderland
(23.5, 38, 62 x 42 inches); 310 NHP, 1500
IHP, 10.5 knots.
6.8.1891: Launched by Bartram and Sons,
Sunderland (Yard No.148) for Thomas
Dunlop and Sons, Glasgow as QUEEN
ANNE.
28.8.1891: Trial trip.
31.8.1891: Registered at Glasgow (84/1891)
in the ownership of Thomas, Thomas junior

and Robert Jack Dunlop.
23.4.1895: Sailed from Akyab on a voyage
to Port Said with a cargo of rice and
disappeared with a crew of 30. Presumed to
have foundered in typhoon.
10.7.1895: Posted missing at Lloyd's.
12.7.1895: Register closed.

20. QUEEN LOUISE (1) 1893-1911
O.N. 102620 3,385g 2,170n
330.0 x 42.5 x 19.6 feet
T.3-cyl. by John Dickinson, Sunderland (24,
39.5, 65 x 42 inches); 250 NHP, 1,250 IHP,
10.5 knots.
12.8.1893: Launched by Bartram and Sons,
Sunderland (Yard No.155) for Thomas
Dunlop and Sons, Glasgow as QUEEN
LOUISE at a cost of £31,800.
15.9.1893: Registered at Glasgow (82/1893)
in the ownership of Thomas and Robert
Jack Dunlop.
20.9.1893: Trial trip.
23.5.1899: Transferred to the Dunlop
Steamship Co. Ltd. (Thomas Dunlop and

Sons, managers), Glasgow.
4.1911: Sold to E. Corentes and G.
Kalagerakis, Piraeus, Greece and renamed
ANASTASIS.
6.4.1911: British register closed.
20.7.1911: Stranded in thick fog on Cape
Roncudo, Spain whilst on a voyage from
Rotterdam to Genoa with a cargo of coal.
6.8.1911: Salvage efforts abandoned.

21. CLAN GRAHAM 1893-1911 Steel four-masted barque
O.N. 102652 2,147g 1,976n
282.9 x 40.4 x 24.6 feet
15.11.1893: Launched by Russell and Co.,
Port Glasgow (Yard No.340) for Thomas
Dunlop and Sons, Glasgow as CLAN
GRAHAM.
18.12.1893: Registered at Glasgow
(128/1893) in the ownership of Thomas and
Robert Jack Dunlop.
5.12.1906: Transferred to the Merito
Shipping Co. Ltd. (Thomas Dunlop and
Sons, managers), Glasgow.

Queen Louise (1). *[Nigel Farrell collection]*

4.1911: Sold to A/S Clan Graham (S. Bruusgaard, manager), Drammen, Norway.
13.4.1911: British register closed.
1914: Sold to A/S Clan Graham (E. Monsen and Co., manager), Tvedestrand, Norway and renamed ASHEIM.
8.7.1917: Captured and sunk by the German submarine U 53 30 miles north west of Inishtrahull whilst on a voyage from Dublin to New York in ballast.

22. CLAN GALBRAITH 1894-1910 Steel four-masted barque

O.N. 102660 2,149g 1,983n
282.9 x 40.4 x 24.6 feet
1.2.1894: Launched by Russell and Co., Port Glasgow (Yard No.347) for Thomas Dunlop and Sons, Glasgow as CLAN GALBRAITH.
17.2.1894: Registered at Glasgow (10/1894) in the ownership of Thomas and Robert Jack Dunlop.
5.12.1906: Transferred to the Merito Shipping Co. Ltd. (Thomas Dunlop and Sons, managers), Glasgow.
23.2.1910: Sold to A/S Clan Galbraith (C. Bech and Co., managers), Tvedestrand, Norway.
11.3.1910: British register closed.
1.1916: Transferred to Bech's Rederi A/S (C. Bech and Co., managers), Tvedestrand.
24.4.1917: Captured and sunk by the German submarine U 70 west of Ireland in position 52.30 north by 14.00 west whilst on a voyage from Philadelphia to Birkenhead with a cargo of lubricating oil and wax.

23. QUEEN OLGA (1) 1894-1910

O.N. 104562 3,347g 2,146n
330.4 x 42.6 x 19.6 feet
T.3-cyl. by John Dickinson, Sunderland (24, 39.5, 65 x 42); 350 NHP, 1,250 IHP, 10.5 knots.
29.8.1894: Launched by Bartram and Sons, Sunderland (Yard No.157) for Thomas Dunlop and Sons, Glasgow as QUEEN OLGA.
15.9.1894: Registered at Glasgow (107/1894) in the ownership of Thomas and Robert Jack Dunlop.
20.9.1894: Trial trip.
30.3.1899: Transferred to the Dunlop Steamship Co. Ltd. (Thomas Dunlop and Sons, managers), Glasgow.
29.12.1910: Sold to W.G. Oates, London.
1911: Sold by the mortgagees, Maritime Securities Ltd., to F. Lukissos and Voyazides Brothers, Andros, Greece and renamed FILOMACHI.
29.7.1911: Britsish register closed.
1915: Sold to Olaf Orvig, Bergen, Norway and renamed HJELTEFJORD.
1916: Sold to A/S Haraldsens Rederi (H. Haraldsen, manager), Skien, Norway.
1918: Sold to A/S D/S Hjeltefjord (Helmer Staubo and Co., managers), Christiana, Norway.
1920: Sold to I.G. Fierro, Gijon, Spain and renamed FLORENTINA.
24.11.1921: Destroyed by fire at Valencia whilst on a voyage from Alexandria with a part cargo of benzene.

Clan Graham was the last sailing ship under the Dunlop flag. *[Monteray Maritime Museum]*

Clan Galbraith (above) under the Norwegian flag with neutrality markings during the First World War. The photograph below shows her stranded on Flying Point Beach near Bridgehampton, Long Island on 22nd July 1916. She was successfully refloated only to be sunk by a U-boat in April 1917. *[Above; John Naylon collection; below: J. and M. Clarkson collection]*

Queen Mary (1) was sold, with sister *Queen Eleanor*, to Italian buyers in 1913.   *[J. and M. Clarkson collection]*

24. QUEEN CRISTINA (1) 1896-1899
O.N. 105985 3,596g 2,291n
344.0 x 45.0 x 18.2 feet
T.3-cyl. by John Dickinson and Sons Ltd.,
Sunderland (24, 40, 66 x 45 inches); 380
NHP, 1,900 IHP, 10.5 knots.
15.2.1896: Launched by Bartram and Sons,
Sunderland (Yard No.162) for Thomas
Dunlop and Sons, Glasgow as QUEEN
CRISTINA.
12.3.1896: Registered at Glasgow (21/1896)
in the ownership of Thomas and Robert
Jack Dunlop.
21.3.1896: Trial trip.
30.3.1899: Transferred to the Dunlop
Steamship Co. Ltd. (Thomas Dunlop and
Sons, managers), Glasgow.
23.12.1899: Wrecked at Lihon Reef off
Queensland in a hurricane in position 17
south by 152 east whilst on a voyage from
Shanghai to Newcastle, New South Wales
in ballast.
2.7.1900: Register closed.

25. QUEEN ELEANOR (1) 1896-1913
O.N. 106019 3,574g 2,270n
344.0 x 45.0 x 18.2 feet
T.3-cyl. by John Dickinson and Sons,
Sunderland (25, 40, 66 x 45 inches); 380
NHP, 1,900 IHP, 10.5 knots.
13.7.1896: Launched by Bartram and Sons,
Sunderland (Yard No.163) for Thomas
Dunlop and Sons, Glasgow as QUEEN
ELEANOR.
11.8.1896: Registered at Glasgow (69/1896)
in the ownership of Thomas and Robert
Jack Dunlop.
15.8.1896: Trial trip.

30.3.1899: Transferred to the Dunlop
Steamship Co. Ltd. (Thomas Dunlop and
Sons, managers), Glasgow.
6.1913: Sold to Figli di Luigi Dufour,
Genoa, Italy and renamed LUIGI.
27.6.1913: British register closed.
7.3.1918: Shelled and driven ashore by
the German submarine U 152 near Cape
Juby, West Africa whilst on a voyage from
Marseilles to Dakar and became a total loss.

26. QUEEN MARY (1) 1897-1913
O.N. 106064 3,564g 2,262n
344.0 x 45.0 x 18.3 feet
T.3-cyl. by John Dickinson and Sons Ltd.,
Sunderland (24.5, 40, 66 x 45 inches); 380
NHP, 1900 IHP, 11.25 knots.
20.2.1897: Launched by Bartram and Sons,
Sunderland (Yard No.165) for Thomas
Dunlop and Sons, Glasgow as QUEEN
MARY.
8.4.1897: Registered at Glasgow (22/1897)
in the ownership of Thomas and Robert
Jack Dunlop.
15.4.1897: Trial trip.
30.3.1899: Transferred to the Dunlop
Steamship Co. Ltd. (Thomas Dunlop and
Sons, managers), Glasgow.
1913: Sold to Figli di Luigi Dufour, Genoa,
Italy and renamed ANGIOLINA.
20.9.1913: British register closed.
1919: Sold to Lloyd Mediterraneo Società
Italiana di Navigazione, Genoa.
1921: Renamed BAGNOLI.
1925: Sold to F. Bennati, Genoa and
renamed DORI.
1925: Sold to La Platense S.A. Marittima,
Genoa.

1926: Sold to P. Consigliere, Genoa.
1926: Sold to William K McKean, Halifax,
Nova Scotia and renamed LARCH.
6.12.1926: Registered at Halifax, Nova
Scotia (18/1926) in the ownership of
William Kirk McKean, lumber merchant.
30.11.1926: Transferred to Tufts Cove
Shipping Co. Ltd., Halifax.
4.1.1927: Sold to Farquhar and Co. Ltd.,
Halifax.
1929: Sold to Compania Del Vapor Larch
Ltda., Panama.
26.3.1929: British register closed.
1.1934: Sold to Metal Industries Ltd.,
Rosyth.
2.2.1934: Arrived at Rosyth.
21.2.1934: Demolition commenced.

27. QUEEN CRISTINA (2) 1901-1907
O.N. 113966 4,268g 2,804n
360.0 x 48.0 x 20.2 feet
T.3-cyl. by North Eastern Marine
Engineering Co. Ltd., Newcastle-upon-Tyne
(23.5, 39, 66 x 48 inches); 341 NHP, 1,800
IHP, 10 knots.
6.3.1901: Launched by Northumberland Ship
Building Co. Ltd., Newcastle-upon-Tyne
(Yard No.89) for the Dunlop Steamship Co.
Ltd. (Thomas Dunlop and Sons, managers),
Glasgow as QUEEN CRISTINA.
9.7.1901: Registered at Glasgow (46/1901)
in the ownership of the Dunlop Steamship
Co. Ltd.
21.10.1907: Wrecked in fog on North Seal
Rocks, Point St. George Reef, near Crescent
City, California whilst on a voyage from San
Francisco to Portland, Oregon in ballast.
8.10.1908: Register closed.

Queen Alexandra (1) left the fleet in 1913 but survived until 1971. *[J. and M. Clarkson collection]*

28. QUEEN ALEXANDRA (1) 1901-1913

O.N. 113970 4,264g 2,788n
360.0 x 48.0 x 20.2 feet
T.3-cyl. by North Eastern Marine
Engineering Co. Ltd., Newcastle-upon-Tyne
(24.5, 40, 68 x 48 inches); 356 NHP.
4.5.1901: Launched by Northumberland
Ship Building Co. Ltd., Newcastle-
upon-Tyne (Yard No.91) for the Dunlop
Steamship Co. Ltd. (Thomas Dunlop and
Sons, managers), Glasgow as QUEEN
ALEXANDRA.
23.7.1901: Registered at Glasgow (50/1901)
in the ownership of the Dunlop Steamship
Co. Ltd.
5.11.1913: Sold to the Gunwell Steamship
Co. Ltd. (George Vincent Craggs, manager),
London.
13.11.1913: Re-registered at London
(146/1913) briefly under original name and
owner.
13.11.1913: Renamed TURNWELL.
3.10.1914: Sold by Edward Asher Cohan
(the mortgagee) to Edward Clouston Thin,
Liverpool.
6.10.1914: Sold to Maritime Investments
Ltd. (Robert Clegg, manager), Liverpool.
1.6.1915: Sold to Leopold H.G. Walford,
London.
8.11.1915: Transferred to the Equinox
Steamship Co. Ltd. (L.H.G. Walford,
manager), London.
19.4.1916: Renamed CRAONNE.
1920: Sold to W. Gonzalez Garra,
Villagracia, Spain and renamed PURA
RASILLA.
23.2.1920: British register closed.
1927: Sold to Compania Naviera Amaya (C.
de Zabala, manager), Bilbao, Spain.
1929: Renamed VICEN.

1934: Sold to Sociedad Metalurgica Duro
Felguerra, Gijon, Spain and renamed
CIANO.
1937: Requisitioned by Spanish Republican
Government and renamed VIRCO V.
6.1937: Found at Bilbao in damaged
condition by Nationalist forces and later
repaired.
1939: Reverted to CIANO and original
owners.
28.7.1971: Demolition commenced at Gijon
by Evies y Trevin.

29. QUEEN HELENA 1904-1919

O.N. 119147 4,224g 2,755n
360.2 x 48.0 x 20.2 feet
T.3-cyl. by North Eastern Marine
Engineering Co. Ltd., Newcastle-upon-
Tyne (24.5, 40, 68 x 48 inches); 362 NHP,
1,900 IHP, 10 knots.
17.5.1904: Launched by Northumberland
Ship Building Co. Ltd., Newcastle-
upon-Tyne (Yard No.112) for the Dunlop
Steamship Co. Ltd. (Thomas Dunlop and
Sons, managers), Glasgow as QUEEN
HELENA.
12.7.1904: Registered at Glasgow
(69/1904) in the ownership of the Dunlop
Steamship Co. Ltd.
24.12.1918: Mined and beached. Later
repaired.
9.10.1919: Sold to General Maritime Trust
Ltd. (R.R. Shankland, manager), London
9.8.1920: Sold to the Guernsey Shipping
Co. Ltd. (Ira Clement Ozanne, manager),
Guernsey.
24.8.1920: Renamed OTTERBURN.
12.11.1920: Re-registered at Guernsey
(10/1920) in the ownership of the
Guernsey Shipping Co. Ltd.
22.11.1923: Beached in Marseilles Roads

following an explosion in a cargo hold
whilst on a voyage from Marseilles to New
York with a cargo of cotton, glycerine, and
potassium chlorate. Burnt out and became
a total loss.
17.3.1924: Register closed.

30. QUEEN AMELIE 1905-1917

O.N. 121257 4,278g 2,782n
372.0 x 48.0 x 20.0 feet
T.3-cyl. by North Eastern Marine
Engineering Co. Ltd., Newcastle-upon-
Tyne (24.5, 40, 68 x 48 inches); 362 NHP,
1,950 IHP, 10 knots.
4.8.1905: Launched by Northumberland
Ship Building Co. Ltd., Newcastle-upon-
Tyne (Yard No.129) for the Dunlop
Steamship Co. Ltd. (Thomas Dunlop and
Sons, managers), Glasgow as QUEEN
AMELIE.
14.9.1905: Registered at Glasgow
(76/1905) in the ownership of the Dunlop
Steamship Co. Ltd.
17.9.1917: Captured, torpedoed and sunk
by the German submarines U 95 and UB
62 in the North Sea 19 miles north north
east from Muckle Flugga, North Unst,
Shetland Islands whilst on a voyage from
Archangel to Dundee with a cargo of flax.
8.10.1917: Register closed.

31. QUEEN ELIZABETH (2) 1907-1919

O.N. 124221 4,225g 2,748n
360.3 x 48.0 x 20.2 feet
T.3-cyl. by Richardsons, Westgarth and Co.
Ltd., Sunderland (25, 41, 69 x 48 inches);
372 NHP, 1,850 IHP, 10 knots.
7.1907: Launched by Northumberland Ship
Building Co. Ltd., Newcastle-upon-Tyne
(Yard No.147) for the Merito Shipping Co.
Ltd. (Thomas Dunlop and Sons, managers),

Glasgow as QUEEN ELIZABETH.
14.9.1907: Registered at Glasgow
(76/1907) in the ownership of the Merito
Shipping Co. Ltd.
18.9.1907: Trial trip.
28.8.1918: Transferred to the Dunlop
Steamship Co. Ltd., Glasgow
2.6.1919: Sold to the Western Counties
Shipping Co. Ltd. (Edwards, Sons and Co.
Ltd., managers), Cardiff for £130,000.
2.3.1922: Renamed VALEMEAD.
3.3.1922: Sold by B.S.T. Ltd. (the
mortgagee) to the Moor Line Ltd. (W.
Runciman and Co. Ltd., managers),
Newcastle-upon-Tyne.
8.3.1922: Re-registered at Newcastle-on-
Tyne (11/1922) in the ownership of the
Moor Line Ltd.
15.3.1922: Renamed NEWTONMOOR.
22.10.1926: Sold to the Arbour Shipping
Co. Ltd. (Howard Houlder, manager),
London.
29.11.1926: Re-registered at London
(180/1926) in the ownership of the Arbour
Shipping Co. Ltd.
7.3.1927: Renamed ORNUS.
12.1927: Sold to S.N. Vlassopulos, Greece
and renamed MARIA.
16.12.1927: British register closed.
7.6.1937: Destroyed by fire at Fernando
Noronha whilst on a voyage from Gdynia
to Rio de Janeiro with a cargo of coal.

32. QUEEN EUGENIE 1909-1917
O.N. 129425 4,358g 2,802n
385.0 x 49.7 x 26.4 feet
T.3-cyl. by North Eastern Marine
Engineering Co. Ltd., Newcastle-upon-Tyne
(24.5, 40, 68 x 48 inches); 374 NHP, 1,750
IHP, 10 knots.
4.8.1909: Launched by Northumberland Ship
Building Co. Ltd., Newcastle-upon-Tyne
(Yard No.163) for the Dunlop Steamship
Co. Ltd. (Thomas Dunlop and Sons, managers),
Glasgow as QUEEN EUGENIE.

Queen Elizabeth (2) at Manchester. *[Nigel Farrell collection]*

6.9.1909: Registered at Glasgow (70/1909)
in the ownership of the Dunlop Steamship
Co. Ltd.
25.3.1917: Torpedoed and sunk by
the German submarine UC 67 in the
Mediterranean 23 miles north north east
from Cani Rocks whilst on a voyage from
New York to Calcutta with general cargo.
The master and 34 crew were lost, but
one apprentice and one gunner were taken
prisoner.
12.6.1917: Register closed.

33. QUEEN MAUD (1) 1909-1919
O.N. 129452 4,344g 2,795n
385.0 x 49.7 x 26.4 feet
T.3-cyl. by North Eastern Marine
Engineering Co. Ltd., Newcastle-upon-
Tyne (24.5, 40, 68 x 48 inches); 376 NHP,
1,750 IHP, 10 knots.
28.10.1909: Launched by Northumberland
Ship Building Co. Ltd., Newcastle-upon-
Tyne (Yard No.164) for the Dunlop
Steamship Co. Ltd. (Thomas Dunlop and

Sons, managers), Glasgow as QUEEN
MAUD.
1.12.1909: Registered at Glasgow
(104/1909) in the ownership of the Dunlop
Steamship Co. Ltd.
6.6.1919: Sold to Union Chartering Co.
Ltd. (William Henry Barwick, manager),
London.
1.3.1920: Sold to General Maritime Trust
Ltd. (R.R. Shankland, manager), London.
24.6.1920: Renamed SPRINGBURN.
9.8.1920: Sold to Guernsey Shipping
Co. Ltd. (Ira Clement Ozanne, manager),
Guernsey.
12.11.1920: Re-registered at Guernsey
(9/1920) in the ownership of the Guernsey
Shipping Co. Ltd.
11.1924: Sold to C. Hadjipateras and
Sons, Chios, Greece and renamed K.
HADJIPATERAS.
6.11.1924: British register closed.
2.5.1932: Wrecked at Punta Vignola,
Sardinia whilst on a voyage from
Marseilles to Chios in ballast.

Queen Eugenie was sunk with heavy loss of life by a U-boat in the Mediterranean during 1917. *[Nigel Farrell collection]*

Queen Maud (1) was the last of seven steamers built for Dunlop on the Tyne between 1901 and 1909. *[Roy Fenton collection]*

34. QUEEN ADELAIDE (2) 1911-1917
O.N. 132993 4,965g 3,196n
405.0 x 53.0 x 27.2 feet
T.3-cyl. by J.G. Kincaid and Co. Ltd.,
Greenock (26, 42, 71 x 48 inches); 428
NHP, 2,300 IHP, 11 knots.
21.10.1911: Launched by R. Duncan and
Co. Ltd., Port Glasgow (Yard No.318) for
the Dunlop Steamship Co. Ltd. (Thomas
Dunlop and Sons, managers), Glasgow as
QUEEN ADELAIDE.
22.11.1911: Registered at Glasgow
(92/1911) in the ownership of the Dunlop
Steamship Co. Ltd.
18.6.1917: Torpedoed and sunk by the
German submarine U 70 in the Atlantic 13
miles north north east from St. Kilda Island,
Outer Hebrides in position 58.40 north
by 08.35 west whilst on a voyage from
Montreal to Leith with a cargo of wheat.
Three of the crew were lost.
18.7.1917: Register closed.

35. QUEEN LOUISE (2) 1912-1922
O.N. 133028 4,879g 3,139n
404.9 x 53.0 x 27.1 feet
T.3-cyl. by North Eastern Marine
Engineering Co. Ltd., Newcastle-upon-Tyne
(26, 42, 72 x 48 inches); 436 NHP, 2,400
IHP, 11 knots.
5.2.1912: Launched by Northumberland
Ship Building Co. Ltd., Newcastle-upon-
Tyne (Yard No.191) for the Dunlop
Steamship Co. Ltd. (Thomas Dunlop and
Sons, managers), Glasgow as QUEEN
LOUISE.
29.3.1912: Registered at Glasgow (31/1912)
in the ownership of the Dunlop Steamship
Co. Ltd.
7.2.1914: Grounded off Squam Beach, New
Jersey. Refloated.
31.3.1917: Torpedoed and damaged in the
English Channel.

1921: Converted to an oil tanker (5,194g,
2,987n).
19.6.1922: Sold to the Cadogan Steam
Ship Co. Ltd. (John Robertson Neil [R.S.
Dalgleish Ltd.], managers), London for
£32,000.
23.1.1924: Grounded on Ponterfyn Point,
Holyhead Bay whilst on a voyage from
Liverpool to Tampico in ballast. Refloated
but found to be beyond economic repair.
27.2.1924: Sold to John Cashmore, Great
Bridge, Staffordshire, metal merchant and
then re-sold for scrap in the USA.
21.3.1924: Register closed.

36. QUEEN MARGARET (2) 1912-1922
O.N. 133093 4,972g 3,197n
405.0 x 53.0 x 27.2 feet
T.3-cyl. by J.G. Kincaid and Co. Ltd.,
Greenock (26, 42, 71 x 48 inches); 415
NHP.

12.11.1912: Launched by R. Duncan and
Co. Ltd., Port Glasgow (Yard No.322) for
the Dunlop Steamship Co. Ltd. (Thomas
Dunlop and Sons, managers), Glasgow as
QUEEN MARGARET.
26.12.1912: Registered at Glasgow
(118/1912) in the ownership of the Dunlop
Steamship Co. Ltd.
28.4.1922: Sold to Barr, Crombie and Co.,
Glasgow.
29.9.1924: Renamed BARRHILL.
21.10.1924: Transferred to the Barr
Shipping Co. Ltd. (Barr, Crombie and Co.,
managers), Glasgow.
28.6.1941: Bombed and sunk by German
aircraft in position 52.50 north by 01.46
east whilst on a voyage from New York to
London with a cargo of 7,000 tons of grain.
Of the 38 crew and 2 gunners, five crew
were lost.
16.8.1941: Register closed.

Queen Adelaide (2) of 1911 was the first Dunlop steamer built on the Clyde since
1890. *[Glasgow University Archives, DC101/1480/Y3]*

37. QUEEN ALEXANDRA (2) 1914-1919

O.N. 136672 4,211g 2,670n
370.0 x 50.9 x 26.2 feet
T.3-cyl. by North Eastern Marine
Engineering Co. Ltd., Newcastle-upon-
Tyne (25, 41, 69 x 48 inches); 371 NHP,
1,800 IHP, 10 knots.
11.3.1914: Launched by Northumberland
Ship Building Co. Ltd., Newcastle-upon-
Tyne (Yard No.218) for Fred Drughorn
Ltd., London as ELFLAND.
30.4.1914: Registered at London (69/1914)
in the ownership of Fred Drughorn Ltd.
12.12.1914: Acquired by the Dunlop
Steamship Co. Ltd. (Thomas Dunlop and
Sons, managers), Glasgow.
16.12.1914: Re-registered at Glasgow
(91/1914) in the ownership of the Dunlop
Steamship Co. Ltd.
16.2.1915: Renamed QUEEN
ALEXANDRA.
22.8.1919: Sold to the Ampleforth
Steamship Co. Ltd. (Charles Cravos,
manager), Cardiff.
25.8.1919: Re-registered at Cardiff
(12/1919) in the ownership of the
Ampleforth Steamship Co. Ltd.
18.3.1920: Sold to the Rhondda Merthyr
Shipping Co. Ltd. (J.A. Thompson,
manager), Cardiff.
27.7.1921: Management transferred to
Cyrus John Evans of the Rhondda Merthyr
Shipping Co. Ltd.
20.8.1924: Sold to the Federated Coal and
Shipping Co. Ltd. (John Edwards Evans,
manager), Cardiff.
8.1924: Sold to George D. Gratsos Co. Ltd.,
Ithaca, Greece and renamed TRITON.
8.9.1924: British register closed.
1939: Sold to Francesco Galli fu Giovanni,
Genoa, Italy and renamed MARIAROSA.
29.2.1940: Torpedoed and sunk by the
German submarine U 20 in position 52.25
north 01.59 east whilst on a voyage from
Marseilles to Hartlepool in ballast. Of her
crew of 29 and a pilot, 12 crew were lost.

38. QUEEN MARY (2) 1915-1917

O.N. 137807 5,658g 3,610n
423.5 x 56.0 x 28.7 feet
T.3-cyl. by Rankin and Blackmore Ltd.,
Greenock (27, 45, 74 x 51 inches); 555
NHP, 2,600 IHP, 11 knots.
18.10.1915: Launched by Russell and
Co., Port Glasgow (Yard No.679) for
the Dunlop Steamship Co. Ltd. (Thomas
Dunlop and Sons, managers), Glasgow as
QUEEN MARY.
23.11.1915: Registered at Glasgow
(44/1915) in the ownership of the Dunlop
Steamship Co. Ltd.
16.4.1917: Torpedoed and sunk by the
German submarine U 60 in the Atlantic
180 miles north west by west from the
Fastnet Rock in position 51.48 north by
14.52 west whilst on a voyage from New
York to Le Havre with general cargo. Nine
members of the crew were lost.
2.5.1917: Register closed.

The crew being rescued from the *Queen Louise* (2) aground off Squam Beach, New Jersey in February 1914. *[Ian J. Farquhar collection]*

Queen Margaret (2). *[Roy Fenton collection]*

Queen Mary (2) in a United States port. She was torpedoed in 1917 after a career of less than two years. *[The Dunlop Family]*

39. COYLET 1920-1922

O.N. 142310 5,522g 3,221n
400.0 x 52.4 x 28.5 feet
T.3-cyl. by North Eastern Marine Engineering
Co. Ltd., Sunderland (27, 44, 73 x 48 inches);
517 NHP, 3,000 IHP, 11.5 knots.
27.10.1917: Launched by Sir J. Laing and

Sons Ltd., Sunderland (Yard No.669) for the
Shipping Controller, London (Hall Brothers,
Newcastle-upon-Tyne, managers) as WAR
RAMBLER.
3.1918: Completed.
21.2.1918: Registered at London (41/1918).
22.9.1919: Sold to the Hindustan Steam

Shipping Co. Ltd. (Common Brothers, managers), Newcastle-upon-Tyne for £175,000.

30.9.1919: Re-registered at Newcastle-on-Tyne (37/1919).

1.10.1919: Renamed WAZIRISTAN.

21.9.1920: Acquired by Thomas Dunlop and Sons, Glasgow for £180,000 to be converted into an oil tanker.

23.9.1920: Re-registered at Glasgow.

24.3.1921: Renamed COYLET

29.3.1921: Transferred to the Coylet Steamship Co. Ltd. (Thomas Dunlop and Sons, managers), Glasgow.

8.2.1922: On fire and abandoned 12 miles west south west of Sand Key, Florida whilst on a voyage from New Orleans to Dunkirk with a cargo of benzene. The crew were picked up by a United States steamer identified as SUROSA.

15.2.1922: Sunk by a United States coastguard cutter.

8.3.1922: Register closed.

Waziristan (above) bought in 1920 and renamed *Coylet*, was the first of Dunlop's ill-fated tanker conversions. *[George Scott collection]*

Queen Eleanor (2) arriving at Avonmouth (above) and as the Italian *Pelorum* (below). She was seized by Argentina during the Second World War and renamed, but reverted to her Italian name and ownership in 1946. *[Above: J. and M. Clarkson, below: FotoFlite]*

40. QUEEN ELEANOR (2) 1924-1938

O.N. 142628 5,271g 3,204n

400.3 x 52.3 x 28.4 feet

T.3-cyl. by John Dickinson and Sons Ltd., Sunderland (27, 44, 73 x 48 inches); 517 NHP, 3,000 IHP, 11.5 knots.

1918: Completed by Bartram and Sons Ltd., Sunderland (Yard No.245) for the Shipping Controller (E. Bigland and Co. Ltd., managers), London as WAR CYGNET.

29.8.1918: Registered at London (310/1918).

1919: Sold to Société Transoceanique de Transports (R. van Hemelryck and Co., managers), Antwerp, Belgium and renamed SIERRA BLANCA.

Queen Olga (2) at Avonmouth. *[J. and M. Clarkson collection]*

9.10.1919: Register closed.
2.1924: Acquired by the Queen Line Ltd. (Thomas Dunlop and Sons, managers), Glasgow and renamed QUEEN ELEANOR.
18.2.1924: Re-registered at Glasgow (11/1924).
24.2.1938: Sold to Alfred Harris Smith, London.
26.2.1938: Re-registered at London (51/1938).
3.1938: Sold to Transmediterranea S.A. di Navigazione, Palermo, Italy and renamed PELORUM.
5.3.1938: British register closed.
10.6.1940: Interned at Necochea.
25.8.1941: Seized by Argentina and renamed RIO CHICO.
1946: Returned to owners and reverted to PELORUM.
1.1953: Broken up at Palermo.

41. QUEEN OLGA (2) 1924-1936
O.N. 142767 5,242g 6,161n
400.0 x 52.3 x 28.5 feet
T.3-cyl. by Caird and Co., Greenock (27,

44, 73 x 48 inches); 517 NHP, 3,000 IHP, 11.5 knots.
7.12.1918: Launched by Caird and Co., Greenock (Yard No.355) for the Shipping Controller (J. Temperley and Co., managers), London as WAR ANCHUSA.
15.1.1919: Registered at London (11/1919).
30.9.1919: Sold to the Temperley Steam Shipping Co. Ltd. (J. Temperley and Co. managers), London.
2.10.1919: Renamed BEMBRIDGE.
9.9.1924: Acquired by the Cadogan Steamship Co. Ltd. (Thomas Dunlop and Sons, managers), Glasgow.
15.10.1924: Re-registered at Glasgow (66/1924).
17.10.1924: Renamed QUEEN OLGA.
11.12.1936: Sold to the Talisman Shipping Co. Ltd. (Monroe Brothers, managers), Liverpool.
11.3.1937: Re-registered at Bristol (1/1937).
11.3.1937: Sold to the Severn Steamship Co. Ltd. (Mark Whitwill (Shipping) Ltd., managers), Bristol.
13.3.1937: Renamed SEVERN LEIGH.

11.1.1938: Transferred to the Kelston Steamship Co. Ltd. (Mark Whitwill (Shipping) Ltd. managers), Bristol.
23.8.1940: Torpedoed and sunk by German submarine U 37 south of Iceland in position 54.31 north by 25.41 west whilst on a voyage from Hull to St. John, New Brunswick in ballast. There were 10 survivors; 32 crew and one gunner were lost.
28.9.1940: Register closed.

42. QUEEN MAUD (2) 1924-1936
O.N. 147886 5,201g 3,188n
400.2 x 52.3 x 28.5 feet
T.3-cyl. by Taikoo Dockyard and Engineering Co. (Hong Kong) Ltd., Hong Kong (27, 44, 73 x 48 inches); 517 NHP.
20.5.1919: Launched by Taikoo Dockyard and Engineering Co. (Hong Kong) Ltd., Hong Kong for E.E. Ambatielos, Argostoli, Greece as EVANGELOS having been laid down as WAR DRIVER for the Shipping Controller.
9.1919: Completed.

Queen Maud (2) was a Hong Kong-built war standard ship which had been repossessed by the British government after its Greek owner could not meet his financial obligations. *[Roy Fenton collection]*

1924: Acquired by the Queen Line Ltd. (Thomas Dunlop and Sons, managers), Glasgow and renamed QUEEN MAUD.
14.3.1924: Registered at Glasgow (15/1924).
5.1936: Sold to Mme. Maria L.C. Marketto, Argostoli and renamed CHRISTOS MARKETTOS.
13.5.1936: British register closed.
1938: Owner re-styled Markettos Steam Ship Co. Ltd.
8.6.1942: Torpedoed and sunk by the Japanese submarine I-20 in the Indian Ocean in position 05.05 south by 40.53 east whilst on a voyage from Durban to Aden with a cargo of 6,039 tons of coal. From her crew of 34 and two gunners, two crew were lost.

Queen Adelaide (3) was the only one of a quartet of Queen motor ships to survive the Second World War (above). In 1951 she was sold to Westralian Farmers Ltd., a company which had chartered a number of Dunlop ships over the years, and renamed *Swanhill* (below). *[Both: J. and M. Clarkson collection]*

43. QUEEN ADELAIDE (3) 1936-1951
O.N. 164093 4,933g 2,993n
418.2 x 55.2 x 25.5 feet
Oil engine 3-cyl. 2SCSA by Barclay, Curle and Co. Ltd., Glasgow; 1,800 BHP, 11 knots.
30.7.1936: Launched by Barclay, Curle and Co. Ltd. Glasgow (Yard No.658) for Queen Line Ltd. (Thomas Dunlop and Sons, managers), Glasgow as QUEEN ADELAIDE at a cost of £88,500.
9.1936: Completed.
1951: Sold to Westralian Farmers Ltd., London and renamed SWANHILL.
1956: Sold to China Shipping Co. Ltd. (John Manners and Co. Ltd. managers), Hong Kong and renamed LONDON BREEZE.
1960: Transferred to the Cambay Prince Steam Ship Co. Ltd. (John Manners and Co. Ltd. managers), Hong Kong and renamed DAIREN.
1964: Sold to Haitong Steamships and Trading Co. Ltd. (Hornbeam Co. Ltd. managers), Hong Kong.
1966: Sold to Lanena Shipping Co. Ltd., Hong Kong (T. Engan, Manila, manager) and renamed AGATE.
1966: Transferred to San Raimundo Compania Navigation S.A., Panama (T. Engan, Manila, manager).
1967: Sold to Express Trader Shipping Co. S.A., Panama (Yusang Shipping Co. Ltd. Hong Kong, managers) and renamed YU LEE.
21.3.1969: Arrived at Kaohsiung for breaking up by Lung Shi Steel and Iron Works Ltd.
20.6.1969: Breaking up commenced.

Queen Adelaide (3)
(right) under Hong
Kong ownership as
Dairen. The general
arrangement drawing
depicts *Queen Adelaide*
(3) and her sister *Queen
Anne* (2). *[Right: J. and
M. Clarkson collection,
below: R. A. Wilson
collection]*

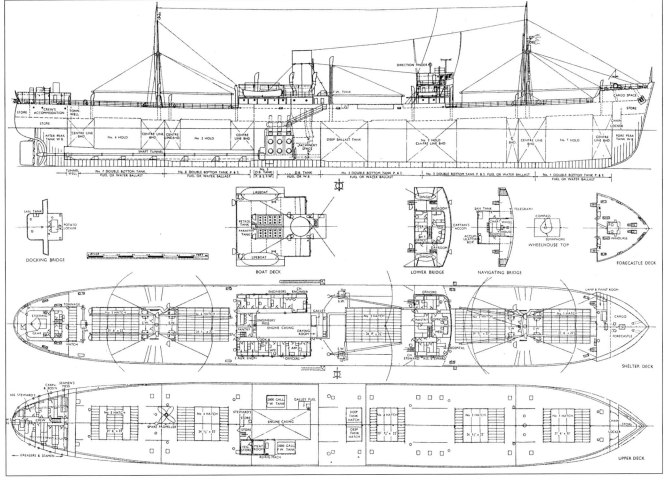

Family members and builder's representatives at the launch of *Queen Victoria* (2) on 15th September 1936. Sir Thomas
Dunlop, 1st Baronet of Woodbourne is on the left with bowler hat. His son Thomas Dunlop is to the left of the bottle to be
broken on the ship. Holding the bottle is his daughter Dorothy Frances Dunlop, then 14 years of age, who launched the ship.
Just behind and to her right is the first Robert Jack Dunlop. The second Robert Jack, owner of the Lomond Shipping Co. Ltd.,
is leaning back on the far right. William Beckett (Billy) Dunlop, Dorothy's brother, is in the right foreground wearing a bowler.
Behind him, and slightly to the right, wearing glasses is Thomas Dunlop, the Baronet's grandson. *[The Dunlop family]*

Two photographs of *Queen Victoria* (2) in Westralian Farmers' colours, the upper in London Docks, the lower sailing from Cape Town. *[Top: George Scott collection, bottom: F. W. Hawks collection]*

44. QUEEN VICTORIA (2) 1936-1942
O.N. 164099 4,937g 2,993n
418.2 x 55.2 x 25.5 feet
Oil engine 3-cyl. 2SCSA by Barclay, Curle and Co. Ltd. Glasgow; 1,800 BHP, 11 knots.
15.9.1936: Launched by Barclay, Curle and Co. Ltd. Glasgow (Yard No.659) for the Queen Line Ltd. (Thomas Dunlop and Sons, managers), Glasgow as QUEEN VICTORIA at a cost of £88,500.
14.10.1936: Registered at Glasgow (41/1936).
28.6.1942: Torpedoed and sunk by the

Japanese submarine I-10 in the Indian Ocean in position 21.15 south by 40.30 east whilst on a voyage from Table Bay to Aden with government stores. All her crew of 48 were lost.
10.9.1942: Register closed.

45. QUEEN MAUD (3) 1936-1941
O.N. 164101 4,976g 3,038n
422.8 x 54.2 x 26.1 feet
Oil engine 3-cyl. 2SCSA by William Doxford and Sons Ltd., Sunderland (520mm x 2,080mm); 1,800 BHP, 11 knots.

29.9.1936: Launched by William Doxford and Sons Ltd. Sunderland for the Queen Line Ltd. (Thomas Dunlop and Sons, managers), Glasgow as QUEEN MAUD at a cost of £90,950.
3.11.1936: Registered at Glasgow (45/1936).
5.5.1941: Torpedoed and sunk by the German submarine U 38 in position 07.54 north by 16.41 west whilst on a voyage from Cardiff to Freetown and Alexandria with coal and government stores. One of her crew of 39 was lost.
20.8.1941: Register closed.

Also in Westralian Farmers' colours, *Queen Maud* (3) (top) was a Doxford 'Economy' type with a compact superstructure, which contrasted with the split superstructure design of her Barclay, Curle-built contemporaries including *Queen Anne* (2) (middle and bottom right). Thomas Dunlop at the launch of the *Queen Anne* (2) at Glasgow in 1937 (bottom left). His wife, Mary Elizabeth Dunlop performed the ceremony and they are accompanied by Thomas's uncle, Robert Jack Dunlop (right). *[Top: F. W. Hawks collection, middle: Roy Fenton collection; bottom left: The Dunlop Family; bottom right: World Ship Society Ltd.]*

111

46. QUEEN ANNE (2) 1937-1943

O.N. 164105 4,937g 2,993n
418.2 x 55.2 x 25.5 feet
Oil engine 3-cyl. 2SCSA by Barclay, Curle and Co. Ltd., Glasgow (520 mm x 2,080 mm); 1,800 BHP, 11 knots.
4.11.1936: Launched by Barclay, Curle and Co. Ltd., Glasgow (Yard No.660) for the Cadogan Steamship Co. Ltd. (Thomas Dunlop and Sons, managers), Glasgow as QUEEN ANNE at a cost of £91,500.
16.12.1936: Registered at Glasgow (50/1936).
10.2.1943: Torpedoed and sunk by the German submarine U 509 in position 34.53 south by 19.51 east whilst on a voyage from Manchester and Table Bay to Aden, Alexandria and Beirut with general cargo. Five of her crew of 44 were lost.
22.3.1943: Register closed.

47. QUEEN VICTORIA (3) 1947-1949

O.N. 180496 7,269g 4,425n
424.0 x 57.1 x 34.8 feet
T.3-cyl. by Worthington Pump and Machinery Corporation, Harrison, New Jersey, USA (24.5, 37, 70 x 48 inches).
31.8.1943: Launched by Bethlehem-Fairfield Shipyards Inc., Baltimore, USA (Yard No.2223) for the United States War Shipping Administration, Washington as JAMES T. EARLE
9.1943: Completed for Lend-Lease bare-boat charter to the Ministry of War Transport, London (Cayzer, Irvine and Co. Ltd., Glasgow, managers) as SAMAYE.
21.4.1947: Acquired by the Queen Line Ltd. and the Cadogan Steamship Co. Ltd. (Thomas Dunlop and Sons, managers), Glasgow and renamed QUEEN VICTORIA.
14.1.1949: Sold to the Charente Steam Ship Co. Ltd. (T. and J. Harrison, managers), Liverpool for £165,000 and renamed HISTORIAN.
19.12.1962: Sold to the Jayanti Shipping

Samaye (above) was acquired by Dunlop to become *Queen Victoria* (3) (below) and seen off Gourock on 27th September 1947. She was sold after less than two years. *[Above: National Waterfront Museum, 1145/1245, below: Roy Fenton collection]*

Queen Anne (3) (below). *[Roy Fenton collection]*

Co. Ltd., Bombay, India and renamed
PARVATI JAYANTI.
6.9.1967: Damaged by Israeli gunfire in
Suez Harbour.
22.2.1968: Grounded at Azenmour, 50
miles from Casablanca, whilst on a voyage
from Alexandria to Bombay with a cargo of
cotton.
23.2.1968: Refloated with serious damage
and subsequently declared a constructive
total loss.
14.4.1968: Arrived under tow at Aviles to
be broken up by Desguaces y Salvamentos
S.A.

48. QUEEN ANNE (3) 1949-1954
O.N. 168465 7,063g 5,020n
430.9 x 56.2 x 35.2 feet
T.3-cyl. by John Readhead and Sons Ltd.,
South Shields (24.5, 39, 70 x 48 inches);
342 NHP, 2,500 IHP, 11 knots.
7.5.1943: Launched by John Readhead and
Sons Ltd., South Shields (Yard No.534)
for the Pachesham Steamship Co. Ltd.
(Runciman (London) Ltd., managers),
London as KELMSCOTT
24.6.1943: Registered at London
(143/1943).
2.3.1949: Acquired by the Queen Line Ltd.
(38 shares) and the Cadogan Steamship Co.
Ltd. (26 shares) (Thomas Dunlop and Sons,
managers), Glasgow.
7.3.1949: Renamed QUEEN ANNE.
11.1954: Sold to Polish Ocean Lines,
Gdynia, Poland and renamed MARIAN
BUCZEK.
26.11.1954: British register closed.
1968: Broken up at Whampoa.

49. QUEEN MAUD (4) 1951-1954
O.N. 168743 7,072g 5,009n
432.2 x 56.3 x 34.2 feet
T.3-cyl. by Harland and Wolff Ltd., Glasgow
(24.5, 39, 70 x 48 inches); 342 NHP.

29.10.1942: Launched by Harland and
Wolff Ltd., Glasgow (Yard No.1168G)
for the Ministry of War Transport
(Counties Ship Management Co.
Ltd., managers), London as EMPIRE
TORRENT.
12.1942: Completed.
1948: Sold to Ernels Shipping Co. Ltd.
(Counties Ship Management Co. Ltd.,
managers), London and renamed ARGOS
HILL.
7.1951: Acquired by the Queen Line Ltd.
and the Cadogan Steamship Co. Ltd.
(Thomas Dunlop and Sons, managers),
Glasgow and renamed QUEEN MAUD.
1954: Sold to Nueva Valencia
Companhia Naviera S.A., Panama (N.J.
Goulandris Ltd., London, managers) and
renamed SCOTIA.
1960: Transferred to the Greek flag and
renamed SKOTIA.
7.1962: Scrapped at Hong Kong.

The only name Dunlop used four
times was *Queen Maud*. The last
of the four is seen above in Dunlop
ownership, as *Argos Hill* (left) and
as *Scotia* (below left and right).
[Top: *Roy Fenton collection, left
and bottom right: World Ship Society Ltd., bottom left: FotoFlite*]

Queen Eleanor (3). *[World Ship Society Ltd.]*

50. QUEEN ELEANOR (3) 1951-1956

O.N. 168425 7,275g 4,988n
428.8 x 56.5 x 35.5 feet
Oil engine 3-cyl. 2SCSA by William
Doxford and Sons Ltd., Sunderland.
20.12.1942: Launched by William Doxford
and Sons Ltd., Sunderland (Yard No.687)
for Nolisment Steam Ship Co. Ltd. (Morel
Ltd., manager), Cardiff as JERSEY HART.
1944: Sold to the Stanhope Steamship Co.
Ltd. (J.A. Billmeir and Co. Ltd., managers),
London.
1945: Renamed STANPARK.
1951: Acquired by the Queen Line Ltd.
(Thomas Dunlop and Sons, managers),
Glasgow and renamed QUEEN ELEANOR.
1956: Sold to the Douglas Steam Ship Co.
Ltd. (Williamson and Co. Ltd., managers),
Hong Kong and renamed INCHDOUGLAS.
14.11.1970: Arrived at Kaohsiung for
breaking up.

Lomond Shipping Co. Ltd.

DUNKELD 1937-1943

O.N. 164118 4,944g 2,994n
418.2 x 55.2 x 25.5 feet
Oil engine 3-cyl. 2SCSA by Barclay, Curle
and Co. Ltd., Glasgow (520 mm x 2,080 mm);
1,800 BHP, 11 knots.
2.4.1937: Launched by Barclay, Curle and
Co. Ltd., Glasgow (Yard No.662) for the
Lomond Shipping Co. Ltd. (Robert J. Dunlop,
manager), Glasgow as DUNKELD at a cost
of £92,000.
1943: Sold to the Stanhope Steamship Co.
Ltd. (J. A. Billmeir and Co. Ltd.), London.
1945: Renamed STANKELD.
1951: Sold to Westralian Farmers Ltd.,
London and renamed SWANBROOK.
1956: Sold to the China Shipping Co. Ltd.
(John Manners and Co. Ltd., managers), Hong
Kong and renamed SYDNEY BREEZE.

1958: Transferred to South Breeze
Navigation Co. Ltd.(John Manners and Co.
Ltd., managers), Hong Kong.
1964: Transferred to San Fernando
Steamship Co. S.A., Panama (John Manners
and Co. Ltd., Hong Kong, managers), and
renamed SAN ERNESTO.
1966: Sold to Oriental Trader Navigation
Co. S.A., Panama (China Pacific Navigation
Co. Ltd., Hong Kong, managers) and
renamed CATHAY TRADER.
1968: Sold to Renown Shipping Co. S.A.,
Panama (Atlantic Shipping and Trading Co.
Ltd., Hong Kong, managers) and renamed
RENOWN TRADER.
8.1.1970: Arrived at Hong Kong for
breaking up by Cheong Wah.
28.1.1970: Breaking commenced.

Dunkeld when new, in the Clyde. *[J. and M. Clarkson collection]*

Vessels managed for the Shipping Controller

M1. WAR LEMUR 1918-1919

O.N. 142429 5,185g 3,152n
400.4 x 52.3 x 28.5 feet
T.3-cyl. by Harland and Wolff Ltd., Belfast
(27, 44, 73 x 48 inches); 518 NHP, 3,000
IHP, 11.5 knots.
9.5.1918: Launched by Harland and Wolff
Ltd., Belfast (Yard No.532) for the Shipping
Controller, London (Thomas Dunlop and
Sons, Glasgow, managers) as WAR LEMUR.
25.5.1918: Registered at London (201/1918).
22.1.1919: Sold to the Cunard Steamship Co.
Ltd., Liverpool.
6.2.1919: Registered at Liverpool (10/1919).
7.2.1919: Renamed VERENTIA.
21.7.1926: Sold to Cree Investment Co. Ltd.
(Andrew Weir and Co., managers), London.
24.9.1926: Registered at London (136/1926).
29.9.1926: Renamed FORERIC.
29.11.1926: Transferred to Bank Line Ltd.
(Andrew Weir and Co., managers), Glasgow.
26.8.1927: Sold to the Buenos Ayres Great
Southern Railway Co. Ltd. (Arthur Holland
and Co. Ltd., managers), London.
29.8.1927: Renamed GALVAN.
22.3.1935: Sold to Kaye, Son and Co. Ltd.,
London.
9.6.1937: Sold to Pedder and Mylchreest
Ltd., London; resold to Chang Shu Chang
(Nisshin Kaiun Shokai K.K., managers),
Tsingtao, China and renamed PEI TAI.
7.10.1937: British register closed.
1938: Sold to Kitagawa Sangyo Kaiun
K.K., Osaka, Japan and renamed HOKUTAI
MARU.
30.3.1944: Bombed and sunk by US carrier-
based aircraft off Babelthuap in the Palau
Islands whilst on a voyage from Palau to
Takao.

War Lemur shortly after her launch at Belfast: note the marks on her hull to help
paint her in camouflage pattern (top). She is seen again with her masts lowered,
presumably to make her less visible to submarines (middle). The final view shows
her as *Galvan*, with modified masts (bottom). *[Top and middle: Ulster Folk and
Transport Museum, 290 and 306, bottom: Ships in Focus]*

M2. WAR LEOPARD 1918-1919

O.N. 142584 5,177g 3,152n
400.4 x 52.3 x 28.5 feet
T.3-cyl. by Workman, Clark and Co. Ltd.,
Belfast (27, 44, 73 x 48 inches); 518 NHP,
3,000 IHP, 11.5 knots.

21.6.1918: Launched by Workman, Clark
and Co. Ltd., Belfast (Yard No.427) for
the Shipping Controller, London (Thomas
Dunlop and Sons, Glasgow, managers) as
WAR LEOPARD.
8.7.1918: Registered at London (254/1918).

7.1919: Sold to Fratelli Bianchi di S, Genoa, Italy and renamed FRATELLI BIANCHI.
5.1.1920: British register closed.
1924: Sold to Società di Navigazione per Transporti Refrigeranti La Polare, Genoa and renamed VILLA ADA.
1927: Sold to the Zinal Steamship Co. Ltd. (Turner, Brightman and Co., managers), London and renamed ZERIBA.
10.5.1927: Restored to register at London (86/1927).
1933: Sold to the Theseus Steamship Co. Ltd. (Rethymnis and Kulukundis Ltd., managers), Syra, Greece and renamed MOUNT CYNTHOS.
15.9.1933: Register closed.
1935: Transferred to Kulukundis Shipping Co. S.A., Syra.
1939: Sold to Yamashita Kisen K.K., Kobe, Japan and renamed MOMOYAMA MARU.
13.3.1943: Bombed and sunk by US aircraft 45 miles north of Wewak, New Guinea in position 02.45 south by 143.20 east.

M3. IRMGARD 1919-1920
O.N. 143151 3,816g 2,305n
362.4 x 50.1 x 23.6 feet
T.3-cyl by A.G. Neptun, Rostock, Germany (25, 41, 69 x 47.25 inches); 327 NHP, 2,100 IHP, 11 knots.
6.1914: Launched by A.G. Neptun, Rostock (Yard No. 339).
5.10.1914: Completed for A.G. Hamburg Bremer Afrika Linie, Bremen, Germany as IRMGARD
10.4.1919: Surrendered to Britain as war reparations.
22.4.1919: Registered at London (188/1919) in the ownership of the Shipping Controller (Thomas Dunlop and Sons, Glasgow, managers) as IRMGARD.
29.10.1920: Sold to the Union Steamship Co. of New Zealand Ltd., Dunedin.
18.11.1920: Re-registered at London (573/1920) as WAIKOUAITI.
15.5.1924: Re-registered at Wellington, New Zealand (5/1924).
28.11.1939: Wrecked near Dog Island Bluff, Foveaux Strait, New Zealand whilst on a voyage from Sydney to Lyttelton with a cargo of steel.
8.1.1940: Register closed

M4. ORISSA 1920-1921
O.N. 144660 3,392g 2,193n
346.9 x 48.7 x 23.1 feet
T.3-cyl. by Wallsend Slipway and Engineering Co. Ltd, Wallsend-on-Tyne (24, 40, 66 x 45 inches); 317 NHP, 1,750 IHP.
29.2.1908: Launched by Chantiers Naval Anversois S.A., Hoboken, Belgium (Yard No.36).
4.4.1908: Completed for Seetransport G.m.b.H., Hamburg, Germany as INGELFINGEN.
1909: Sold to Dampfschiffs Union A.G., Hamburg.
23.11.1912: Sold to Rhederic AG von 1896, Hamburg and renamed ORISSA.
4.8.1914: Seized by the Russian government

at St. Petersburg and allocated to the Imperial Russian Navy as the transport AZ.
12.1918: Recovered by owners.
8.7.1920: Surrendered to Britain as war reparations.
21.7.1920: Registered at London (403/1920) in the ownership of the Shipping Controller, London (Thomas Dunlop and Sons, Glasgow, managers) as ORISSA.
23.3.1921: Sold to the Byron Steamship Co. Ltd. (M. Embiricos Ltd., managers), London.
14.4.1921: Re-registered at London (165/1921) and renamed MAID OF CORFU.
5.1924: Sold to N.D. Bogiazides and Co., Andros, Greece and renamed DIMITRIOS N. BOGIAZIDES.
6.6.1924: British register closed.
3.1939: Sold to Alba Steamship Co. Ltd., Panama (S.G. Embiricos Ltd., London, managers) and renamed ALBA.
5.1940: Detained while under repair at Antwerp by German forces.

23.12.1941: Seized by Germany.
5.1942: Placed in German government service as RAUENTHALER
22.4.1942: Managers became Atlas Levante Linie A.G., Bremen, Germany.
15.8.1942: Renamed AQUILA.
8.11.1944: Bombed and sunk by RAF Coastal Command aircraft off Midtgulen whilst on a voyage from Bergen to Boden.

Vessels managed for the Ministry of War Transport/ Ministry of Shipping

M5. GUDRUN MAERSK 1940-1944
O.N. 166299 2,294g 1,344n
327.2 x 46.2 x 17.9 feet
Oil engine 4SCSA 6-cyl. by A/S Burmeister & Wain's Maskin- og Skibsbyggeri, Copenhagen, Denmark (24.8 x 51.18 inches), 3,000 IHP, 13 knots.

The New Zealand steamer *Waikouaiti* was formerly the *Irmgard*. After being surrendered to Britain in 1919 she was registered under the British flag until sold to the Union Steamship Company in 1920 and renamed. *[Ian J. Farquhar collection]*

Dimitrios N. Bogiazides, seen at Montevideo in 1932, was managed for just over a year as the *Orissa. [J. and M. Clarkson collection]*

116

1.1937: Completed by Odense Staalskibsverft ved A.P. Moller, Odense (Yard No.63) for D/S A/S af 1912 (A.P. Moller, manager), Copenhagen, Denmark as GUDRUN MAERSK.

15.4.1940: Brought into Bombay after being intercepted by British warships and subsequently requisitioned.

19.8.1940: Registered at Liverpool (18/1940) in the ownership of the Ministry of War Transport (Thomas Dunlop and Sons, managers).

25.9.1944: Management transferred to T. and J. Brocklebank, Liverpool.

1946: Returned to owners.

3.6.1946: British register closed.

1955: Sold to D/S Hetland A/S (Basse and Co., managers), Copenhagen and renamed SANDAA.

1962: Sold to Naviera Dorhex Ltda., Monrovia, Liberia (Joaquin Ponte Naya S.A., Corunna, Spain, managers), and renamed MATEO.

1964: Sold to Seven Seas Shipping Corporation, Monrovia (Niksa Sekulovich, Lugano, Switzerland, manager).

1966: Sold to Evia Compania Naviera S.A., Panama (E. Kastrinos and J. Psiakis, Piraeus, Greece, managers) and renamed MAYA under the Greek flag.

1968: Renamed OLYMPIC.

1974: Renamed UNIFORCE.

1975: Sold to Richmond Shipping Co. Ltd., Monrovia (Gloriosa Primera Companhia Naviera S.A., Piraeus) and renamed LIBERTY under the Greek flag.

1975: Sold to Costamare Shipping Co. S.A. (V. Constantakopoulos), Piraeus and renamed CARMEN.

1975: Sold to Cerolane Shipping Co. Inc., Monrovia (Naftilos Shipping Co. Ltd., Piraeus, managers) and renamed APOLLO under the Greek flag.

8.1979: Broken up at Laurion.

Gudrun Maersk, the first ship put under Dunlop management in the Second World War. *[World Ship Society Ltd.]*

M6. BORNHOLM 1940-1945

O.N. 165254 3,177g 1928n
326.2 x 50.1 x 20.8 feet
Oil engine 4SCSA 6-cyl. by A/S Burmeister & Wain's Maskin- og Skibsbyggeri, Copenhagen, Denmark (550 x 1,500 mm); 1,600 IHP, 10 knots.

28.11.1929: Launched by A/S Burmeister & Wain's Maskin- og Skibsbyggeri, Copenhagen (Yard No.570) for A/S Det Dansk-Franske Dampskibsselskab (A N Petersen and E Hahn-Petersen, managers), Copenhagen, Denmark as BORNHOLM.

1940: Brought into Halifax, Nova Scotia after being intercepted by British warships and subsequently requisitioned.

24.7.1940: Registered at Aberdeen (3/1940) in the ownership of the Ministry of Shipping, London (Thomas Dunlop and Sons, Glasgow, managers).

12.1945: Returned to owners.

9.1.1946: British register closed.

1954: Sold to A/B Kronvik Shipping Co.

O/Y (Gunnar Erickson, manager), Vasa, Sweden.

4.5.1957: Sprang a leak in heavy weather in the North Atlantic and sank in position 36.40 north by 48.30 west whilst on a voyage from San Felieu to Wilmington, Delaware with a cargo of fluorite.

M7. FORT MISSANABIE 1943-1944

O.N. 169617 7,147g 4,244n
424.7 x 57.2 x 34.9 feet
T.3-cyl. by Dominion Engineering Co. Ltd., Lachine, Quebec, Canada (24.5, 37, 70 x 48 inches, 229 NHP, 2,500 IHP, 10 knots.

15.7.1943: Completed by Marine Industries Ltd., Sorel, Quebec (Yard No. 119).

8.10.1943: Registered at London (247/1943) in the ownership of the Ministry of War Transport, London (Thomas Dunlop and Sons, Glasgow, managers) as FORT MISSANABIE.

19.5.1944: Torpedoed and sunk by the German submarine U 453 off Calabria in

The *Fort Missanabie* was torpedoed and sunk in May 1944 after only eight months' service. *[J. and M. Clarkson collection]*

position 38.20 north by 16.28 east whilst on a voyage from Taranto to Augusta in ballast (ship broke in two with fore part sinking immediately; aft part the next day while in tow).
3.7.1944: Register closed.

M8. FORT ASPIN 1944-1946
O.N. 169981 7,161g 4,222n
424.6 x 57.2 x 34.9 feet
T.3-cyl. by Canadian Allis Chalmers Ltd., Montreal, Quebec, Canada (24.5, 37, 70 x 48 inches); 229 NHP, 2,500 IHP, 11 knots.
27.1.1944: Completed by Prince Rupert Drydock and Shipyard (Grand Trunk Pacific Development Co. Ltd.), Prince Rupert, British Columbia, Canada (Yard No. 52).
3.10.1944: Registered at London (316/1944) in the ownership of the Ministry of War Transport, London (Thomas Dunlop and Sons, Glasgow, managers) as FORT ASPIN.
15.7.1946: Transferred to the Ministry of Transport.
17.7.1946: Sold to the Canadian Ministry of Reconstruction and Supply, Ottawa (Park Steamship Co. Ltd., Montreal, managers).
6.8.1946: Re-registered at Montreal (58/1946).
22.8.1946: Sold to the Triton Steamship Co. Ltd., Montreal (Goulandris Brothers, London, managers).
23.9.1946: Renamed TRIPORT.
1950: Sold to Companhia Maritima del Este S.A., Panama (Goulandris Bros (Hellas) Ltd., Piraeus, managers) and renamed HERON.
16.8.1950: British register closed.
1960: Renamed TINOS.
1963: Renamed EVERGREEN.
1967: Broken up at Kaohsiung.

M9. EMPIRE FREETOWN 1945-1946
O.N. 180350 7,132g 5,033n
443.1 x 57.0 x 27.3 feet
Oil engine 2SCSA 3-cyl. by William Doxford and Sons Ltd., Sunderland (600 x 2,320 mm).
29.1.1945: Launched by Burntisland Shipbuilding Co. Ltd., Burntisland (Yard No.288) for the Ministry of War Transport, London (Thomas Dunlop and Sons, Glasgow, managers) as EMPIRE FREETOWN.
1946: Sold to B.J. Sutherland and Co. Ltd., Newcastle-upon-Tyne and renamed INVERNESS.
10.1953: Sold to Turnbull Scott Shipping Co. Ltd. (Turnbull, Scott and Co., managers), London and renamed REDGATE.
1.1963: Sold to Marvalia Naviera S.A., Panama (Pateras Shipbrokers Ltd., London, managers) and renamed AGIA ELPIS.
1964: Management transferred to Poseidon Shipping Agencies Ltd., London.
1967: Transferred to the Southern Cross Shipping Co. Ltd., Famagusta, Cyprus (Poseidon Shipping Agencies Ltd., London).
1968: Sold to China Machinery Import-Export Corporation.
25.6.1968: Left Singapore Roads for demolition at Shanghai.
30.7.1968: Arrived Shanghai.

Fort Aspin. [National Maritime Museum P22639]

Empire Freetown (upper middle) was managed until 1946 when she was sold by the Ministry of War Transport to B. J. Sutherland and Co. Ltd. Renamed *Inverness* (lower middle) she is seen at Cape Town in August 1951. In 1953, following her sale to other British buyers she was renamed *Redgate* (bottom) and is seen in a South Wales port in June 1959. [Ship in Focus]

James Craig - 134 years young

Thomas Dunlop traded in the *Clan Macleod* as part payment to Russell and Co. for the *Clan Buchanan* in 1887. In 1888 Russell sold her another Glasgow owner who in turn in 1900 sold her to J. J. Craig of Auckland, New Zealand. Craig renamed her *James Craig* in 1905, the name which she holds to this day. Following a further sale in 1911 she was converted to a coal hulk. Sold again in 1918 she was re-rigged and returned to service.

Top: *James Craig* began her long association with southern Tasmania when she made four voyages from mainland ports in 1920 and 1921 under the ownership of local company H. Jones and Company. Having arrived with general cargo from Melbourne the previous day, she was appropriately dressed for the Hobart Regatta on 1st February 1921. *[Maritime Museum of Tasmania]*

Middle left: In the Hobsons Bay Dock and Engineering Company's floating dock at Williamstown (a suburb of Melbourne) between 25th and 28th July 1921. This was the ship's last visit to Melbourne in commercial service having arrived on 9th July and later sailed on 20th September. Her next visit was in January 2006, 84 years later. *[Cliff Gibson collection]*

Middle right: *James Craig* became a coal hulk for the second time in her career when the Catamaran Coal Mining Company, a company associated with H. Jones and Company, acquired her in 1925. She was to use this same slip on Hobart's Domain several times during the early stages of her restoration half a century later. *[Maritime Museum of Tasmania]*

Bottom left: *James Craig* as a coal hulk anchored off the coal loader in Recherche Bay, Tasmania in January 1934. *[Lindsay Rex/Melbourne Grammar School]*

Bottom right: *James Craig* aground at the east side of The Pigsties, Recherche Bay, Tasmania on 22nd April 1962 where she had drifted ashore after breaking her moorings in a 1930s storm. She lay here for over forty years until recovered by the Sydney Maritime Museum. The Pigsties is the description of this area at the north end of Recherche Bay. *[Lindsay Rex]*

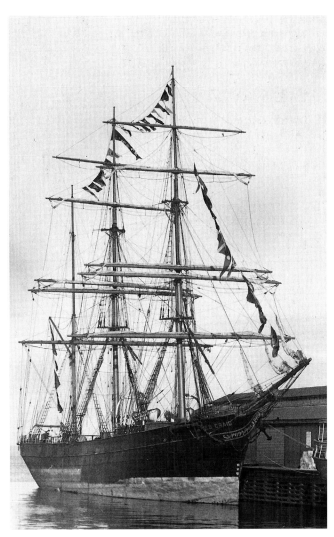

Top left: The tug *Sirius Cove* (165/1958) towed the *James Craig* to Hobart from Recherche Bay on 28th May 1973. Late that afternoon, and almost at the end of their 100 kilometre/60 mile journey, both vessels proceeded upriver through the Tasman Bridge to a temporary mooring in Prince of Wales Bay. She was later slipped, plates removed and repaired, the hull cleaned and checked and then taken to the old Powder Jetty. *[Rex Cox]*

Top right: Alongside the Powder Jetty in December 1974, the berth provided for her by the Hobart Marine Board just upstream from the Domain Slip, with restoration work underway. *[Rex Cox]*

Middle left: *James Craig* sank at these moorings on 23rd August 1975 but was raised four days later. Hobart's Tasman Bridge can be seen in the background. *[Maritime Museum of Tasmania]*

Middle right: Now in much happier circumstances at The Domain moorings, Hobart in January 1980 looking much more spic and span with the light grey hull colour she received around the middle of 1978, the *James Craig* lay here for most of the time until towed to Sydney in January 1981. Restored and fitted with engines she was officially re-commissioned by the Sydney Maritime Museum, now renamed the Sydney Heritage Fleet, at Wharf 7, Pyrmont, Sydney on 12th November 2000. *[Lindsay Rex]*

Lower middle and bottom: *James Craig* on 24th February 2001, ten to fifteen miles off Sydney Heads, on the first day on which full sail had been set since restoration. The flag of the Sydney Maritime Museum is at the mainmast and the P&O (sponsors) flag flies at the mizzen. Since re-commissioning *James Craig* has sailed interstate on three occasions having visited Hobart in February 2005 and Melbourne in January and February 2006 and again two years later. She has also sailed on the New South Wales coast north to Newcastle and south to Eden on several occasions. Regular day sails are made off the Sydney Heads, perhaps of the order of one hundred such sails having been made by early 2008. *[Both: Lindsay Rex] [All captions by Lindsay Rex and Rex Cox]*

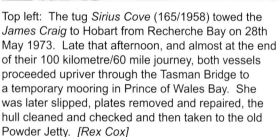

RICHARD B. CHELLEW
CHELLEW NAVIGATION CO. LTD.

Tony Atkinson

Richard Berryman Chellew was born in 1856, the first child of William and Elizabeth Chellew. Both William (1829-1916) and his wife, born Elizabeth Berryman, had been brought up in the Cornish fishing village of St. Ives, but after marrying they moved up the county to Devoran on the River Fal south of Truro. Here, William established himself as a timber merchant, importing timber mainly from Scandinavia for use as a building material, in boat building and as props for the tin mines. The vessels that brought in timber sailed from the Devoran valley with the minerals mined there.

Richard Chellew and his younger brother John were educated at the Davies Academy, Truro and the North Devon County School, West Buckland. When Richard left school at age 16 in 1872 he was sent to work in Plymouth with timber merchants R.R. Bailey where he learnt book-keeping and other office skills. After two years working in Plymouth, Richard joined the family business in Truro.

Sail and steam

In 1877, William Chellew in partnership with the Devoran shipbuilder John Stephens built the 107-ton ketch *Hetty*. Over the next 20 years, William was to take shares in a number of Cornish sailing vessels. Richard, however, became interested in steam, recognising that it would herald the demise of sail. For a long period he tried to steer his father away from sail towards the iron steamers that could carry a much larger cargo, carry it faster and without relying on the wind. Richard was ambitious: many years later his younger brother recalled that Richard once said he had three ambitions, to become a shipowner, a millionaire and to marry Miss Jane Trefusis. He succeeded in the first, and if not a millionaire he was to become seriously wealthy, but it was impossible for a tradesman like him to marry into the wealthy Trefusis family.

On 12th September 1882 William, Richard and a third family member, James Chellew, registered the Cornwall Steamship Co. Ltd. to own the new steamer *City of Truro*, which was to be built by John Readhead and Co. at South Shields. Details were given in reports in the 'Royal Cornwall Gazette.' These claimed that the original builder had failed, but there is no suggestion of this in the history of Readheads, a successful company which had just established what was to be a lasting relationship with another Cornish shipowner, Edward Hain. The claim in the newspaper was probably made to cover the Chellews' inability to sell all the shares in time, or that negotiations broke down when Readhead was unwilling to build for the

£18,000 mentioned in the new company's prospectus. In the event, Chellews revised the prospectus to increase the capital and gave the order to William Gray at Hartlepool.

The *City of Truro* was launched on 4th October 1883 and a month later delivered to the owning company, the Cornwall Steamship Co. Ltd. Following sea trials the customary inventory was made to check that the builders had fulfilled the contract. The inventory would be checked by representatives of the owners and the builders, each placing a tick alongside every item. Only when this had been done was the steamer handed over. The Cornwall County Records Office has the leather-bound inventory book of one of Chellew's later steamers, the *Penwith*, built at Hayle.

The *City of Truro* left Hartlepool on her maiden voyage on 24th November 1883 loaded with rails for Naples, where she arrived on 15th December. Following discharge she sailed to the Black Sea to load a cargo of grain for London at

Hetty, one of William Chellew's first ventures into shipowning, loading china clay at Newquay about 1919. Formerly a schooner, she was now rigged as a ketch. *[Author's collection]*

City of Truro in rough seas, painted by an unknown artist. *[Author's collection]*

Sulina on the Danube. Her second voyage was with coal for the Admiralty from Cardiff to Port Said. She again loaded grain at Sulina, this time for Bristol. The local paper noted that these first two voyages had made a profit of £513 after running expenses and wages had been paid.

At the second Annual General Meeting of the Cornwall Steamship Co. Ltd. in October 1884, Richard Chellew reported that the whole capital of £25,000 had been subscribed, with 500 shares at £50 each allotted to 93 shareholders. During construction of *City of Truro* the 950 shares at £20 mentioned in the original prospectus had been revised to 500 shares at £50. From this capital they had paid £22,250 to William Gray and Co., the builders, leaving £2,000 still due, for which the builders received a bill of exchange.

Expansion of the fleet

After a gap of about five years, Chellew's fleet began to expand with four more steamers: the *Duke of Cornwall*, *Duchess of Cornwall*, *Cornubia* and *Pencalenick*. Once again, Readheads were reported as being about to build the *Duke of Cornwall*, but again the order went to William Gray. Like all steamers ordered by Richard Chellew, each was registered in the ownership of a newly-floated single-ship company. From the *Pencalenick*, all new Chellew ships bore Cornish place names with the prefix, *Pen-*. At the same time, Edward Hain of St Ives was using the prefix *Tre-*, and the less well known William Badcock, also of St. Ives, later had a small fleet with names beginning *Pol-* to indicate their Cornish connection, including *Polurrian* and *Poldhu*.

Duke of Cornwall, completed in 1888, at Bristol. *[Nigel Farrell collection]*

Richard Chellew said later in his life that it had been a struggle to raise the money for the *City of Truro*, but share issues for subsequent ships had been over-subscribed. This was only partly true. In the prospectus for the owning company, the Cornwall Steamship Co. Ltd., investors were promised profits of between 15% and 25%, and even this high figure was increased to 20% to 30% in an announcement in the local paper. But for its first three years, it seems that the company paid no dividends, the ship's earnings being used to meet the final payments to the builders. Only in its fourth year of trading were modest dividends totalling £1,000 paid. Although this approach may have been financially prudent, the investors were not getting their promised profits, and Chellew found it difficult to raise the money for his next company, the Duke of Cornwall Steamship Co. Ltd. In December 1887, when only 260 of its 500 shares had been taken up, he had to re-issue his prospectus. However, helped by dividends totalling almost £3,500 on the next year's trading by *City of Truro*, all the remaining shares in the new company were sold. Chellew's subsequent ventures were frequently over-subscribed. For instance, in a short note in the 'Royal Cornwall Gazette' for 7th November 1900, which a week earlier had advertised a prospectus to raise money to build the *Penlee*:

'Mr R.B .Chellew was glad to advise the columns of the local press that the 1,000 shares of £50 each to raise £50,000 for the new steamship *Penlee* were all subscribed within a few days, and in the main by his old shareholders'. In 1912 shares in his Penolver Steamship Co. Ltd. sold out within three days of his issuing a prospectus.

Clearly the ease with which he could raise capital suggests that Chellew had built up a sufficiently good reputation as a steamship manager that subscribers saw shares in his new companies as excellent investments. This was particularly admirable since Chellew seems to have had no previous experience in steamship management before floating his first company in 1883. Chellew and his family would take some of the shares in each single-ship company, but also benefited from fees paid by the companies to them as managers. In 1888 R.B. and W.

Chellew and Co. was set up to manage the day to day running of their ships, with Richard and William Chellew as partners. Just how well Chellew was succeeding was apparent from figures presented at the 1894 annual general meeting. Those who had originally invested in the Cornwall Steamship Co. Ltd., owners of the *City of Truro*, had received dividends of £174 19s 3d for each £50 share; three and a half times their original investment. In the past year the *City of Truro* had made another £22 12s 11d for each shareholder. The *Duke of Cornwall* of 1888 had also done well, paying dividends of £50,875 over her career to date - more than two and three quarter times her original cost.

Chellew's ships had been built by Grays at Hartlepool or on the Wear in the case of the *Pencalenick*. In October 1889 he placed a contract with Harvey and Company of Hayle for the sister ships *Penwith* and *Penpol*. The latter was launched by a Mrs. Rawlings, wife of one of the major shareholders, in July 1890. These were the largest vessels to have been built in Cornwall, but it seems that the local yard could not compete on delivery times with shipbuilders in the north east to whom Chellew went for all his subsequent ships.

With most of the company's vessels loading coal in South Wales, an office was opened in Cardiff where Richard's younger brother John Chellew was appointed office manager. In time this became more important than the Truro office. William E. Hinde (1878-1956) was a significant Cardiff shipowner who began his career at Chellew's Cardiff office in 1893. In 1903 Hinde left to set up on his own and had a long and successful career as manager of the Portfield Steamship Co. Ltd. and a number of other South Welsh shipping-related businesses.

Richard Chellew was clearly doing well from his shipowning. In the spring of 1897 he purchased 3 Strangways Terrace, Truro, in easy walking distance of his offices in Boscawen Street. But only a few months later in October 1897 he bought the old freehold mansion of Tregolls, once the seat of Sir Samuel Spry, for £3,000. The property had not been occupied for some time and needed thorough restoration and renovation. In 1901 Chellew bought for £5,000 the Tremorvah Estate, comprising a house situated in the midst of 45 acres of park-like grounds; the

Penpol, the second of two sisters built at Hayle and one of the few ships to be broken up there. *[Nigel Farrell collection]*

purchase included two lodges, and three farms plus gardener's cottages.

But not all of his ventures prospered. In response to suggestions from shareholders that the company should invest in a mutual insurance scheme, in 1898 Richard Chellew formed the Truro Mutual Marine Insurance Association Ltd., both to insure his own fleet of ships and those of other shipowners, with his father William Chellew as Chairman. Unfortunately, it did not survive long and in February 1901 it was reported that the venture was experiencing heavy losses, and its operations were scaled down, and at the same time William Chellew retired from the business.

Consolidation: proposed and rejected

In 1902, at the urging of several major shareholders, it was proposed that the companies managed by Richard Chellew be liquidated, and the ships transferred to one new company with a nominal capital of £350,000 in 35,000 shares of £10 each. It was pointed out such an amalgamation offered many advantages. It would lead to great savings in insurance, spread the shareholders' interest over the whole fleet, make the investment of a more permanent character, make the shares more negotiable by converting them into smaller sums, disposing of the least remunerative ships when appropriate, utilise the reserve funds (now standing at £36,000) for new and modern tonnage, and ensure the equalisation and more regular payment of dividends. For the purposes of the proposal, the fleet was valued as follows:

Duke of Cornwall	£15,500
Duchess of Cornwall	£15,500
Cornubia	£16,500
Pencalenick	£14,500
Penwith	£17,500
Penpol	£18,500
Pendarves	£20,520
Pendennis	£22,500
Pendeen	£23,500
Penmount	£24,500
Penare	£33,500
Penlee	£41,500
Total value	£264,020

It was intended that shareholders would receive in return for their current holding an equivalent amount in £10 shares in the new company. The remainder of shares - the difference between the £350,000 and £264,020 - would be issued to build new tonnage. The proposal was circulated to all shareholders, but although there was a six-to-one majority in favour, Richard Chellew appears to have had cold feet and decided to withdraw the proposal, wanting greater unanimity.

Chellew built up his fleet considerably in the first decade and a half of the 20th century. He was one of a relatively small number of ship owners to experiment with the Doxford Turret, adding two to his fleet, the *Penvearn* in 1906 and the *Penrose* in 1908. All vessels were registered in the ownership of single ship companies, most of which were split into 1,000 relatively low denomination shares with the total capital being equivalent to the contract price of the vessel in question – thus the capital of the Penrose Steamship Co. Ltd. was £36,000 divided into 1,000 shares of £36 each. This system was maintained even as asset prices rose for the larger vessels built just before the war, the Penmorvah Steamship Co. Ltd. of 1913, for example, being capitalized at £52,500 divided once again into 1,000 shares. With the companies maintaining separate existences as far as paying dividends was concerned, there tended to be only general references to the fleet as a whole in each new prospectus. One exception, however, was that for the Turret *Penrose*, which was specifically introduced as a replacement for the *Pencalenick*.

The Cornish-built *Penwith* in the Avon Gorge. Note the sail on the foremast, and the well deck forward. In January 1912, Richard Chellew received a telegram from Las Palmas that the *Penwith* had sunk but her crew were safe. She had been on a voyage from Hornillo to Cardiff with iron ore, having sailed on the 14th December. *Penwith* had last been seen passing Cape St. Vincent, and it was feared that she and all her crew had been lost in the Bay of Biscay during a storm. It was now known that on the 21st December she lost her rudder, and for nearly a week lay helpless. On the 28th December the Russian steamer *Hektor* was sighted, and Captain Tregarthen abandoned the ship. Last to leave was the second engineer Mr Yates who opened the sea valves to scuttle the vessel so that it would be of no danger to other shipping. *[J. and M. Clarkson]*

Pencalenick's voyages 1903

By the beginning of the twentieth century the Chellew fleet had grown to eleven ships, all tramping to the Mediterranean, Black Sea and the Baltic. Richard Chellew liked to advertise his fleet and how it was doing, and in every weekly issue of the 'Royal Cornwall Gazette' was a list showing the last known position of each vessel and the cargo it was carrying. The local shareholders could check on their investment, and how their vessel was employed. From the copies from December 1902 to December 1903, it is possible to trace one year's tramping of the *Pencalenick*. Her voyage starts from her home port, as near as a vessel of her size could get to Truro, on the buoy at Maggoty Bank, just downstream from Malpas.

Date	Port: arrivals and departures
22nd December 1902	Arrived at Maggoty Bank, Malpas from Constantinople.
15th January 1903	Sailed from the River Fal for Barry, South Wales.
18th January	Arrived Barry to load coal for the Admiralty.
23rd January	Sailed for Malta.
8th February	Arrived Malta and discharged her coal.
9th February	Sailed for Varna, Bulgaria.
15th February	Arrived Varna to load barley.
18th February	Sailed for Falmouth.
20th February	Passed Constantinople.
8th March	Arrived Falmouth to discharge.
12th March	Sailed for Cardiff.
13th March	Arrived Cardiff to load coal for the Admiralty.
24rd March	Sailed for Piraeus.
14th April	Arrived Piraeus, where part of her cargo was discharged, and sailed same day for Sulina.
18th April	Arrived Sulina to finish discharging.
22nd April	Sailed for Odessa.
29th April	Arrived Novorossysk from Odessa to complete loading of grain.
3rd May	Passed Constantinople for Dunkirk.
20th May	Arrived Dunkirk to discharge.
3rd June	Arrived Newport, South Wales to load coal for the Admiralty.
9th June	Sailed for Constantinople.
26th June	Arrived Constantinople where cargo was transhipped to units of the British Mediterranean fleet
6th July	Arrived Nicolaieff to load Russian grain.
21st July	Sailed Gibraltar for Manchester.
29th July	Arrived Manchester to discharge.
8th August	Sailed Swansea for Sfax, with coal for the Admiralty
20th August	Arrived Sfax, Tunisia to discharge.
2nd September	Passed Constantinople for Azoff (Azov), to load grain.
6th September	Arrived Taganrog (on the River Don), Russia to load grain.
16th September	Passed Constantinople for United Kingdom.
25th September	Sailed Gibraltar for Portishead.
3rd October	Arrived Portishead.
12th October	Arrived Newport to load coal for Volo, Greece for the Admiralty.
16th October	Sailed for Volo.
31st October	Arrived Volo.
10th November	Sailed Volo for Azoff.
17th November	Arrived Temruk, Ukraine to load grain.
25th November	Sailed Temruk for United Kingdom.
29th November	Passed Constantinople for Plymouth.
10th December	Passed Algiers for Plymouth.
19th December	Arrived Plymouth to discharge. Laid over in Plymouth for maintenance and painting and sailed on 23rd January 1904 for Swansea to load coal for the Admiralty.

In October 1904 the *Pencalenick* was stopped in the Bay of Biscay by the Russian cruiser *Ural*, and boarded by an officer who examined the ship's papers. After an hour's delay she was allowed to proceed on her voyage from Cardiff to Malta with Admiralty coal. The Captain of the *Pencalenick* noticed that the cruiser stopped another steamer about seven miles off his vessel. On arrival at Malta the *Pencalenick* was ordered to follow the British Mediterranean Fleet which had moved to the eastern Mediterranean. The Russian Black Sea Fleet was preparing to break out into the Mediterranean, and it was thought that this could lead to conflict between the Greeks who backed the Russians and the Turks who did not. By coincidence, earlier that month in the North Sea the *Aldebaran*, the former *City of Truro*, had been fired on by Russian warships who thought she was a Japanese battleship sent around the world to stop the Baltic Fleet sailing to relieve the Russian Pacific fleet at the time blockaded in Vladivostok. But the *Aldebaran* was eventually discovered not to be a warship or Japanese and allowed to sail on. The following day the Russians fired on and damaged British fishing vessels in the North Sea, believing them to be Japanese torpedo boats. *[World Ship Photo Library]*

During September 1912, Richard Chellew was being driven to Tremorvah, his home in Truro, following a visit to one of his vessels in Falmouth, when his car was involved in an accident in the dark. He was badly injured, and from then on was confined to a wheel chair. This did not curtail his activities, however, as it is said that he was invited by Lord Inchcape, Chairman of P&O, to accompany him to the opening of the Panama Canal. *[Author's collection]*

War and rumours of war

A short note in the 'Royal Cornwall Gazette' for 14th July 1914 advised the company's shareholders that R.B. Chellew had received a telegram stating that the Admiralty were seeking 'spot' boats on time charter, and that it was rumoured they intended taking over tonnage already fixed out. The note explained that this meant that ships in port would be time chartered to follow the fleet, and those already loaded with coal for foreign ports might be commandeered for the same purpose. It is interesting to note here that the average cargo ship of the day could carry 2,500 tons of coal; it would need ten such cargoes to keep the British Mediterranean Fleet at sea for a day.

In view of the trade from the Baltic to the UK, it was no surprise that when war was declared on 4th August 1914 over 90 ships were trapped in Swedish and Russian Baltic ports, including four Chellew ships.

Three of the trapped ships belonged to A.M. Sutherland of Newcastle-upon-Tyne. In the summer of 1915 he discussed, with Swedish masters visiting the Tyne, the possibility of bringing the ships out. In October his friends in Gothenburg agreed that for a fee of £1,000 plus expenses Swedish crews would sail them inside territorial waters to Gothenburg, where they would be returned to British crews, sent out via Norway.

The Admiralty arranged escorts across the North Sea. Sutherland was Vice-Chairman of the North of England

Pensilva, completed at West Hartlepool in 1913. *[Author's collection]*

War Risk Association who gave cover, and Lloyd's underwriters insured marine risks.

Sutherland intended to bring his *Dunrobin* (3,617/1903) out first, but it was late in the season, she was caught in ice at Lulea and had to wait until the summer of 1916. Other owners took up his offer to bring out their ships, including Chellew who had four bottled up. The first to escape, from ice free ports, were *Ryde* (3,556/1907), *F.D. Lambert* (2,195/1892) and *Gitano* (1,179/1913) in December 1915. A rival scheme only attempted to bring out one ship. *Adams* (2,223/1887) was captured by German torpedo boats, but later released.

By the end of July 1916, 29 ships had been recovered despite attempts by German naval units to catch them. A Swedish gunboat protected territorial waters, but that month a Swedish minefield was laid which stopped the route unless ships ventured into international waters. Chellew's *Penmount* arrived on the Tyne on 5th July, but *Pendennis* sailed from Gothenburg and was captured by *U 48* off the Norwegian coast on 6th July. Her crew was interned in Gefangenenlager, Frankfurt.

Pressure from the British Government saw the minefield removed in May 1917, after which sailings again commenced and a further 54 ships were brought out. Chellew's *Penpol* and *Pendeen* had been requisitioned in July 1916 to serve Allied needs in the Baltic. *Penpol* was captured by *UC 57* in the Gulf of Bothnia on 19th June 1917 and *Pendeen* escaped from the Baltic in September 1917 to be taken up as Admiralty collier number 1779.

War loss claims were paid on *Pendennis* and *Penpol*. Handed back in January 1919 they were registered to the Shipping Controller until sold to new owners.

Chellew's *Penmount* and *Pendennis*, plus Headlam's *Ryde*, frozen into the harbour at Sundsvall, Sweden during the First World War. *[Author's collection]*

Some 350,000 deadweight tons of shipping, valued at £5 million, was released at a cost of little over £300,000. Many were later war losses, but with the high rate of sinkings they were valuable additions to the war effort.

The company lost five other ships during the First World War. First was the *Cornubia*, captured and sunk off Cartegena by an Austro-Hungarian submarine on the 15th September 1915. The worst loss was the *Duchess of Cornwall*, torpedoed on 11th April 1917 with the loss of 23 lives. Her loss was closely followed by that of *Penhale*, torpedoed off Ireland on 18th May 1917, with one life lost. Sinkings continued into 1918, with *Penvearn* torpedoed in the Irish Sea on 1st March again with heavy loss of life, and *Penhallow* torpedoed in the Mediterranean on 12th June with no casualties.

Like many other British shipowners, Chellew was able to take advantage of high wartime freight rates to make handsome profits. However, returns varied depending on whether vessels were free to trade on the highly inflated commercial market or were under government charter. One of the most profitable vessels, the *Penmount*, paid a dividend of £10 per share in December 1916, one of £2 in March 1917, another of £3 in June 1917 and yet another of £3 in September 1917, a total return of more than 50% on each £31 share in less than a year. By contrast, the *Penare* and the *Penlee* each paid a total dividend of only £7 over the same period. Chellew also registered significant capital gains on insurance payments for vessels lost. The *Penhallow*, for example, had cost £51,000 to build in 1913, but was insured for £94,500 when sunk.

Late in the war, Chellew was given management of vessels by the Shipping Controller. The ships concerned were relatively small steel steamers building for British account in Canadian yards on the Great Lakes. Four were completed before the Armistice, and two more in 1919. With a typical flourish, Richard Chellew announced in the 'Royal Cornwall Gazette' that these vessels were being built under supervision of Chellew staff and would be managed from Truro. He listed six, including the *War Karma*, but there was clearly a change of mind and *War Badger* was allocated to Chellew instead. Management in most cases was for only a matter of months.

Wealthy shipowners were expected to make philanthropic gestures to help the war effort, and Richard Chellew maintained the Chellew Ward at the Royal Naval Hospital, Truro and gave assistance to a military hospital in Camborne.

Reorganisation and sale

In 1918 Richard had all the vessels re-registered under one company, the R.B. Chellew Steam Navigation Co. Ltd. This was a reorganisation and renaming of one of Chellew's existing companies, the Pengreep Steamship Co. Ltd. In August 1918 the new company's 11 ships were valued at £485,492. Chellew's rekindled enthusiasm for amalgamation may have been explained by his eagerness to retire from the business. His father, William Chellew, had died on the 28th January 1916, at his home at Point, Truro, and Richard had no sons to whom he could pass his business.

Rumours of a sale for £1 million reached the 'Falmouth Packet' in July 1920. Chellew denied this, and insisted the fleet was not for sale and the offices in Truro and Cardiff would carry on as usual. What had been sold, he insisted, were his management shares. Aged 63, in bad health and confined to a wheelchair, Chellew had been advised by his doctor to retire from business. The transaction was confirmed later that month at the Annual General Meeting when Richard Chellew announced that he had sold all his shares in the management company R.B. Chellew and Co. to Frank Shearman of Tiverton. Owning the management company gave Shearman control of how the ships were run, but without a majority stake in the owning company, R.B. Chellew Steam Navigation Co. Ltd., he could not dictate whether, for instance, the fleet would be sold. This was a situation that was to endure for many years, with no one individual or organisation holding sway over the Chellew business.

Frank Shearman's background was in ship repairing and engineering. Born at Newport in 1879, he had worked at his father's repair yard in Cardiff, and served an apprenticeship in various yards in Sunderland, before going to sea as an engineer. In 1902, with his father seriously ill, he came ashore to manage the business of John Shearman and Co. Ltd. at Cardiff and Barry, which he later expanded to Avonmouth and Newport. In 1912 he acquired a controlling interest in Mountstuart Dry Docks Ltd., the major ship repairers at Cardiff, and in 1916 took over the repair works of Mordey,

The *Penhale* of 1911 had only a short life as she was torpedoed and sunk in May 1917. Only one crew member was killed but the master was taken prisoner. *[Author's collection]*

Penhale delivered in January 1924. *[Nigel Farrell collection]*

Carney and Co. Ltd. at Newport, a company with a history of both shipbuilding and ship owning. At some point he also joined the Chellew board, probably on the understanding that he would eventually assume control.

The day-to-day running of the business was entrusted to Frederick C. Perman. He had joined Chellew in the Cardiff office in 1893, moved to Truro in 1898 and as head clerk effectively ran that office by 1918. He joined the board in 1920. Despite Chellew's assurances that the Truro office would remain open, it was not long before the new management ended the Cornish connection, and from 1921 the company was run from 47 Stuart Street, Cardiff.

Richard Berryman Chellew, founder of the company, died at his home Tremorvah on Good Friday 1929 at the age of 72. His estate was valued at £667,380, and in his will he left a silver galleon to the Truro Museum and £100 towards a stained glass window at Feock Church where his father and mother were buried. Richard's younger brother John Chellew, who had run the Cardiff office until 1918, died at his home in Falmouth on 28th May 1936; he was 76.

After Richard Chellew
As if the death of Richard Chellew signalled the start of a new era, in September 1929 the directors of R.B. Chellew Steam Navigation Co. Ltd. decided to rename the company the Chellew Navigation Co. Ltd. A new management company, the Chellew Steamship Management Co. Ltd., had been set up in March 1927 with a modest capital of £1,000. This company had an agreement to manage the ships belonging to the Chellew Navigation Co. Ltd.

But if this was a new era, it was not to be a particularly profitable one with the difficulties encountered by all shipping companies during the years between the wars. In 1928, for instance, R.B. Chellew Steam Navigation Co. Ltd.

Frank Shearman. *[Amgueddfa Cymru - National Museum Wales 86.123/60]*

had made a profit of just £17,878 and a dividend of only 6p per share was to be paid. Although the Cornish connection was severed, new and second hand ships continued to be given names beginning *Pen-* and Chellew's funnel and houseflag were unchanged.

In 1930 Frank Shearman resigned as manager of the Chellew Navigation Co. Ltd. for what were described as personal reasons. He sold his shares to Mackintosh and Co. (Gibraltar) Ltd. for almost £36,000. This company belonging to Gibraltar merchant John Mackintosh was the largest shareholder but it did not have a controlling interest in the Chellew Navigation Co. Ltd.. However, it did own all the shares in Chellew Steamship Management Co. Ltd. which gave them control of operations. Shearman's place as manager was taken by board member Frank C. Perman, who acquired a modest shareholding in the company. The head office moved again, this time to Bevis Marks House, London.

Under Shearman four new ships had been added to the fleet during the 1920s, but the new regime was much more cautious. Indeed, the only addition to the fleet during the early 1930s came about through an exchange with Swansea owners Ambrose, Davies and Mathews Ltd. Their *Brynymor* of 1929 became Chellew's second *Pensilva*, whilst the first *Pensilva* dating from 1913 became *Brynymor*. In 1936 and 1937, three Gibraltar-registered ships were transferred to the company from the Calpean Shipping Co. Ltd., a company associated with Mackintosh and Co. These included two relatively new steamers built at Burntisland. A Doxford 'Economy' type motor ship, building for Calpean, was also registered with Chellew on completion, the only motor vessel the company was ever to own. No explanation for these transfers has been found, and none of the four ships took traditional *Pen-* names.

Pengreep of 1914 laid up during the depression of the 1930s. *[Nigel Farrell collection]*

Frederick Perman continued to run both the Chellew Navigation Co. Ltd. and the Chellew Steamship Management Co. Ltd. throughout the Second World War. Again, losses were heavy, with *Pensilva* (2) lost in 1939, *Pengreep* captured and *Statira* lost in 1940, *Justitia* in 1941, *Penrose* in 1942 and *Penolver* in 1943. These were to some extent offset by management of seven ships for the Ministry of War Transport, but three of these were sunk by enemy action.

The loss of the *Penolver* on 19th October 1943 was unusual enough to be worthy of special attention. Although U-boats had been extensively involved in offensive minelaying in British coastal waters in the early months of the war, it was rare for them to be so employed in distant waters later in the submarine campaign. One exception was *U 220*, a specialized Type XB minelayer, which laid a field off the coast of Newfoundland on 9th October 1943. Ten days after it was laid, the field claimed two victims, the *Penolver* and the United States steamer *Delisle* (3,478/1919). *U 220* did not return from this, her first and only combat mission. On 28th October she was surprised on the surface by two aircraft from the escort carrier USS *Block Island* and sunk with all

hands some 1,000 miles north of the Azores.

The share ownership in Chellew Navigation Co. Ltd. changed during the war years, with Mackintosh and Co. gradually disposing of their holding. Major new shareholders were members of the London-Greek Chandris family and companies which they controlled. But again, no single shareholder had a controlling interest in Chellew Navigation Co. Ltd., although Perman acquired all the shares in Chellew Steamship Management Co. Ltd. Perhaps in response to the bombing of London, offices were moved back to Cardiff, returning to London in September 1945.

A welcome return to the traditional Chellew naming policy came in 1947 with the purchase of the Liberty *Samnebra*, which had been managed since 1946, and was renamed *Pentire.* The early postwar years were profitable ones for the company, with dividends of 11¼% being paid in 1946, 1947 and 1948, up from 7½% in most wartime years.

Frederick Perman died in harness during March 1948. He was by then the largest single shareholder, although the various Chandris interests held more shares overall. Perman had been involved with Chellew for a remarkable

The *Auretta* of 1936 on 15th November 1938, was the first of the three ships transferred from the Calpean Shipping Co. Ltd. *[Roy Fenton collection]*

The *Pensilva* of 1929 became the company's first loss in the Second World War when she was torpedoed, shelled and sunk in the bay of Biscay in November 1939. *[Nigel Farrell collection]*

Two funerals and a battle: *Pendeen* in the River Plate

Chellew's *Pendeen* passed the Recalada Light Vessel at 12.30pm on 12th December 1939, and hauled down her wireless aerial in accordance with Argentina's neutrality rules. For almost a fortnight her master, Captain John Owen Jones, had been complaining of severe headaches and had run a temperature, but he turned out to attend to the formalities of port entry in Buenos Aires Roads.

The pilot who boarded the *Pendeen* next day reported having heard heavy gunfire out to sea, but this did not prepare the officer of the watch for what happened next. 'Look what's coming astern!' he shouted to the helmsman as the *Admiral Graf Spee* quickly overhauled them. The crew rushed on deck, and from barely 50 yards away could clearly see the shell holes in the German warship's superstructure. Edgar Thompson, the surprised helmsman, recalls being given a tot of rum after coming off watch.

On *Pendeen's* arrival at Dorsena Sud, an ambulance was waiting to take the master to the British hospital, but he slipped into unconsciousness and died of what was diagnosed as meningitis. He was buried in the British cemetery.

First officer John Alun Jones, the late captain's cousin, was subsequently appointed master of *Pendeen*, but the major drama was played out in the River Plate. *Admiral Graf Spee* sailed from Montevideo and on the evening of 18th December sank when her remaining ammunition was detonated. Two days later, in the Buenos Aires Naval Barracks where his crew were interned, Captain Hans Langsdorff shot himself. Edgar Thompson and a sizeable number of others from *Pendeen's* crew attended Langsdorff's funeral, honouring an opponent who had sunk nine British merchant ships but had behaved with honour and compassion to their crews.

Captain John Alun Jones enjoyed a long career with Chellew, having joined the *Pencarrow* as third officer in January 1930. He was master of the managed *Fort Maisonneuve* at the Anzio landings and when sunk by a magnetic mine in the River Scheldt in December 1944. He remained with the company until the end, commanding Chellew's last ship, the *Eskglen*. Both he and his late cousin, Captain John Owen Jones, were Welsh bards, accomplished in the ancient *cynghanedd* tradition of poetry.

Pendeen at Cardiff. *[Amgueddfa Cymru - National Museum Wales 998/1092]*

Chellew ships at war. The *Pengreep* had an eventful war. After capture and renaming by the Vichy French she was retaken by the Allies, brought to Newport, South Wales and given the name *Empire Fal* (above). Her end came in July 1945 when she was scuttled with a cargo of poison gas shells. Nothing unusual was reported about the *Penhale* during the Second World War, seen below at Halifax, Nova Scotia, Canada in December 1943. However, judging by her appearance she was not having an easy war. *[National Maritime Museum P22286 and P.23753]*

55 years, and it had made him a relatively wealthy man. As well as holding a number of other directorates in the shipping industry, he had been Chairman of the Cardiff and Bristol Channel Shipowners' Association in 1928, and held positions in the Chamber of Shipping and the Shipping Federation. The fleet's management was taken over by fellow director Baden H. Roberts, who was also a long standing Chellew employee, having joined the company in 1915.

During 1952 both the management company and shares in the shipping company were sold to Cory Brothers and Co. Ltd. of Cardiff. The management was strengthened with the appointment of William Evans and John Davies as directors of Chellew Steam Navigation Co. Ltd., and Evans was also appointed chairman with Baden Roberts becoming his deputy. The company once again returned to Cardiff.

Once again, the new management could control the ships but not the shareholders. There was disagreement amongst the latter about whether the fleet should be rebuilt or the company and its assets sold off at a time of relative prosperity for shipping. Those wanting to take the money won the argument. In September 1954, an offer was accepted from the Eskgarth Steamship Co. Ltd. for the whole of the issued share capital of the Chellew Navigation Co. Ltd. The fleet was now down to three ships, two of which were over 30 years old. The *Pendeen* (2) and *Penhale* (2) were sold, both to Turkish owners, and one more was added to the fleet, the *Eskglen*. But early the following year the *Eskglen* was transferred to the Esk Shipping Co. Ltd. and the final Chellew ship, the Liberty *Pentire*, was sold. On 20th December 1955 the Chellew Navigation Co. Ltd. was wound up. The business begun in Truro by Richard Berryman Chellew had long outlived him, and in his name had operated around 40 ships over 72 years. It was fitting that its last vessel, the *Pentire*, had continued Chellew's naming and colour scheme.

Derivations of Chellew names

After the *Pencalenick* joined the Chellew fleet in 1890 it was decided all vessels would have names with the prefix Pen-, meaning in Cornish 'head, top or end'. Using this prefix Richard Chellew was able to use many Cornish names of headlands, houses, villages and creeks. Names are listed in alphabetical order.

City of Truro Truro is the county town of Cornwall, situated at the head of the River Fal. Truro became a city in 1877, and is dominated by the 19th century cathedral.

Cornubia The name given by the Romans to the area west of the River Tamar, now Cornwall. It is thought to derive from the Latin cornu, meaning 'horn shaped'.

Duchess of Cornwall This title is held by the wife of the heir to the throne.

Duke of Cornwall The title is held by the eldest son of the reigning monarch. Much of Cornwall and the Isles of Scilly are owned by the Duchy of Cornwall, including Dartmoor Prison, giving the duke his annual income.

Penare In Cornish means 'high headland'. There are numerous Penares, but the ship may have been named after a small hamlet and headland overlooking St. Austell Bay or, more likely, the estate and house on the southern side of the Helford River on the Lizard peninsula.

Pencalenick In Cornish 'a place where a holly tree grows' or 'holy place'. Richard Chellew took the name from the large house and estate east of Truro on the banks of the Tresillian River.

Pencarrow 'Stag's head'. There are a number of Pencarrows, with the most likely candidate being the large house and estate near Egloshayle, north of Bodmin.

Pendarves Means 'oak tree'. The village of Pendarves is to the south of Camborne on the main road to Helston in the once-rich tin mining area of Cornwall. There is also a Pendarves Island in Watergate Bay, north east of Newquay.

Pendeen 'Headland with a fort'. The village of Pendeen and Pendeen lighthouse are on the north coast of Penwith about three miles north east of St Just. The Pendeen is surrounded by desolate gorse-covered moorland open to the prevailing Atlantic winds.

Pendennis Translated as 'headland with a castle', this name is very appropriate as Pendennis Castle stands on the western side of the River Fal. The castle was built during the reign of Henry VIII to guard the harbour entrance against seaborne attack. Pendennis Point on which the castle stands protects Falmouth harbour from westerly and south westerly gales.

Pengreep A large house situated off the road between Redruth and Falmouth, and near the villages of Stithians, Ponsanooth and Lanner.

Penhale 'End of a marsh'. Of over 20 Penhales, the ship's name may come from the village, headland, disused army camp and mine with this name on the north Cornish coast between Perranporth and Newquay.

Penhallow Also translates as 'end of a marsh'. Penhallow is a small village north of Truro on the road between Redruth and Newquay.

Penlee 'Headland with a slab of stone'. Penlee is a small hamlet on the western side of Mount's Bay, near the ports of Penzance and Newlyn. It is remembered for the loss of the lifeboat *Solomon Browne* during an attempt to rescue the crew of the coaster *Union Star* in hurricane force winds on 19th December 1981. Both vessels were lost with all on board.

Penmorvah The ship probably took its name from Penmorvah House at Budock Water, Falmouth.

Penmount Literally means 'top hill, head hill'. In Richard Chellew's time Penmount was a hamlet and large estate of 140 acres to the north cast of Truro. The large house with its garden is today a crematorium.

Penolver 'Headland with a lookout'. Penolver is a large house on the banks of the River Fal south of Truro, near where Richard Chellew spent his childhood.

Penpol Means 'creek end'. Penpol is a hamlet on the north bank of the Devoran River, which flows into the River Fal, and besides which Richard Chellew was brought up. There are 13 Penpols or Penpolls in Cornwall.

Penrose 'End of heath or moorland'. Of the eight Penroses, the most likely origins are a village on the north Cornish coast between Newquay and the Camel estuary or a large house and farm near Maenporth on the western side of Falmouth Bay.

Pensilva The village of Pensilva is in the east of Cornwall, on the road between Callington and Liskeard.

Pentire Simply means 'headland'. At Newquay, headlands on the sides of the Gannel River are East and West Pentire Point, and a local beach is called Pentire Beach. The next river along the north coast, the Camel, also has a Pentire Point.

Penvearn The only Penvearn found is a small house and farm at Cury, south of Helston on the Lizard Peninsula.

Penwith The Cornish translation is 'far end, furthest point or extremity'. Penwith is the area of Cornwall west of a line from Hayle on the north coast (where the steamer Penwith was built) to Marazion on the south coast.

FLEET LIST

1. CITY OF TRURO 1883-1897 Iron

O.N. 86129 1,767g 1,141n
257.0 x 34.8 x 19.7 feet
C. 2-cyl. by Thomas Richardson and Sons, Hartlepool; 150 NHP.
4.10.1883: Launched by William Gray and Co., West Hartlepool (Yard No. 282).
11.1883: Completed.
23.11.1883: Registered in the ownership of the Cornwall Steamship Co. Ltd., Truro as CITY OF TRURO.
24.11.1883: Left West Hartlepool on her maiden voyage for Naples with a cargo of rails.
1888: R.B. and W. Chellew became managers.
5.4.1897: Register closed on sale to C.A. Banck, Helsingborg, Sweden and renamed ALDEBARAN.
1898: Owners became Rederiaktieb Astrea (C.A. Banck, managers), Helsingborg.
1918: Sold to G. Carlsson, Gothenburg, Sweden.
1.10.1918: Torpedoed and sunk by the German submarine UB 112 seven miles and 250° from the Wolf Rock whilst on a voyage from Marbella to Ayr with a cargo of iron ore. The entire crew was lost.

2. DUKE OF CORNWALL 1888-1922

O.N. 92237 1,704g 1,081n
260.5 x 36.6 x 18.2 feet
T.3-cyl. by Central Marine Engineering Company, West Hartlepool; 150 NHP.
12.4.1888: Launched by William Gray and Co., West Hartlepool (Yard No. 339).
7.6.1888: Registered in the ownership of the Duke of Cornwall Steamship Co. Ltd. (R. B.

City of Truro as the Swedish *Aldebaran* at Kockum's shipyard, Malmo in 1902. *[Author's collection]*

and W. Chellew, managers), Truro as DUKE OF CORNWALL.
14.6.1888: Completed.
5.1891: Collided with the Austrian steamer ETTORE (1,967/1874) at Alexandria, Egypt. Badly damaged and remained at Alexandria for over a month before proceeding to UK for dry docking and permanent repairs.
29.8.1912: Ran aground outside Holmsund whilst on a voyage to Cardiff with pit props.
12.9.1912: Refloated and later docked at Oskarshamn for repairs.
1.7.1916: Taken up by the French Government for the carriage of steel for the manufacture of shells, between United Kingdom and France.
31.1.1917: Became Expeditionary Force

Transport No. C0816, carrying stores from London to Dunkirk, and ammunition from Southampton to Rouen.
16.3.1918: Became Royal Navy Collier No. 2120.
7.1.1920: Owners became R.B. Chellew Steam Navigation Co. Ltd., Truro.
10.8.1920: Manager became Frank Shearman.
31.10.1922: Sold to Arcos Ltd., London.
27.4.1923: Sold to Stuart H. Biscoe, London.
20.8.1923: Sold to the Apollo Steamship Co. Ltd. (McNabb, Rougier and Co. (Italy) Ltd., managers), London.
9.11.1925: Manager became Candido Camalich, London.
25.3.1926: Register closed when sold to

Duke of Cornwall in the Avon. *[E.N. Taylor]*

Sicula Carboni S.a.S., Catania, Italy and renamed CLAUDIA.

1929: Sold to A.P. Synodinos (Synodinos Brothers, managers), Athens, Greece and renamed MAIOTIS.

27.4.1941: Bombed and sunk at Aegion. Later salvaged but then scuttled at Trieste, Italy in April 1945.

3.1947: Raised and towed to Venice and broken up in 1949.

3. DUCHESS OF CORNWALL 1889-1917

O.N. 95904 1,720g 1,080n
260.5 x 36.6 x 18.3 feet
T.3-cyl. by Central Marine Engine Works, West Hartlepool.

2.5.1889: Launched by William Gray and Co., West Hartlepool (Yard No. 356).

1889: Registered in the ownership of the Duchess of Cornwall Steam Ship Co. Ltd. (R. B. and W. Chellew, managers), Truro as DUCHESS OF CORNWALL.

7.1889: Completed.

12.1890: Ran ashore near Dunraven Head, Swansea. Refloated within a week and docked at Cardiff.

7.9.1915: Became Expeditionary Force Transport No. 8126.

11.4.1917: Torpedoed and sunk by the German submarine UC 26 five miles north of Pointe de Barfleur, France whilst on a voyage from London to Le Havre.

23 members of the crew were lost.

4.5.1917: Register closed.

4. CORNUBIA 1889-1915

O.N. 95905 1,736g 1,107n
260.0 x 36.6 x 18.2 feet
T.3-cyl. by Central Marine Engine Works, West Hartlepool; 150 NHP, 750 IHP, 9 knots.

29.11.1889: Launched by William Gray and Co. Ltd., West Hartlepool (Yard No. 377).

19.12.1889: Registered in the ownership of the Cornubia Steamship Co. Ltd. (R.B. and W. Chellew, managers), Truro as CORNUBIA.

12.1889: Completed.

16.3.1904: Ran ashore at Dedeagatch, Greece.

24.3.1904: Refloated with little damage.

9.9.1915: Captured by the German submarine U 39 and sunk by gunfire 75 miles south east by south of Cartagena, Spain in position 36.46 north by 00.15 east whilst on a voyage from Alexandria and Cartagena to the Clyde with a cargo of beans.

16.2.1916: Register closed.

Top: *Duchess of Cornwall* in the Avon. *[J. and M. Clarkson]*
Middle: a distressed *Duchess of Cornwall* in Falmouth Harbour, 26th December 1912. She had put back after being damaged in heavy weather during a voyage from Swansea to Leghorn with coal. *[Author's collection]*
Below: *Cornubia*. *[J. and M. Clarkson]*

5. PENCALENICK 1889-1907

O.N. 95456 1,879g 1,223n
265.0 x 37.0 x 17.4 feet
T.3-cyl. by William Doxford and Sons, Sunderland; 150 NHP.

21.7.1888: Launched by William Doxford and Sons, Sunderland (Yard No. 178).

8.1888: Completed for Jackson Brothers and Cory, London as CHAMOIS.

10.1889: Acquired by the Pencalenick Steamship Co. Ltd. (R.B. and W. Chellew, managers), Truro.

1.3.1890: Renamed PENCALENICK.

12.8.1904: Stopped by the Russian cruiser URAL in position 36.37 north by 07.50 west whilst on a voyage from Cardiff to Malta with a cargo of coal for the Royal Navy. After her papers were inspected she was allowed to proceed.

17.10.1907: Register closed on sale to Rederi A/B Urania (B.O. Borjesson, manager), Helsingborg, Sweden and renamed URANIA.

11.1914: As a result of a stranding on 2.11.1913 sold to Rederi A/B Nordkap (Carl W. Winck, managers), Helsingborg, Sweden and renamed OSMAN.

1918: Sold to Rederi A/B Felix (O.H.W. Dalman, manager), Gothenburg, Sweden.

6.1919: Sold to Rederi A/B Tertia (Ivor Lignell, managers), Gothenburg and renamed MAJA.

5.1921: Sold to Aug. Bolten, Wm. Miller's Nachfolgers, Hamburg, Germany and renamed BOLIVAR.

16.6.1925: Sold to Rederi A/B Tertia (Ivor Lignell, managers), Gothenburg and renamed MAJA.

7.1926: Sold to Rederi A/B Hilding (Filip Hultman, manager), Gothenburg and renamed MAJ.

1932: Manager became Harry Trapp, Gothenburg.

5.3.1933: Ran aground at Klitmöller, Jutland whilst on a voyage from the Tyne to Gothenburg. Later refloated, but declared a constructive total loss.

5.1933: Sold for breaking up to Lindholmen-Motala A/B, Gothenburg.

6. PENWITH 1890-1911

O.N. 95907 2,001g 1,268n
270.0 x 36.9 x 18.9 feet
T.3-cyl. by Harvey and Co. Ltd., Hayle; 156

Pencalenik as the Swedish *Osman*. [Author's collection]

NHP, 1,000 IHP, 9.5 knots.

3.7.1890: Launched by Harvey and Co. Ltd., Hayle (Yard No. 148).

8.1890: Completed.

30.8.1890: Registered in the ownership of the Penwith Steamship Co. Ltd. (R.B. and W. Chellew, managers), Truro as PENWITH.

28.12.1911: Abandoned and later sank in the Bay of Biscay in position 45.40 north by 11.18 west whilst on a voyage from Hornillo to Cardiff with a cargo of 2,550 tons of iron ore. The crew of 22 was rescued and taken to Las Palmas.

20.1.1912: Register closed.

7. PENPOL 1891-1917

O.N. 95908 2,033g 1,285n
276.0 x 36.9 x 19.0 feet
T.3-cyl. by Harvey and Co. Ltd., Hayle; 156 NHP.

12.12.1890: Launched by Harvey and Co. Ltd., Hayle (Yard No. 149).

2.1891: Completed.

11.2.1891: Registered in the ownership of the Penpol Steamship Co. Ltd. (R.B. and W. Chellew, managers), Truro as PENPOL.

3.1.1901: Driven ashore in gale force winds between Port Talbot and Briton Ferry, and refloated the following day with no

damage.

3.1911: Collided with and sank a Turkish steamer reported as the KARA KUSH off Yombournon in the Bosphorus. The PENPOL was virtually undamaged and was able to proceed.

8.1914: Trapped in the Baltic and placed under Russian Government control.

19.6.1917: Captured in the Gulf of Bothnia by the German submarine UC 57 and taken to Libau. She was subsequently used as an army transport.

9.1.1919: Arrived in the Tyne.

10.4.1919: Owners became the Shipping Controller (Coastal Trading Office), London (E.R. Newbigin, Newcastle-upon-Tyne, manager).

11.5.1921: Sold to Alexander Shipping Co. Ltd. (Capper, Alexander and Co., managers), London.

8.6.1921: Renamed MALMESBURY.

19.2.1925: Sold to British Lines Ltd. (Stuart H. Biscoe, manager), London.

10.3.1925: Register closed following sale to Stuart H. Biscoe and E .Gerachi, London, who registered her in Catania, Italy as CARMELO POLIZZI.

1926: Renamed ANAPO.

1927: Sold to T.W. Ward Ltd., Sheffield and broken up at Hayle, Cornwall.

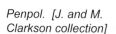

Penpol. [J. and M. Clarkson collection]

Penpol. [Author's collection]

8. PENDARVES 1892-1925

O.N. 99156 2,669g 1,706n
299.5 x 40.1 x 20.5 feet
T.3-cyl. by Thomas Richardson and Sons,
Hartlepool; 250 NHP, 933 IHP, 9 knots.
10.8.1892: Launched by Sir Raylton Dixon
and Co., Middlesbrough (Yard No. 366)
having been laid down for Farrar, Groves
and Co. Ltd., London.
9.1892: Completed.
29.9.1892: Registered in the ownership of the
Pendarves Steamship Co. Ltd. (R.B. and W.
Chellew, managers), Truro as PENDARVES.

9.12.1915: Taken up as Royal Navy Collier
No. 229.
24.7.1916: Taken up as Royal Navy Collier
No. 229.
15.9.1916: Placed on White Sea service.
27.11.1916: Time chartered to the Hudson's
Bay Company, London.
7.1.1920: Owners became R.B. Chellew
Steam Navigation Co. Ltd., Truro.
10.8.1920: Manager became Frank
Shearman.
17.3.1925: Register closed when sold to
Kirtatas Brothers, Andros, Greece and

renamed AIKATERINI M. GOULANDRIS.
1929: Sold to Veli Zade Moustafa Faik Bey,
Istanbul, Turkey and renamed VELIZADE.
1931: Sold to Kalkavan Zadé Riza ve
Mahdumu Ismail (Vapurculuk Sirketi),
Istanbul, Turkey and renamed USKUDAR.
1939: Owners became Kalkavanoglu Mehmet
Riza ve Mahdumu Ismail (Vapurculuk
Sirketi), Istanbul.
1941: Owners became Kalkavan, Riza ve
Ismail Oglu (Vapurculuk Sirketi), Istanbul.
6.1951: Demolition began at Spezia, Italy.

Pendarves. [J. and M. Clarkson]

9. PENDENNIS 1897-1916

O.N. 108015 2,123g 1,348n
290.0 x 42.2 x 19.1 feet
T.3-cyl. by Central Marine Engine Works, West Hartlepool; 200 NHP, 1,000 IHP, 9 knots.

6.3.1897: Launched by William Gray and Co. Ltd., West Hartlepool (Yard No. 533).
4.1897: Completed.
12.4.1897: Registered in the ownership of the Pendennis Steamship Co. Ltd. (R.B. and W. Chellew, managers), Truro as PENDENNIS.
10.7.1898: Towed the French steamship GUADIANA (2,581/1888) to Gibraltar after its tailshaft had broken. A salvage award of £1,000 was made.
8.1914: At Sundsvall, Sweden on the outbreak of the First World War.
8.7.1916: Captured by the German submarine U 48 in the North Sea about 60 miles west of Stavanger and taken into Borkum Roads.
10.1916: Became a collier for the Imperial German Navy.
14.1.1919: Arrived in the Tyne.
10.4.1919: Owners became the Shipping Controller, London (E.R. Newbigin, Newcastle-upon-Tyne, manager).
24.3.1921: Sold to the Board of Trade, London.
11.5.1921: Sold to Samuel Thubron (John Winlo and Stanley Walker, managers), North Shields.
26.5.1921: Sold to the Pendennis Steamship Co. Ltd. (Wilson and Armstrong, managers), London.
19.10.1923: Register closed when sold to Mikel Sandberg and Co., Riga, Latvia and renamed SKAUTS.
6.1940: Seized by the Soviet Union in Baltic waters and became military transport number 549.

10.1940: Owners became Latviyskoye gosudarstvyennoye morskoye parok-hodstvo, Riga.
30.11.1941: Sunk in position 60.00 north by 29.33 east in the Gulf of Finland after being attacked by German aircraft.
16.11.1947: Wreck lifted and broken up.

'Thrilling experience of a Cornish Steamer'

Under this headline the 'Royal Cornwall Gazette' for 30th January 1913 reported the following.

'While on passage from Malta to Sulina, the steamer *Pendennis*, of Falmouth, owned by Chellew & Co., Truro and Cardiff, had a very exciting experience.

Among the islands of Tenendos, near the entrance to the Dardenelles during early morning she was approached by two vessels that turned out to be Greek destroyers who asked the steamer to identify itself and destination. The Chief Officer Mr F. C. Hitchens from Feock, who happened to be on watch, gave the vessel's name and destination which satisfied the Greeks who then retired.

At daybreak the ship was surrounded by warships, to port Turkish Naval vessels including cruisers and destroyers, and to starboard Greek naval ships which as they approached one another began to open fire with the *Pendennis* in the middle.

The *Pendennis* then made full speed towards the entrance to the Dardanelles leaving the sea battle astern. As she passed the entrance

into the Dardanelles she was passed by more Turkish warships including battleships going out into the Aegean. It was reported later that, seeing the entire Turkish fleet, the Greeks made a hasty retreat'.

10. PENDEEN (1) 1899-1922

O.N. 109218 2,108g 1,342n
290.0 x 42.0 x 19.2 feet
T.3-cyl. by Central Marine Engine Works, West Hartlepool; 200 NHP, 1,000 IHP, 9 knots.

15.11.1898: Launched by William Gray and Co. Ltd., West Hartlepool (Yard No. 575).
2.1899: Completed.
22.2.1899: Registered in the ownership of the Pendeen Steamship Co. Ltd. (R.B. and W. Chellew, managers), Truro as PENDEEN.
4.1911: Went ashore whilst entering West Hartlepool, damaging her bottom.
8.1914: In the Baltic at the outbreak of the First World War and placed under Russian Government control.
1916: Broke out of the Baltic and returned to the United Kingdom.
9.8.1917: Became Royal Navy Collier No. 1779
3.1919: Returned to owners.
7.1.1920: Owners became R.B. Chellew Steam Navigation Co. Ltd., Truro.
10.8.1920: Manager became Frank Shearman.
5.5.1922: Register closed on sale to Rederi A/B Helsingborg (Otto Hillerstrom, manager), Helsingborg, Sweden and renamed CITOS.
22.3.1928: Wrecked on Cabezus Shoal, near Tarifa, Spain whilst on a voyage from New Orleans to Alexandria with a cargo of timber.

Pendennis. [J. and M. Clarkson]

11. PENMOUNT 1900-1928

O.N. 109221 2,314g 1,483n
302.5 x 43.2 x 19.7 feet
T.3-cyl. by Central Marine Engine Works, West
Hartlepool; 220 NHP, 1,100 IHP, 9 knots.
16.1.1900: Launched by William Gray and Co.
Ltd., West Hartlepool (Yard No. 602).
2.1900: Completed.
10.2.1900: Registered in the ownership of the

Pendeen in the Avon (top).
She was built at West
Hartlepool under the supervision of Captain Thomas
Christopher and the owner's
younger brother, John
Chellew (1860-1936). John
later became office manager
at Cardiff. *[J. and M. Clarkson collection]*
Penmount ashore in the
Avon during 1916 (right)
and approaching Rotterdam
(below). *[Author's collection;
Ships in Focus]*

Penmount Steamship Co. Ltd. (R.B. and W.
Chellew, managers), Truro as PENMOUNT.
8.1914: At Sundsvall, Sweden on the outbreak
of the First World War.
7.1916: Broke out of the Baltic and returned
to Hull.
5.3.1918: Taken up as Royal Navy Collier
No. 206
2.7.1919: Returned to owners.

7.1.1920: Owners became R.B. Chellew Steam
Navigation Co. Ltd., Truro.
10.8.1920: Manager became Frank Shearman.
6.7.1928: Register closed when sold to the
Latvian Government - Valsts Kugu Parvalde
(State Shipping Board), Riga and renamed
BARTA.
6.1940: Seized by the Union of Soviet Socialist
Republics in Baltic waters.
10.1940: Owners became Latviyskoye
Gosudarstvyennoye Morskoye Parokhodstvo,
Riga.
1941: Owners became Baltiyskoye
Gosudarstvyennoye Morskoye Parokhodstvo,
Leningrad.
21.9.1941: Bombed and beached near
Kronstadt.
31.3.1944: Refloated.
1945: Owners became Latviyskoye
Gosudarstvyennoye Morskoye Parokhodstvo,
Riga
1945: Known to be in service but fate
unknown.
1960: Deleted from 'Lloyd's Register'.

Above: the *Penare* in the Avon and, below, as the Latvian *Gaisma* at Cardiff about 1936. *[Above: J. and M. Clarkson collection, below: Amgueddfa Cymru - National Museum Wales, Hansen collection 732/H1003]*

Above: *Penlee.* [Tom Rayner]
Below: *Penvearn,* Chellew's first Turret deck steamer. *[Nigel Farrell collection]*

12. PENARE 1900-1924

O.N.109225 3,078g 1,973n
325.0 x 48.1 x 21.9 feet
T.3-cyl. by Blair and Co. Ltd., Stockton-on-Tees; 220 NHP, 1,100 IHP, 9 knots.
11.10.1900: Launched by Ropner and Son, Stockton-on-Tees (Yard No. 376).
11.1900: Completed.
17.11.1900: Registered in the ownership of the Penare Steamship Co. Ltd. (R.B. and W. Chellew, managers), Truro as PENARE
10.8.1914: Taken up as Royal Navy Collier No. 160.
20.3.1917: Expeditionary Force Transport No. 8061, carrying military stores from Avonmouth to Alexandria.
9.5.1917: To Indian Government to carry wheat from Bombay to Italy.
27.10.1917: Expeditionary Force Transport No. 8061, carrying hay across the English Channel.
7.1.1920: Owners became R.B. Chellew Steam Navigation Co. Ltd., Truro.
10.8.1920: Manager became Frank Shearman.
11.8.1924: Register closed when sold to N.M. Eustathiou and Co., Syra, Greece and renamed MARIETTA.
1929: Sold to Kugniecibas Akcij Sabiedriba

'Jura' [Jura Shipping Co. Ltd.] (Fr. Karklins, manager), Ventspils, Latvia and renamed GAISMA.
7.1940: Seized by the Union of Soviet Socialist Republics.
22.6.1941: Sunk by the German motor torpedo boats S 59 and S 60 off Windau, east of Gotland, in the opening minutes of Operation Barbarossa.

13. PENLEE 1901-1919

O.N. 109228 3,775g 2,451n
340.0 x 48.0 x 25.8 feet
T.3-cyl. by Blair and Co. Ltd., Stockton-on-Tees; 280 NHP, 1,400 IHP, 9 knots.
5.3.1901: Launched by Ropner and Son, Stockton-on-Tees (Yard No. 381).
5.1901: Completed.
29.5.1901: Registered in the ownership of the Penlee Steamship Co. Ltd. (R.B. and W. Chellew, managers), Truro as PENLEE.
11.3.1917: Taken up as Royal Navy Collier No. 1503.
28.5.1917: Taken up as an Expeditionary Force Transport, carrying hay and oats to the French Channel ports.
23.8.1917: Taken up as Royal Navy Collier No. 1503.

12.10.1917: Taken up as an Expeditionary Force Transport, carrying hay and oats to the French Channel ports.
13.11.1917: Taken up by the Indian Government to carry steel and oats.
2.2.1918: Taken up as Expeditionary Force Transport No. D 180, carrying British hay and oats to the British Army in France.
1.11.1918: Taken up as Royal Navy Collier No. 1503.
12.3.1919: Caught fire in position 47.10 north by 14.46 west during a voyage from Cienfuegos to Liverpool with a cargo of sugar.
20.3.1919: Abandoned by her crew in position 47.12 north by 13.07 west. The crew was rescued by the United States steamer JULIA LUCKENBACH (8,151/1917) which had been standing by, and were landed at Bordeaux.
16.4.1919: Register closed.

14. PENVEARN 1906-1918

O.N. 120212 3,710g 2,377n
342.1 x 46.6 x 24.7 feet
T.3-cyl. by William Doxford and Sons Ltd., Sunderland; 313 NHP, 1,350 IHP, 9½ knots.
23.2.1906: Launched by William Doxford and Sons Ltd., Sunderland (Yard No. 354).
19.3.1906: Registered in the ownership of the Penvearn Steamship Co. Ltd. (R.B. and W. Chellew, managers), Truro as PENVEARN.
18.2.1916: Taken up as Royal Navy Collier No. 1040.
14.10.1916: Taken up as Royal Navy Collier No. 1040.
14.11.1916: Taken up as an Expeditionary Force Transport, carrying wheat from the River Plate to the British Army in France.
30.6.1917: Taken up as Royal Navy Collier No. 1040.
28.7.1917: Returned to owners, next voyage from Cuba to Liverpool with a cargo of sugar.
7.12.1917: Taken up as Royal Navy Collier No. 1040.
1.3.1918: Torpedoed and sunk by the German submarine U 105 in the Irish Sea 15 miles off South Stack, Holyhead whilst on a voyage from Barrow to Barry Roads in ballast. 21 members of her crew were lost.
7.3.1918: Register closed.

Penrose was Chellew's second Turret steamer. *[J. and M. Clarkson]*

15. PENROSE (1) 1908-1927
O.N.124608   3,882g 2,463n
350.0 x 49.1 x 23.9 feet
T.3-cyl. by William Doxford and Sons Ltd., Sunderland; 314 NHP, 1,450 IHP, 9½ knots.
14.4.1908: Launched by William Doxford and Sons Ltd., Sunderland (Yard No. 396).
*30.5.1908:*Registered in the ownership of the Penrose Steamship Co. Ltd. (R.B. and W. Chellew, managers), Truro as PENROSE.
11.4.1916: Taken up as Royal Navy Collier No.870.
16.6.1916: Returned to owners, cargo of sugar from Cuba to Bristol.
17.10.1916: Taken up as Royal Navy Collier No.870.
30.12.1916: Returned to owners, cargo of wheat from the River Plate to Liverpool.
23.3.1917: Taken up as Royal Navy Collier No.870.
10.5.1917: Indian Government Service, cargo of grain to Italy.
25.7.1917: Taken up as Royal Navy Collier

No.870.
4.1919: Returned to owners.
7.1.1920: Owners became R.B. Chellew Steam Navigation Co. Ltd., Truro.
10.8.1920: Manager became Frank Shearman.
28.11.1927: Register closed when sold to John N. Goulandris, Andros, Greece and renamed ADELFOTIS.
1934: Sold to P. and W. McLelland Ltd., London.
9.1934: Arrived at Bo'ness to be broken up.

16. PENHALE (1) 1911-1917
O.N. 128438   3,712g 2,330n
350.0 x 50.0 x 23.6 feet
T.3-cyl. by Central Marine Engine Works, West Hartlepool; 335 NHP, 1,400 IHP, 9 knots.
10.10.1911: Launched by William Gray and Co. Ltd., West Hartlepool (Yard No. 795).
11.1911: Completed.
7.11.1911: Registered in the ownership

of the Penhale Steamship Co. Ltd. (R.B. and W. Chellew, managers), Truro as the PENHALE.
1.10.1914: Taken up as Royal Navy Collier No. 346.
12.11.1914: Returned to owners.
21.2.1915: Chased by a German submarine three miles off Holyhead, Anglesey, but managed to keep her stern towards the U-boat and escaped.
7.1.1916: Taken up as Royal Navy Collier No. 346.
28.12.1916: Taken up as Royal Navy Collier No. 346.
18.5.1917: Torpedoed and sunk by the German submarine U 46 in position 52.48 north by 12.15 west, 72 miles north west by north of Tearaght Island, County Kerry, whilst on a voyage from Halifax to Queenstown with a cargo of sugar. One member of the crew was killed and the captain taken prisoner.
15.6.1917: Register closed.

Penhale in a Finnish port. *[Roy Fenton collection]*

17. PENOLVER 1912-1943

O.N. 133334 3,721g 2,338n

350.0 x 50.0 x 23.6 feet

T.3-cyl. by Central Marine Engineering Works., West Hartlepool; 336 NHP, 1,409 IHP, 9 knots.

18.5.1912: Launched by William Gray and Co. Ltd., West Hartlepool (Yard No. 806).

6.1912: Completed.

21.6.1912: Registered in the ownership of the Penolver Steamship Co. Ltd. (R.B. and W. Chellew, managers), Truro as PENOLVER.

7.9.1914: Taken up as Royal Navy Collier No. 293.

6.1.1915: Taken up as Royal Navy Collier No. 293 (in June and November 1916 made two voyages to the White Sea for railway timbers).

4.3.1917: French Government Service No. F 618 for the carriage of timber from Canada to France.

17.4.1917: Wheat cargo from Baltimore to France.

5.7.1917: Expeditionary Force Transport No. 618, for the carriage of railway materials from England to France.

6.9.1917: Taken up as Royal Navy Collier No. 293.

26.3.1918: Military nitrate cargoes.

25.6.1918: Taken up as Royal Navy Collier No. 293.

25.7.1918: Sugar cargo from Cuba to Liverpool.

12.10.1918: Taken up as Royal Navy Collier No. 293.

15.11.1918: Sugar cargo from Cuba to Liverpool.

30.1.1919: Taken up as Royal Navy Collier No. 293.

15.3.1919: For Government account loaded two cargoes of wheat from the River Plate, then returned to owners for commercial trading.

7.1.1920: Owners became R.B. Chellew Steam Navigation Co. Ltd., Truro.

10.8.1920: Manager became Frank Shearman.

10.10.1929: Owners became Chellew Navigation Co. Ltd., Cardiff.

11.8.1930: Manager became Frederick C. Perman.

19.10.1943: Mined and sunk in position 47.19 north by 52.27 west, near Harbour Grace, Newfoundland whilst on a voyage from Cabana to Sydney, Nova Scotia with 5,300 tons of iron ore. 24 of the 37 crew and 3 of 4 gunners were lost.

24.2.1944: Register closed.

This page: three photos of *Penolver*, the top with her topmasts struck, and others without the white hull line. *[Ships in Focus; Author's collection; J. and M. Clarkson]*

18. PENSILVA (1) 1913-1931

O.N. 133342   4,316g 2,714n

365.2 x 50.8 x 26.0 feet

T.3-cyl. by Central Marine Engine Works, West Hartlepool; 371 NHP, 1,603 IHP, 9 knots.

10.3.1913: Launched by William Gray and Co. Ltd., West Hartlepool (Yard No. 824).

22.5.1913: Registered in the ownership of the Pensilva Steamship Co. Ltd. (R.B. and W. Chellew, managers), Truro as PENSILVA.

5.1913: Delivered.

26.10.1914: Taken up as Royal Navy Collier No. 399.

27.3.1915: Cargo of sugar from Cuba to Liverpool.

27.5.1915: Taken up as Royal Navy Collier No. 399.

17.10.1915: French Government Service as a transport from Marseilles to Salonika, moving the Army of the Orient.

7.1.1916: Returned to owners.

19.4.1916: Taken up as Royal Navy Collier No. 399.

9.5.1916: Returned to owners.

3.1.1917: Taken up as Royal Navy Collier No. 399.

7.2.1917: Returned to owners.

8.5.1917: Taken up as Royal Navy Collier No. 399.

28.8.1917: Wheat cargoes from the United States to United Kingdom.

3.12.1917: Taken up as Royal Navy Collier No. 399.

22.1.1918: Cargoes of sugar from Cuba to United Kingdom.

4.5.1918: Attacked by gunfire from a German submarine in the Irish Sea. Returned fire and escaped.

4.5.1918: Taken up as Royal Navy Collier No. 399.

28.6.1918: Wheat cargo from the River Plate to Bristol.

15.9.1918: Timber transport from Canada to United Kingdom.

15.1.1919: Taken up as Royal Navy Collier No. 399.

3.1919: Three cargoes of sugar from Cuba to United Kingdom for the British Government, then returned to commercial trading.

7.1.1920: Owners became R.B. Chellew Steam Navigation Co. Ltd., Truro.

10.8.1920: Manager became Frank Shearman.

10.10.1929: Owners became Chellew Navigation Co. Ltd., Cardiff.

11.8.1930: Manager became Frederick C. Perman.

3.8.1931: Sold to the Brynymor Steamship Co. Ltd. (Ambrose, Davies and Mathews, managers), Swansea.

28.9.1931: Renamed BRYNYMOR.

3.3.1932: Register closed when sold to Atlantska Plovidba d.d., Susak, Yugoslavia and renamed SLOGA.

16.10.1943: Wrecked off Long Point, Newfoundland whilst on a voyage from Aguathuna to Sydney, Nova Scotia with a cargo of limestone.

19. PENHALLOW 1913-1918

O.N. 133343   4,318g 2,707n

365.0 x 50.8 x 26.0 feet

T.3-cyl. by Central Marine Engine Works, West Hartlepool; 371 NHP, 1,603 IHP, 10 knots.

20.5.1913: Launched by William Gray and Co. Ltd., West Hartlepool (Yard No. 828).

7.1913: Completed.

24.7.1913: Registered in the ownership of the Penhallow Steamship Co. Ltd. (R.B. and W. Chellew, managers), Truro as PENHALLOW.

29.8.1914: Taken up as Royal Navy Collier No. 301.

26.10 1914: Returned to owners.

14.1.1915: Taken up as a Royal Navy Collier No. 301.

30.10.1915: Taken up as Royal Naval commissioned ship.

19.6.1917: Taken up as Royal Navy Collier No. 301.

14.7.1917: Cargo of sugar from Cuba to Liverpool.

30.9.1917: Taken up as Royal Navy Collier No. 301.

1.4.1918: Cargo of wheat from Argentina to the Clyde.

12.6.1918: Torpedoed and sunk by German submarine UB 48 52 miles north west of Cape Caxine, Algeria on a voyage from Buenos Aires to Italy with a cargo of grain. One crew member was lost.

14.8.1918: Register closed.

20. PENMORVAH 1913-1936

O.N. 133347 4,323g 2,711n

365.2 x 50.8 x 26.0 feet

T.3-cyl. by Central Marine Engine Works, West Hartlepool; 371 NHP, 1,603 IHP, 10 knots.

1.9.1913: Launched by William Gray and Co. Ltd., West Hartlepool (Yard No. 833).

10.1913: Delivered.

27.10.1913: Registered in the ownership of the Penmorvah Steamship Co. Ltd. (R.B. and W. Chellew, managers), Truro as PENMORVAH.

Pensilva. [Tom Rayner]

12.4.1914: Taken up as Royal Navy Collier No. 307.

5.12.1915: Cargoes from Cuba to Liverpool.

4.3.1916: Taken up as Royal Navy Collier No. 307.

21.3.1916: Returned to owners.

31.3.1917: Attacked in the English Channel, torpedo missed.

7.1.1920: Owners became R.B. Chellew Steam Navigation Co. Ltd., Truro.

10.8.1920: Manager became Frank Shearman.

10.10.1929: Owners became Chellew Navigation Co. Ltd., Cardiff.

11.8.1930: Manager became Frederick C. Perman.

11.1.1936: Register closed when sold to Società Anonima Co-operativa di Navigazione Garibaldi, Genoa, Italy and renamed LUIGI RAZZA.

18.4.1943: Sunk by allied aircraft at Porto Torres, Sardinia. Later salvaged.

1946: Renamed ANTONINO STRAZZERA.

1947: Owners became Società Co-operativa di Navigazione Garibaldi A.R.L.,Genoa, Italy and renamed PIETRO GORI.

1955: Sold to F. Italo Croce, Genoa, Italy and renamed EZILDA CROCE.

21.7.1959: Arrived at Savona, Italy to be broken up by A.R.D.E.M.

31.10.1959: Demolition completed.

Penmorvah (top) and as *Pietro Gori* (middle) and *Ezilda Croce* (bottom). *[J. and M. Clarkson (2); author's collection]*

Pengreep. [P. Rasmussen, Author's collection]

21. PENGREEP 1914-1941

O.N. 133349 4,806g 3,007n
402.0 x 52.0 x 26.9 feet
T.3-cyl. by Richardsons, Westgarth and Co. Ltd., Hartlepool; 402 NHP, 1,900 IHP, 10 knots.

8.4.1914: Launched by Irvine's Shipbuilding and Dry Docks Co. Ltd., West Hartlepool (Yard No. 540).

5.1914: Completed.

14.5.1914: Registered in the ownership of the Pengreep Steamship Co. Ltd. (R.B. and W. Chellew, managers), Truro as PENGREEP.

28.9.1914: Taken up as Royal Navy Collier No. 343.

2.12.1914: Returned to owners.

17.11.1916: Taken up as Royal Navy Collier No. 343.

21.12.1916: Cargo of wheat from Australia to the United Kingdom.

6.5.1917: Taken up as Royal Navy Collier No. 343.

7.6.1917: Cargo of wheat from Canada to United Kingdom.

5.8.1917: Taken up as Royal Navy Collier No. 343.

6.9.1917: Cargo of wheat from the United States of America to United Kingdom.

9.12.1917: Taken up as Royal Navy Collier No. 343.

16.2.1918: To French Government service, to carry grain from Karachi to France.

9.4.1918: Cargo of wheat from Karachi to Bristol.

8.5.1918: Expeditionary Force Transport from Bombay to Karachi.

22.5.1918: Cargo of wheat from Karachi to United Kingdom.

5.9.1918: Taken up as Royal Navy Collier No. 343.

17.12.1918: Cargo of wheat from Australia to United Kingdom.

7.1.1920: Owners became R. B. Chellew Steam Navigation Co. Ltd., Truro.

10.8.1920: Manager became Frank Shearman.

10.10.1929: Owners became Chellew Navigation Co. Ltd., Cardiff.

11.8.1930: Manager became Frederick C. Perman.

6.1941: Seized by Vichy French forces at Casablanca and renamed STE. JACQUELINE.

11.1942: Recaptured by the Allies in Morocco in unseaworty condition, but later repaired.

20.4.1943: Registered in the ownership of the Ministry of War Transport (Chellew Navigation Co. Ltd., managers), London.

10.5.1943: Renamed EMPIRE FAL.

5.1945: Sailed from Lisbon to Immingham with a cargo of shells believed to have originated in Italy.

2.7.1945: Scuttled north west of Scotland with a cargo of poison gas shells too dangerous to discharge.

9.7.1945: Register closed.

22. PENCARROW 1921-1952

O.N. 137213 4,841g 2,955n
402.0 x 52.0 x 26.8 feet
T.3-cyl. by Richardsons Westgarth and Co. Ltd., Hartlepool.

25.1.1921: Launched by Irvine's Shipbuilding and Dry Dock Co. Ltd., West Hartlepool (Yard No. 608).

7.1921: Completed.

18.7.1921: Registered in the ownership of the R.B. Chellew Steam Navigation Co. Ltd. (Frank Shearman, manager), Cardiff as PENCARROW.

10.10.1929: Owners became Chellew Navigation Co. Ltd., Cardiff.

11.8.1930: Manager became Frederick C. Perman.

3.12.1952: Register closed when sold to Compania Maritima Tees S.A., Panama (Arthur Jurgenthal, Stockholm, manager) and renamed AVON.

1955: Sold to Compania Navegacion Staras S.A., Panama (S.G. Embiricos Ltd., London) and renamed STARAS.

27.7.1959: Demolition commenced at Hirao, Japan.

Four scenes from *Pencarrow's* 38-year career. She is seen arriving at Avonmouth (opposite bottom), on the Mersey 19th August 1950 (this page top); without the white hull stripe (middle) and as Arthur Jurgenthal's *Avon*, one of two Chellew ships to carry this name in later life (bottom). *[J. and M. Clarkson (3); Ships in Focus collection]*

Pendeen (2) seen with a white line on a somewhat work-stained hull (top) and entering Avonmouth with a plain black hull (middle). *[Author's collection; J. and M. Clarkson]*

23. PENDEEN (2) 1923-1954

O.N. 146381 4,174g 2,481n
375.0 x 51.2 x 24.7 feet
T.3-cyl. by Blair and Co. Ltd., Stockton-on-Tees; 386 NHP, 1,900 IHP, 10 knots.
4.4.1923: Launched by Irvine's Shipbuilding and Dry Dock Co. Ltd., West Hartlepool (Yard No. 612).
5.1923: Completed.
24.5.1923: Registered in the ownership of the R.B. Chellew Steam Navigation Co. Ltd. (Frank Shearman, manager), Cardiff as PENDEEN.
10.10.1929: Owners became Chellew Navigation Co. Ltd., Cardiff.
11.8.1930: Manager became Frederick C. Perman.
18.1.1954: Register closed when sold to Sadikzade Rusen Ogullari Vapurculuk Komandit Sirketi, Istanbul, Turkey and renamed MUSTAFA.
1958: Owners became Sadikzade Rusen Ogullari Kollektif Sirketi, Istanbul.

1960: Owners became Sadan Sadikoglu Silepcilik Isletmesi, Kollektif Sirketi, Istanbul.
15.5.1961: Demolition commenced at Halic, Turkey by the owner.

24. PENHALE (2) 1924-1954

O.N. 146388 4,071g 2,451n
377.5 x 51.5 x 23.8 feet
T.3-cyl. by George Clark Ltd., Sunderland; 317 NHP, 1,350 IHP, 9¼ knots.
22.11.1923: Launched by Sir John Priestman

Penhale (2) with a full timber cargo, 25th July 1953. Note how the derricks are stowed upright. *[J. and M. Clarkson collection]*

Penhale (2) with a plain black hull, at Cardiff. *[Amgueddfa Cymru - National Museum Wales, 1002/1104]*

and Co., Southwick, Sunderland (Yard No. 286).
1.1924: Completed.
7.1.1924: Registered in the ownership of the R. B Chellew Steam Navigation Co. Ltd. (Frank Shearman, manager), Cardiff as PENHALE.
10.10.1929: Owners became Chellew Navigation Co. Ltd., Cardiff.
11.8.1930: Manager became Frederick C. Perman.
10.1.1954: Register closed when sold to Sadikzade Rusen Ogullari, Istanbul, Turkey and renamed PREVEZE.

1959: Owners became Sadikzade Rusen Ogullari Vapurculuk Komandit Sirketi, Istanbul, Turkey.
25.6.1961: Arrived at Beograd, Yugoslavia to be broken up by Slobodna Plovidba.

25. PENROSE (2) 1928-1942
O.N. 160949 4,393g 2,630n
412.2 x 53.0 x 25.3 feet
T.3-cyl. by John Dickinson and Sons Ltd., Sunderland; 413 NHP, 1,940 IHP, 10 knots.
17.7.1928: Launched by W. Dobson and Co., Newcastle-on-Tyne (Yard No. 229).

8.1928: Registered in the ownership of the R.B. Chellew Steam Navigation Co. Ltd. (Frank Shearman, manager), Cardiff as PENROSE.
10.10.1929: Owners became Chellew Navigation Co. Ltd., Cardiff.
11.8.1930: Manager became Frederick C. Perman.
3.9.1942: Torpedoed and sunk by German submarine U 107 in position 38 north by 9 west off the Portuguese coast whilst on a voyage from Lisbon to southern Spain in ballast. Two of her crew of 39 and 6 gunners were lost.
11.12.1942: Register closed.

Penrose (2) at Avonmouth. *[J. and M. Clarkson collection]*

Pensilva (2) on 26th March 1935. [J. and M. Clarkson]

26. PENSILVA (2) 1931-1939

O.N. 143999 4,258g 2,640n
382.3 x 51.4 x 25.1 feet
T.3-cyl. by David Rowan and Co. Ltd.,
Glasgow; 331 NHP, 1,623 IHP, 10½ knots.
19.10.1929: Launched by Burntisland
Shipbuilding Co. Ltd. Burntisland (Yard
No.156).
11.1929: Completed.
23.11.1929: Registered in the ownership of
the Brynymor Steamship Co. Ltd. (Ambrose,
Davies and Mathews Ltd., managers),
Swansea as BRYNYMOR.
29.8.1931: Acquired by the Chellew
Navigation Co. Ltd. (Frederick C. Perman,
manager), London.
3.9.1931: Renamed PENSILVA.
19.11.1939: Torpedoed, shelled and sunk by
the German submarine U 43 in position 46.51
north by 11.36 west in the Bay of Biscay

whilst on a voyage from Durban to Dunkirk
with a cargo of 6,985 tons of maize.
28.11.1939: Register closed.

27. ENSIGN 1936

O.N. 139451 2,327g 1,261n
290.0 x 40.7 x 19.2 feet
T.3-cyl. by North Eastern Marine Engineering
Co. Ltd., Sunderland; 218 NHP, 1,200 IHP,
10 knots.
1916: Launched by Sir John Priestman and
Co., Sunderland (Yard No. 255).
7.1916: Completed.
24.7.1916: Registered in the ownership
of the Uskside Steamship Co. Ltd. (R.W.
Jones and Co. Ltd., managers), Newport as
USKMOUTH.
1.6.1927: Sold to Ensign Shipping Co. Ltd.
(Dunn and Co. Ltd., managers), Newport
for £22,500.

7.7.1927: Renamed ENSIGN.
23.2.1933: Sold to Constants (South Wales)
Ltd. (Martin Constant, manager), London
for £7,000.
10.6.1933: Renamed WROTHAM.
19.12.1934: Sold to Calpean Shipping Co.
Ltd. (John Mackintosh, manager), Gibraltar.
19.1.1935: Renamed ENSIGN.
28.2.1936: Acquired by the Chellew
Steamship Management Co. Ltd. (Frederick
C. Perman, manager), London.
12.11.1936: Sold to Constants (South Wales)
Ltd. (Martin Constant, manager), London.
9.1.1937: Renamed SELLINGE.
16.2.1939: Manager became Halford
Constant.
6.9.1943: Mined off Hurd Bank, Malta, seven
miles and 62 degrees from Dellimara Point
whilst on a voyage from Catania to Malta in
ballast, but arrived at Malta later that day.

Uskmouth, later to become Chellew's *Ensign. [National Maritime Museum P.13610]*

Auretta. [Nigel Farrell collection]

5.2.1944: Sunk at Bari, Italy as part of a breakwater.

5.4.1944: Register closed.

23.4.1946: Refloated.

1947: Sold to Achille Onorato du Vincenzo, Naples, Italy, repaired and returned to service as SILVIA ONORATO.

2.1.1948: Ran aground west south west of the East Goodwins whilst on a voyage from Rijeka to Rotterdam with a cargo of lead ore. Broke in two and became a total loss.

28. AURETTA 1936-1941

O.N. 153734 4,564g 2,766n

424.0 x 56.0 x 25.1 feet

T.3-cyl. with exhaust-driven turbine driving a steam compressor by David Rowan and Co. Ltd., Glasgow; 283 NHP, 1,550 IHP, 10½ knots.

18.6.1935: Launched by Burntisland Shipbuilding Co. Ltd., Burntisland (Yard No. 186).

8.8.1935: Registered in the ownership of Calpean Shipping Co. Ltd., Gibraltar as AURETTA.

9.1935: Completed.

1.5.1936: Acquired by the Chellew Steamship Management Co. Ltd. (Frederick C. Perman, manager), London.

6.2.1941: Sold to William H. Cockerline and Thomas C. Jackson, Hull.

26.2.1945: Mined and sunk in position 51.24 north by 02.49 east, 11 miles north of Ostend, Belgium whilst on passage from London to Antwerp with military stores. From her crew of 41 and 7 gunners, 2 were lost.

14.5.1945: Register closed.

29. JUSTITIA 1936-1940

O.N. 153736 4,562g 2,767n

424.0 x 56.0 x 25.1 feet

T.3-cyl. with exhaust-driven turbine driving a steam compressor by David Rowan and Co. Ltd., Glasgow; 333 NHP, 1,550 IHP,

10½ knots.

1939: Compressor removed; 283 NHP.

12.9.1935: Launched by Burntisland Shipbuilding Co. Ltd., Burntisland (Yard No. 187).

5.10.1935: Registered in the ownership of the Calpean Shipping Co. Ltd., Gibraltar as JUSTITIA.

11.1935: Delivered.

17.7.1936: Acquired by the Chellew Steamship Management Co. Ltd. (Frederick C. Perman, manager), London.

22.11.1940: Torpedoed by German submarine U 100 in position 55 north by 13.10 east about 80 miles west of North Aran Island whilst on a voyage from Savannah and Sydney, Nova Scotia for London with 5,161 tons of lumber, 2,248 tons of steel, 40 tons of turpentine and 300 tons of sundries. From her crew of 38 and 1 gunner, 13 were lost.

23.11.1940: Last seen afloat at 12:05.

24.3.1941: Register closed.

Justitia in Australian waters. [J. and M. Clarkson collection]

The short-lived Doxford motorship *Statira*. [*Author's collection*]

30. STATIRA   1937-1940
O.N. 165381   4,852g 2,920n
423.4 x 54.2 x 26.1 feet
3-cyl 2SCSA oil engine by William Doxford and Sons Ltd., Sunderland; 388 NHP, 1,800 BHP, 2,060 IHP, 11 knots.
1936: Launched by William Doxford and Sons Ltd., Sunderland (Yard No. 630) for Calpean Shipping Co. Ltd., Gibraltar as STATIRA.
1.1937: Completed
8.1.1937: Registered in the ownership of the Chellew Steamship Management Co. Ltd., (Frederick C. Perman, manager), London.
3.8.1940: Bombed 38 miles north of Stornaway, whilst on a voyage from Masulipatam to London with 1,200 tons of

manganese ore, 1,100 tons of oilcake, and 6,400 tons of groundnuts. Her crew of 31 was rescued.
7.8.1940: Beached in Glumaig Bay still on fire.
9.8.1940: Scuttled to extinguish fire. Later raised and taken to Rothesay Bay for her cargo to be discharged. Declared a constructive total loss
29.10.1940: Register closed.
7.10.1943: Demolition completed at Troon.

31. PENTIRE   1947-1955
O.N. 169655   7,270g 4,451n
441.8 x 57.1 x 34.8 feet
T.3-cyl. by General Machinery Corporation, Hamilton, Ohio, USA; 276 NHP, 2,500 IHP,

10½ knots.
12.9.1943: Keel laid.
10.10.1943: Launched by Bethlehem-Fairfield Shipyard Inc., Baltimore, Maryland, USA (Yard No. 2247) for the United States War Shipping Administration, Washington, USA as LYON G. TYLER.
18.10.1943: Completed and bare-boat chartered to the United Kingdom.
3.12.1943: Registered in the ownership of the Ministry of War Transport, London (Cayzer, Irvine and Co. Ltd., Glasgow, managers) as SAMNEBRA.
30.4.1946: Owners became the Ministry of Transport (Frederick C. Perman, manager), London.
22.8.1947: Register closed on return to

Pentire. [*FotoFlite/Author's collection*]

United States War Shipping Administration, Washington.

4.9.1947: Registered in the ownership of the Chellew Navigation Co. Ltd. (Frank C. Perman, manager), London as PENTIRE.

4.9.1948: Manager became Baden H. Roberts.

23.7.1955: Register closed when sold to Cia. de Navegacion Gaviota S.A., Panama (Mario Zoboli, Genoa, Italy) and renamed CUACO.

18.6.1963: Arrived Hirao, Japan to be broken up.

5.12.1963: Demolition commenced by Matsukura Co. Ltd., Tokyo.

32. ESKGLEN 1954-1955

O.N. 148816 7,333g 4,222n
447.8 x 56.3 x 35.6 feet
T.3-cyl. by John Readhead and Sons Ltd., South Shields; 352 NHP.

10.7.1944: Launched by John Readhead and Sons Ltd., South Shields (Yard No. 542) for the Ministry of War Transport, London having been laid down as the EMPIRE PITCAIRN.

1944: Completed for the Royal Navy as the maintenance ship HMS MORAY FIRTH.

12.1947: Sold to Stag Line Ltd., South Shields, converted to a dry cargo ship by

Tyne Dock and Engineering Co. Ltd., South Shields and renamed LINARIA.

2.4.1948: Commenced trading.

1954: Acquired by Chellew Navigation Co. Ltd. (Chellew Steamship Management Ltd., managers) and renamed ESKGLEN.

1955: Owners became Esk Shipping Co. Ltd.

1961: Sold to Fortune Shipping Co. Ltd. (World Wide (Shipping) Ltd. (Y.K. Pao),

managers), Hong Kong and renamed MARINE FORTUNE.

1962: Sold to Herald Shipping Co. Ltd. (World Wide (Shipping) Ltd. (Y.K. Pao), managers), Hong Kong.

8.6.1967: Arrived at Yokosuka, Japan to be broken up

Top: Another view of *Pentire*, light, in London Docks. *[Ships in Focus]*

Middle: *Linaria*, later *Eskglen*. *[FotoFlite/Roy Fenton collection]*

Bottom: *Eskglen in* Esk Shipping's colours. *[J. and M. Clarkson]*

Managed ships

M1. WAR ISIS 1918-1919

O.N. 142469 2,231g 1,343n
251.0 x 43.8 x 21.6 feet
T.3-cyl by Port Arthur Ship Building Co. Ltd.,
Port Arthur, Ontario, Canada; 147 NHP, 1,250
IHP, 10.5 knots.
4.1918: Launched by Port Arthur Ship
Building Co. Ltd., Port Arthur, Ontario,
Canada (Yard No. 19).
5.1918: Delivered.
26.6.1918: Registered in the ownership of
the Shipping Controller, London (Richard B.
Chellew, Truro, manager) as WAR ISIS.
21.7.1918: Taken up as Royal Navy Collier
No. 2284.
6.1919: Control passed to the Director of
the Royal Indian Marine after intended sale
to British India Steam Navigation Co. Ltd.,
London as WAREPA fell through.
20.7.1920: Sold to Société Maritime et
Commerciale du Pacifique, Paris, France and
renamed CLAUDEGALLUS.
1926: Sold to Compagnie Nationale de
Navigation, Bordeaux, France.
1929: Sold to Revel Shipping Co. Ltd.,
Tallinn, Estonia and renamed TORNI.
1930: Company restyled Tallinn Shipping
Co. Ltd.
17.12.1940: Registered in the ownership of
the Ministry of Shipping, London (Rodney
Steamship Co. Ltd., Newcastle-upon-Tyne,
managers).
9.4.1941: Owners became the Ministry of
War Transport, London.
3.2.1947: Owners became the Ministry of
Transport, London (Pelton Steamship Co.
Ltd., Newcastle-upon-Tyne, managers).
27.11.1950: Register closed on return to
Tallinna Laevauhisus, Stockholm, registered
under Compania Maritimi Trema S.A.,
Panama (Arthur Jurgenthal, Stockholm) and
renamed TREMA.
1957: Renamed AVON.
11.11.1962: Sold to Rudolf Harmstorf
Wasserbau und Travewerft GmbH, Lübeck.
10.1.1963: Breaking up began at Lübeck.

M2. WAR OSIRIS 1918-1919

O.N. 142663 2,2264g 1,342n
251.0 x 43.8 x 21.7 feet
T.3-cyl. by Port Arthur Ship Building Co.
Ltd., Port Arthur, Ontario, Canada; 147 NHP,
1,250 IHP, 10.5 knots.
5.1918: Launched by Port Arthur Ship
Building Co. Ltd., Port Arthur, Ontario,
Canada (Yard No. 20).
7.1918: Delivered.
2.10.1918: Registered in the ownership of
the Shipping Controller, London (Richard B.
Chellew, Truro, manager) as WAR OSIRIS.
20.9.1918: Taken up as Royal Navy Collier
No. 236
2.2.1919: Sold to Société Anonyme de
Navigation 'Les Armateurs Francais', Paris,
France and renamed COLMAR.
1929: Sold to Herlof Andersens Rederi A/S,
Kristiansand, Norway and renamed LISTO.

War Isis in London under her final name, *Avon.* Arthur Jurgenthal had previously given the name to Chellew's *Pencarrow. [J. and M. Clarkson]*

The Norwegian *Listo,* briefly managed by Chellew as *War Osiris. [World Ship Society Ltd.]*

16.2.1943: Mined and sunk near Spodsbjerg,
Denmark on a voyage from Narvik to Emden,
whilst under German control.

M3. WAR HATHOR 1918-1919

O.N. 142692 2,264g 1,342n
251.0 x 43.8 x 20.7 feet
T. 3-cyl by Port Arthur Ship Building Co.
Ltd., Port Arthur, Ontario, Canada; 147 NHP,
1,200 IHP, 10.5 knots.
1918: Launched by Port Arthur Ship Building
Co. Ltd., Port Arthur, Ontario, Canada (Yard
No. 20).
8.1918: Delivered.
24.10.1918: Registered in the ownership of
the Shipping Controller, London (Richard
B. Chellew, Truro, manager) as WAR
HATHOR.
17.10.1918: Control passed to DRIM.
15.2.1919: Expeditionary Force Transport.
11.3.1920: Sold to British India Steam
Navigation Co. Ltd., London for £88,900.

12.8.1920: Renamed WARLA.
21.4.1934: Sold to Chung Wei Steamship
Co., Shanghai, China for £3,700 and renamed
YUAN CHAN.
1937: Sunk by Chinese forces as a blockship
across the mouth of Kiangyin Harbour, during
the Sino-Japanese War.
1941: Broken up.

M4. WAR HORUS 1919

O.N. 142758 2,266g 1,351n
251.0 x 43.8 x 20.7 feet
T.3-cyl by the Port Arthur Ship Building Co.
Ltd., Port Arthur, Ontario, Canada; 157 NHP,
1,500 IHP, 11.5 knots.
1918: Launched by Port Arthur Ship Building
Co. Ltd., Port Arthur, Ontario, Canada (Yard
No. 30).
10.1918: Delivered.
31.12.1918: Registered in the ownership of
the Shipping Controller, London (Furness,
Withy and Co. Ltd., Halifax, Nova Scotia,

Empire Drum was photographed at New York on 20th April 1942, about to set out on her final voyage. She was torpedoed just four days later. *[US Coast Guard]*

managers) as WAR HORUS.

14.5.1919: Manager became Richard B. Chellew, Truro.

7.10.1919: Register closed on sale to Filippo Baglietto, Genoa, Italy and renamed EMMA.

1924: Sold to Societa Italiana di Navigazione Lloyd Marittimo., Livorno, Italy and renamed GIUSEPPI SONCINO.

1925: Sold to Mutual Shipping Interests Ltd., London.

1926: Sold to Yuyei Shokai, Japan and resold to Sukeo Kudo, Tokyo, Japan and renamed TOSHU MARU.

1928: Sold to Abe Shokai K.K., Kobe, Japan.

1944: Sold to Asahi Kisen K.K., Kobe.

1954: Sold to Nihon Senpaku Kogyo K.K., Tokyo, Japan.

22.2.1961: Demolition completed at Osaka, Japan by Rinko Seitetsu K.K.

M5. WAR WEASEL 1919

O.N. 143349 2,243g 1,315n
251.0 x 43.5 x 22.9 feet
Two steam turbines by British Westinghouse Electric and Manufacturing Co. Ltd., Manchester direct geared to a single screw; 1,250 SHP, 10 knots.

1919: Launched by British American Shipbuilding Co. Ltd., Welland, Ontario, Canada (Yard No.2).

18.7.1919: Registered in the ownership of the Shipping Controller, London (Richard B. Chellew, Truro, managers) as WAR WEASEL.

17.9.1919: Register closed on sale to Compagnie Generale Transatlantique, Paris, France and renamed ORNE.

1930: Sold to Société Commerciale de Navigation Maritime 'Navmar', Paris, France.

1933: Sold to L. Lescurat, St. Jean de Lus, France

1934: Sold to Caledonickel Société Anonyme, Noumea, New Caledonia.

1947: Sold to T. Suen, Shanghai, China and renamed HUO FONG.

1948: Sold to Chang An Steam Navigation

Co., Shanghai and renamed AN HSING.

1956: Reported to have been broken up.

M6. WAR BADGER 1919-1920

O.N. 143428 2,243g 1,315n
251.0 x 43.5 x 22.9 feet
Two steam turbines by British Westinghouse Electric and Manufacturing Co. Ltd., Manchester direct geared to a single screw; 1,250 SHP, 11¼ knots.

1919: Launched by British American Shipbuilding Co. Ltd., Welland, Ontario, Canada (Yard No.2).

19.9.1919: Registered in the ownership of the Shipping Controller, London (Richard B. Chellew, Truro, managers) as WAR BADGER.

17.10.1919: Register closed on sale to Société Anonyme de Navigation 'Les Armateurs Francais', Paris, France and renamed RIBEAUVILLE.

1929: Sold to Maura y Aresti, Bilbao, Spain and renamed ZALLA.

1936: Broken up at Bilbao, Spain.

According to a press release by Richard Chellew, the WAR KARMA, also built by the Port Arthur Ship Building Co. Ltd., was to be managed by him for the Shipping Controller, but registration documents show that when registered on 4.1.1919 the managers were Furness Withy and Co., Halifax.

M8. EMPIRE DRUM 1942

O.N. 169012 7,244g 5,099n
442.9 x 56.5 x 35.5 feet
Oil engine 2SCSA by William Doxford and Sons Ltd., Sunderland; 301 NHP, 2,500 BHP, 2,860 IHP, 12 knots.

19.11.1941: Launched by William Doxford and Sons Ltd., Sunderland (Yard No. 684).

27.2.1942: Registered in the ownership of the Ministry of War Transport, London (Chellew Navigation Co. Ltd., Cardiff, managers) as EMPIRE DRUM.

3.1942: Delivered.

24.4.1942: Torpedoed and sunk by the

German submarine U 136 in position 37.00 north by 69.15 west whilst on a voyage from New York to Table Bay and Alexandria with Government stores including explosives. Her crew of 35 plus six gunners were rescued.

28.5.1942: Register closed.

M9. OCEAN HONOUR 1942

O.N. 16882 7,173g 4,278n
441.5 x 57.0 x 34.8 feet
T. 3-cyl. by the General Machinery Corporation, Hamilton, Ohio, USA; 505 NHP, 2,000 BHP, 2,500 IHP, 12 knots.

7.2.1942: Launched by the Todd-Bath Ship Building Corporation, South Portland, Maine (Yard No. 5).

5.1942: Completed.

12.6.1942: Registered in the ownership of the Ministry of War Transport, London (Chellew Navigation Co. Ltd., Cardiff, managers) as OCEAN HONOUR.

16.9.1942: Sunk by torpedo and gunfire from the Japanese submarine I-29 in the Indian Ocean in position 12.48 north by 50.50 east whilst on a voyage from Liverpool to Aden and Alexandria via Durban with 6,000 tons of Government stores including motor transport. Fifteen of her crew of 45 and five of her eight gunners were lost.

17.10.1942: Register closed.

M10. FORT SIMPSON 1942-1947

O.N. 168354 7,133g 4,222n
441.6 x 57.2 x 34.8 feet
T. 3-cyl. by Canadian Allis-Chalmers Ltd., Montreal, Canada.; 229 NHP, 2,500 IHP, 10 knots.

21.7.1942: Launched by North Van Ship Repairs Ltd., North Vancouver, British Columbia (Yard No. 108) for the United States War Shipping Administration, Washington, USA.

11.9.1942: Completed and bareboat chartered

4.12.1942: Registered in the ownership of the Ministry of War Transport, London (Chellew Navigation Co. Ltd., Cardiff,

Fort Simpson. [Ships in Focus]

managers) as FORT SIMPSON.
6.11.1947: Register closed on return to the United States Maritime Commission and laid up.
1948: Sold to 'Italia' Societa per Azioni di Navigazione, Genoa, Italy and renamed ATLANTA II.
1949: Renamed ATLANTA.
1951: Sold to Marritima Capodorso S.p.A. (Fratelli d'Amico, manager), Rome, Italy.
21.1.1966: Arrived at Vado Ligure to be broken up by A.R.D.E.M.

M11. EMPIRE NERISSA 1943-1946
O.N. 168751 7,076g 4,769n
432.2 x 56.2 x 34.2 feet
T. 3-cyl. by Harland and Wolff Ltd., Govan.
23.12.1942: Launched by Harland and Wolff Ltd., Govan (Yard No. 1169).
23.2.1943: Delivered to the Ministry of War Transport, London (Chellew Navigation Co. Ltd., Cardiff, managers) as EMPIRE NERISSA.
4.1946: Management transferred to Johnston Warren Lines Ltd., Liverpool.
1949: Sold to Claymore Shipping Co. Ltd., Cardiff and renamed DAYDAWN.

4.1950: Converted to burn oil.
1954: Sold to Steamship Induna Co. Ltd. (Maclay and McIntyre Ltd., managers), Glasgow and renamed LOCH DON.
1959: Sold to Maritenia Shipping Co. Ltd., Schaan, Lichtenstein (Kvarnerska Plovidba, Rijeka, Yugoslavia, managers) and renamed KRALJEVICA under the Yugoslav flag.
1961: Owners became Jugoslavenska Linijska Plovidba, Rijeka, Yugoslavia.
24.6.1966: Arrived at Spilt to be broken up by Brodospas.

M12. FORT MAISONNEUVE 1943-1944
O.N. 168459 7,128g 4,240n
424.5 x 57.2 x 34.9 feet
T. 3-cyl. by Dominion Engineering Works Ltd., Lachine, Quebec, Canada; 229 NHP, 2,500 IHP, 10 knots.
14.11.1942: Launched by United Shipyards Ltd., Montreal, Quebec (Yard No. 3) for the Dominion of Canada, Ottawa, Canada for bareboat charter to the Ministry of War Transport as FORT MAISONNEUVE
6.5.1943: Delivered.
22.6.1943: Registered in the ownership

of the Ministry of War Transport, London (Chellew Navigation Co. Ltd., Cardiff, managers).
15.12.1944: Mined and sunk in the Scheldt in position 51.24.09 north by 03.21.20 east, 105 degrees and 8.5 miles from the NF14 buoy whilst on a voyage from New York via The Downs to Antwerp with 6,142 tons of general cargo including explosives. From her crew of 48 and 12 gunners, four members of he crew were lost.
4.1.1945: Register closed.

M13. FORT TICONDEROGA 1943-1946
O.N. 169736 7,130gt 4,263n
440.5 x 57.2 x 34.9 feet
T. 3-cyl. by Dominion Engineering Works Ltd., Lachine, Quebec, Canada; 229 NHP, 2,500 IHP, 10 knots.
6.11.1943: Launched by United Shipyards Ltd., Montreal, Quebec (Yard No. 223) for the Dominion of Canada, Ottawa, Canada for bareboat charter to the Ministry of War Transport, London (Chellew Navigation Co. Ltd., Cardiff, managers) as FORT TICONDEROGA.

A United States Coast Guard view of the *Empire Nerissa* dated 12th December 1943. *[Ian J. Farquhar collection]*

Fort Ticonderoga during management by Cunard. *[Ships in Focus]*

7.12.1943: Delivered.
11.1.1946: Damaged by a mine in the Adriatic in position 44.35 north by 13.55 east whilst on a voyage from Port Said to Trieste.
12.1.1946: Arrived at Trieste and subsequently repaired.
17.5.1946: Management transferred to Cunard White Star Ltd., Liverpool.
7.1948: Returned to the Canadian Government.
1948: Sold to Ivor Shipping Co. Ltd. (Quebec Steamship Lines Ltd., managers), Montreal, Canada and renamed IVOR ISOBEL.
1950: Transferred to British registry and Chandris (England) Ltd., London became managers.
1955: Sold to Novor Shipping Co.

Ltd. (George E. Nicoletta, manager), Montreal.
(Chandris (England) Ltd., London, remain agents).
1956: Renamed NOVOR ISABEL.
1958: Sold to Ocean Tramping Co. Ltd. (Far East Enterprising Co. Ltd.), Hong Kong and renamed HEREFORD.
1959: Transferred to the People's Republic of China, Peking and renamed HOPING WU SHI 1.
1967: Renamed ZHAN DOU 51.
1973: Transferred to China Ocean Shipping Co.
1979: Transferred to Government of the People's Republic of China (Bureau of Maritime Transport Administration), Shanghai.
1985: Reported broken up.

M14. EMPIRE GOODWIN   1945-1946
O.N. 169528 7,192g 5,004n
447.8 x 56.2 x 34.4 feet
T. 3-cyl. by Fairfield Co. Ltd., Govan.
6.8.1945: Launched by William Hamilton and Co. Ltd., Port Glasgow (Yard No. 466).
12.1945: Delivered to the Ministry of War Transport, London (Chellew Navigation Co. Ltd., Cardiff, managers) as EMPIRE GOODWIN.
10.4.1946: Sold to the Denholm Line Steamers Ltd. (J. and J. Denholm Ltd., managers), Greenock.
1947: Renamed GARVELPARK.
1958: Sold to Trans Oceanic Steamship Co. Ltd., Karachi, Pakistan and renamed OCEAN ENSIGN.
25.1.1971: Breaking up began by M.M. Bakshi, Gadani Beach, Pakistan.

Garvelpark, formerly the *Empire Goodwin. [FotoFlite]*

GLOVER BROTHERS

W.A. Laxon

There are many cases of two brothers together in business. Three brothers together in the first generation of a firm is rarer, but the London shipowning and shipbroking firm of Glover Brothers was one such. The Glover family was of County Durham stock, the father of the brothers, Terrot Glover, being an alderman and thrice mayor of South Shields. He began his career as a stonemason, but later became an auctioneer. He and his wife, Ann, were members of the non-conformist community of South Shields and their family of eight sons (two daughters died at an early age) was brought up in a strict, God-fearing household.

Despite the rising prominence of their home town as a shipping and shipbuilding centre, the early careers of the Glover boys pointed in other directions. The third child, Robert, was a clerk in the District Bank at Hartlepool, while the sixth, John, became a chemist's apprentice. Notwithstanding his youth, it was John who made the break at the age of 18 when he took a sea passage to London to seek his fortune. Starting out as an office boy, he then joined a firm of shipping agents and shipbrokers as a chartering clerk. He rapidly acquired an intimate knowledge of the business and became a key employee, such that he felt in a position to name his own terms. These included a partnership for himself and that the present partners should abandon their frequent absences from the business and over-indulgence in withdrawal of much-needed capital. Not surprisingly, such plain speaking did not endear Glover to his employers and, although his worth was recognised in the offer of a considerable increase in salary, a partnership was flatly refused.

After six years in the metropolis John Glover felt sufficient confidence in his own experience and abilities not to accept this rebuff and he persuaded his older brother, Robert, to come south to join him. With the aid of founding capital of £500 lent by their father, Glover Brothers opened its doors for business at 9 Eastcheap early in 1853. Despite Robert's seniority in years John, with his hard won experience of the London shipping world, was and remained the senior partner. The new firm relied in its early years on an effective combination of John's shipbroking and chartering background, Robert's financial expertise and the north east coast connections of the family. It was a success from the start, grossing nearly £2,500 in commissions in the first year and enabling John to become engaged to Louisa Moser, a union which was to last for over 60 years.

Although the income fluctuated, the gross receipts of the firm never fell below £1,800 per annum over the first 10 years and in the halcyon year of 1860 reached £3,300. By then the firm's expanding business required larger premises and a move had been made to 34 Great St Helens where it remained for some 20 years. The sound economic basis of their enterprise encouraged the brothers to embark on a path which had been taken by so many other similar firms and cross the divide from shipbroking and chartering to shipowning. However, unlike the majority who began with cheap second hand tonnage, the Glovers ordered a new ship. Not surprisingly they turned to their home territory on the north east coast, placing the order with the Sunderland yard of Peverill and Co. The vessel was a composite barque of 534 tons whose chosen name of *W.E. Gladstone* reflected the brothers' political leanings.

They ran her mainly in the Indian and Far East trades where she gave them 15 years of satisfactory service before being sold to a Swansea owner. In January 1867 she was joined by the small wooden barque *Dione* of 1857, which came on the market cheaply and was acquired by Robert Glover in his own name although run with the rest of the partnership fleet. Later that year came a slightly larger vessel than *W.E. Gladstone*, the 585-ton composite barque *Jungfrau*, also a Sunderland product but this time from Doxford's yard on the opposite bank of the Wear. She gave 13 years of service until sold to Swansea owners in 1880. Size increased once more when the brothers returned to Doxfords in 1868 for the 665-ton *Inarime*. Delivered in February 1869, she proved a less rewarding investment as she was lost on her maiden voyage to China.

Notwithstanding this setback, the success of their two other sailing ships encouraged the Glover brothers to venture into steam. In 1869 they placed an order with the Sunderland yard of Iliff, Mounsey and Co. for a flush-decked steamer which was launched in February 1870 as the *Titian*, the only artist in a fleet otherwise consistently named after poets. Although she met with early disaster when heavily damaged in collision in 1871, her iron hull was found to be still sound and she was repaired to resume service. This early setback did little to affect her longevity for after being sold in 1880 a later owner converted her to a tanker in 1886 and her final destruction by fire did not come until 1911 when she had passed her fortieth year.

For their second steamer the brothers returned to their home town, placing the order with Softley and Co. of South Shields. Delivered in June 1874, the *Dante* followed the Italian association of the first steamer, but this time with a poet. She marked a considerable improvement in economy over the pioneer, being fitted with compound engines, and with the tonnage increased to 1,743 gross. Unfortunately her career was short, as she was lost in collision in St George's Channel in December 1875. In the meantime a third steamer had joined the fleet in 1874, this time from the West Hartlepool yard of E. Withy and Co. with whom Robert had had dealings during his time with the District Bank across the harbour at Hartlepool. She introduced the name of a British poet, *Milton*, a practice, with three exceptions, to which the Glovers remained faithful for all their later ships. Her career was as long and as profitable as the *Dante's* was short for she remained in the fleet until 1899 and then served three more owners under the Spanish flag before becoming a collision victim in 1925.

Three brothers

But 1874 was to prove a more momentous year in a quite different direction. Septimus Glover, the ninth child and seventh son of Terrot and Ann, had not followed his elder brothers to London but had established himself in business at West Hartlepool, becoming a successful shipowner in his own right. The ties of blood, or perhaps the prospect of strength through joint pooling of resources, persuaded him to join his siblings in that year, thus completing the first generation of Glovers in the business. Septimus brought with him four modern steamers, the *Amazon*, *Himalaya*, *Burlington* and the larger *Annan*.

The brothers' quest for modern tonnage continued with the acquisition of the year-old *Bengal* in the same year and the completion to their own order of the *Ossian*. However, the sailing vessels still beckoned, as the eight-year old barque *Ocean Rover* was purchased in 1875. A further steamer of similar size to the *Ossian*, the *Homer* was delivered in 1877, but her service to Glovers was brief as in December 1878 she went missing in the North Atlantic. It may be coincidence, but it was to be over 20 years before a subsequent Glover ship received the name of a foreign poet.

Broadening interests

Meanwhile the Glover interests had expanded in other directions. In 1872 John became a member of the committee of Lloyd's Register of Shipping, followed by underwriting membership at Lloyd's in March 1874. This latter move was made at the suggestion of Fred Bolton, later to be the founder of the Bolton Steam Ship Company and, like John Glover, a member of the Union Chapel in Upper Street. Bolton formed a syndicate at Lloyd's for which he himself was the active underwriter and John was joined on it as a name (as the non-active underwriting members were called) by his brother Robert, and his brother-in-law, John Moser. In addition, Fred Bolton himself became a name in 1878. The underwriting business was soon showing healthy returns. Fred Bolton also attended to the insurance of the Glover ships and when he turned to shipowning in 1885 Glovers became his chartering brokers. This interlocking of activities was a forerunner of the eventual merger of the Glover and Bolton interests 60 years later.

In 1877 John Glover took the chair at the first meeting of the Chamber of Shipping, becoming its President in 1880. Septimus had also lost no time in adjusting to London, becoming honorary secretary of a committee of the Baltic Exchange established in 1878 to draft a standard charter party for vessels in the Black Sea grain trade, then one of the staples of the British tramp fleet.

An even more important development was the association with the Mercantile Steamship Co. Ltd. which had been formed in 1871 to take over the business of John A. and Charles R. Dunkerly, originally from Hull. The Dunkerlys already had associations with the Glovers as brokers and both John and Robert became initial shareholders in and directors of the new company. After dabbling in the liner trades in the early 1870s the company had stagnated and it was Thomas Birkin, a major shareholder, who had joined the Bolton underwriting syndicate in 1875, who persuaded John Glover to give it a new impetus by becoming chairman and managing director soon after. Larger and more efficient ships of simple tramp design were ordered, and the Mercantile ships with their alphabetical sequence of river names soon became a very efficient enterprise. Although Glovers handled the chartering of the Mercantile fleet, it remained independently run from its own premises at 12 St Mary Axe, even though its trades were similar to those of the brothers' own ships, and both fleets shared a common grey hull colour and plain black funnel. Following Robert's retirement, Septimus Glover took his place on the Mercantile Steamship board.

A wholly steam fleet

1880 could be regarded as a turning point for the Glovers' shipowning interests as all the remaining sailing ships were sold in that year while over the following 18 months three larger steamers were built to the brothers' order. William Gray and Co. delivered the *Shelley* and *Wordsworth* in 1881 and 1882 respectively, both of which were to give 25 years of satisfactory service to the firm. In contrast the Withy-built *Burns* of 1882 was lost when only just over a year old. Perhaps because of this experience she remained the only Glover ship to carry the name of a Scottish poet. Her replacement in 1885 was the *Shakespear* whose name was to be the cause of endless comment. The reason for the dropping of the final letter e was very simple. In those days all communication where speed was important was by cable, and cable companies charged any word with more than 10 letters as 2 words. Omitting the final e ensured a considerably reduced cable bill for the *Shakespear* over her 26 years with the firm as did the specification of triple-expansion engines result in a greatly reduced coal bill for her owners.

Wordsworth of 1882 approaching Bristol. *[Nigel Farrell collection]*

During the construction of these ships a second generation of Glovers had joined the firm. The first to be admitted as a partner was Howard Glover, son of John, in 1874, followed by his cousin Ernest, son of Septimus, in 1882. On the other side of the coin, the eldest of the founding brothers, Robert, had retired in 1888 leaving the two father and son combinations in control.

Two new ships, the *Byron* and *Tennyson*, were delivered from Thompsons in 1889 and 1894 respectively, the former introducing a new profile by abandoning the well deck for a flush-deck design. The friendship and business relationships between the Glover and Bolton families took on a more personal basis at this time when George Pearse, whose sister had married Fred Bolton, married John Glover's daughter and joined the staff of Glover Brothers. Moreover the offices of the two firms were now on adjoining floors of the building at 88 Bishopsgate (renumbered as 57 in 1910), Glovers being on the first floor and Boltons on the second.

Limited liability

The year 1898 brought a change which mirrored a development in the ownership pattern of both small and large tramp fleets. Hitherto Glovers had followed the general fashion with ownership of their fleet being held directly, the investors taking up one or more 64th shares. This had the attraction of providing a return solely related to the performance of each individual ship, and also confined the outfall of a disaster to those investing in the ship concerned. As ship prices increased, the cost of a 64th share rose proportionately and the attractions of limited liability loomed larger, while a changing fiscal and taxation regime also favoured the corporate structure. In 1898 the individual partnerships for each ship were wound up and the six ships were transferred into a single company whose shares were issued in exchange for the previous direct ownership. The distinctive form of the Shakespear name was chosen for the new company and the Shakespear Shipping Company Ltd. remained the owning vehicle for all subsequent steamers. It needs emphasising that the new concern was simply an owning entity. Day to day management of the fleet remained with the partners of Glover Brothers in exactly the same way as before.

Two new ships which reflected the increasing size of tramps were delivered from Thompson's yard in 1899 and 1902. The *Milton* replaced the 1874 ship of the name which had been sold at the end of 1898, while an even more marked rise came with the *Ovid*, the last foreign poet name to be chosen.

John Glover had been knighted in 1900, the first man from South Shields to receive that honour. As the new century progressed he took a less active part in the business but remained a partner even though his younger brother, Septimus, retired in 1906.

The driving forces in the firm were now Howard, in charge of the shipbroking side, and Ernest whose realm was in ship management. Howard followed his father's interest in Lloyd's Register of Shipping, being a long time Chairman of

its Classification Committee. He was also actively involved with the Shipping Federation, the Chamber of Shipping, served as a member of the Port of London Authority and as a Joint Honorary Treasurer of King George's Fund for Sailors of which he was a founding spirit. On the retirement of Septimus, he took his place as a director of the Mercantile Steamship Company. Ernest's domain was the Baltic Exchange where he was Chairman for four years, but he was also President of the Chamber of Shipping and Honorary Treasurer of the British Sailors' Society. The cousins were joined in partnership in 1902 by Ernest's younger brother, Fred, who had been originally destined for the medical profession. His fluctuating state of health prevented him from taking as wide interests as his partners and his activities were largely confined to those of the firm.

The Glovers found the attractions of shipbroking and agency greater than those of shipowning in the first decade of the twentieth century, and when the *Shelley* and *Wordsworth* were sold in 1906 they were not replaced. In fact it was not until the sale of the *Shakespear* in 1911 that a new vessel of the same name was ordered from Thompson's yard. Her size of only 3,466 tons reflected the difficulties that had been faced in the lean years of finding profitable employment for the larger *Ovid*, but she was otherwise a thoroughly up-to-date vessel of three-island design with four hatches in the two well decks either side of a long centrecastle. A generally similar vessel, the *Wordsworth*, was on order from Gray's yard at West Hartlepool at the outbreak of the First World War and was delivered in March 1915. In 1913 a third generation of Glovers appeared in the firm when John's grandson, Cedric, became a partner. Two other of his grandsons, Ronald Glover and Kenneth Pearse, were also working for the partnership in 1914, but regrettably both were to be killed on active service.

Demands of war

The war made many other demands on both partners and staff of the firm. Ernest Glover was a member of the Advisory Committee in the Transport Department of the Admiralty from 1915, and then joined the Ministry of Shipping from its inception as Director of its Ship Management Branch. For these services he was knighted in 1918 and became a baronet in 1920. Fred Glover was sent to Gibraltar as the Ministry of Shipping Representative there, leaving Howard to carry on the firm's business virtually single-handed as Sir John had retired in 1917 from the firm he had founded and Cedric was serving in the Army with the Intelligence Corps.

Glovers second ship of the name, the *Shakespear* of 1912. *[Nigel Farrell collection]*

So far as the fleet was concerned, the war dealt less harshly with the Glover ships than with many other tramp fleets. Of the four ships owned in August 1914, only the *Ovid* of 1902 became a casualty when she was torpedoed and sunk off Suda Bay on 25th November 1917. Much more serious was the loss of the almost brand new *Wordsworth* which survived for only two years before being captured and sunk by the German raider *Wolf* in the Indian Ocean in March 1917. As a result of the sale of the *Tennyson* in 1915 the Shakespear Shipping Co. Ltd. emerged at the Armsitice with only its namesake ship and the elderly *Milton* of 1899. But there was much other work to keep the firm busy. It had already managed four captured German ships for the British Admiralty between 1914 and 1916, followed by two vessels

The *Duchess of York,* one of the paddle steamers which was managed by the company from 1919 until 1921 when she was was sold back to her original owners, the Southampton, Isle of Wight and South of England Royal Mail Steam Packet Co. Ltd. Renamed *Duchess of Cornwall* in 1928 she lasted until 1950 when broken up at Northam. *[J. and M. Clarkson collection]*

requisitioned from Norwegian owners from 1917. Through Ernest Glover's position with the Ministry of Shipping the firm agreed to manage eight wooden ships being constructed in Canadian yards for the Shipping Controller. Fortunately its connection with those financial and commercial disasters ceased in 1920. No fewer than 14 war-built steel ships were also put under Glover's management, two of which had been built in Canada. Ernest Glover also undertook the management on behalf of the Shipping Controller in 1918 and 1919 of three ships that had been damaged by enemy action until their return to their owners in 1919 following completion of repairs: Clan Line's *Clan Graham* , the Royal Mail Steam Packet Company's *Asturias*, and the tramp steamer *Quito*. Elder, Dempster's elderly steamer *Teneriffe* joined them after the Admiralty decided it had no need for her as a blockship. Another Admiralty cast-off was the bulk carrier *August Belmont*, which had been converted to a tanker. Glovers accepted the management in 1919 of four ex-German ships surrendered to British control. A remarkable procession of vessels then passed through Glovers' books, including two

hopper barges and two paddle steamers. Ernest Glover also assumed management of a cargo liner originally ordered in 1915 from Sir Raylton Dixon and Co. as the Federal Line's *Norfolk* but whose construction had not reached the launching stage by the end of the war. She eventually entered the New Zealand Shipping Company fleet in January 1921 as the *Hurunui* without Glover ever having had her in other than nominal control. These were later joined by four ships built for the Shipping Controller with War names, but which had been sold to commercial concerns who had defaulted on payment, so that they returned to the Shipping Controller or its successor the Board of Trade for sale. Two of these had been built in Canada and two in Hong Kong, whilst yet another war-built ship put under Glover's control had been built in Shanghai. These ships passed rapidly to other owners.

Post-war co-operation with Boltons
In post-war years a longer lasting management connection was formed in connection with four ships previously owned by the West Russian Steamship Company Ltd. of St Petersburg.

With her fine array of masts, the *Daghild* was managed by Glovers for eight months from November 1916. *[B. and A. Feilden/J. and M. Clarkson collection]*

All had escaped from Bolshevik control and in 1920 were transferred to the British-registered Ornis Shipping Co. Ltd. with Glover Brothers as managers. This arrangement continued until 1924 when the real owners recognised that their exile from their homeland was permanent and took over control themselves. In the meantime both Glovers and Boltons had again moved together to larger though still rather traditional premises at 16 St Helens Place.

The four Glover partners had not been neglectful of their own fleet, acquiring from the Shipping Controller in 1920 and 1921 four of the surrendered German ships, which became *Shelley*, *Keats*, *Wordsworth* and *Ovid*. All were more liner than tramp tonnage and only the last and newest, Hamburg Amerika's *Altmark* of 1911, which became the *Shelley*, was German built. The Glovers were fortunate in that the purchase of these ships was arranged after the bull freight

The former German steamer *Elbe* was aquired in 1920 and named *Wordsworth (3)* (above). The *Spenser* (below) was acquired from Trinder, Anderson in 1924. *[Above: Nigel Farrell collection, below: Roy Fenton collection]*

market of the first part of 1920 had collapsed, so that they were acquired at the reduced prices then prevailing, but of course the charters obtainable for them were on a similarly lower scale. By careful management the firm weathered the storm, and in 1923 disposed of the elderly *Milton* for further trading. Another escaped Russian ship was bought in April of that year to replace her but was resold advantageously the following month. More permanent replacements, again more of the liner type, were secured in 1924 when the *Errol* and *Montrose* were acquired from Trinder, Anderson's Australind Steam Shipping Co. Ltd. to become the *Spenser* and *Milton*.

As trade picked up in the mid 1920s, the Glovers returned to the building berth for the first time in ten years but now deserting their traditional north east coast builders for the Port Glasgow yard of Robert Duncan and Co. Ltd., probably due to the Bolton connection. The *Shakespear* was delivered in November 1926, her predecessor of 1912 having been disposed of to Japanese owners only a few months earlier. The new ship was a sister of the *Reynolds*, completed for Boltons the following year, and featured a long bridge deck with short wells at numbers 1 and 5 hatches and a generally higher specification than the average tramp with a view to

Milton (3) (above) was the second ship acquired from Trinder, Anderson in 1924. The *Chaucer* (below) entered the fleet in 1929 when completed at Port Glasgow. *[Above: George Scott collection, below: F. W. Hawks collection]*

attracting liner company charters. Her success in service led to the placing of a similar dual order for two slightly larger ships from the same yard which entered the fleets in 1929. The Glover vessel was the *Chaucer* while her Bolton sister was the *Romney*. In the meantime a joint move to adjoining floors of a building was again made in 1928 when Glovers and Boltons took over premises at Bevis Marks House. The Depression of 1929 found the Glover fleet with eight ships, six second hand and two nearly new and purpose built. The former had just been put through expensive surveys absorbing some £60,000 from which little return was received. Only the new ships were to survive the financial storm, all the second hand tonnage being sold for demolition between 1932 and 1934.

Adapting to changing times

The same period saw considerable change on shore. Fred Glover died in 1929, followed by Ernest in June 1934. The two surviving partners, Howard and his son Cedric, felt the need to adapt the business to changing conditions and in 1935 the partnership gave way to a new company, Glover Brothers (London) Ltd. with Howard as Chairman and Cedric as a director. They were joined on the board by three long-serving staff members, Charles Bird who had first joined the firm in 1916, Victor Young and Brian Turner whose association dated from 1921 and 1924 respectively. It was in this form that the two companies faced the outbreak of the Second World War in 1939. Its effect was catastrophic on an enterprise which had never really recovered fully from the Depression. It was symptomatic of the situation that when Louis Bolton, who in 1939 had ordered two new ships for his own company from Lithgows, took the precaution of reserving two berths for similar ships for the Shakespear Company, Howard Glover immediately repudiated the action and accused Bolton of 'criminal stupidity' in ordering newbuildings at the time.

This reaction typified the negative outlook of those in charge of the business.

By this time Howard Glover's health had already deteriorated and he came to the London office infrequently. Cedric Glover rejoined the Army while Charles Bird and Victor Young were both recruited by the Ministry of Shipping (later the Ministry of War Transport) leaving only Brian Turner to carry on. With such reduced manpower and only two owned ships plus two managed for the Ministry, the problems were enormous and in November 1940 the decision was made to sell the Shakespear Shipping Co. Ltd. to the South American Saint Line which was desperate for tonnage to replace losses. In fact their acquisition of the two Shakespear ships did little to resolve their needs as both ships were soon lost to enemy action, the *Shakespear* on 5th January 1941 before she had actually been handed over to the new management and the *Chaucer* but six months later.

The sale of the shipowning company was the beginning of the end for Glovers as an independent entity. Brian Turner had joined the Army in 1942 following the loss of the second of the managed *Empire* ships, and at the end of that year the long-standing association with Boltons reached its logical conclusion when the Bolton Steam Shipping Co. Ltd. acquired the whole of the capital of Glover Brothers (London) Ltd. Howard retired from the board in 1943, with Louis Bolton becoming chairman and Charles Bird the managing director. Glovers never became shipowners again, concentrating instead on the ship chartering and insurance broking businesses. On his return from war service, Cedric Glover became a director of the Bolton Steam Shipping Co. Ltd., but did not actively become involved in the Glover subsidiary again. He retired in 1970. Together with the Boltons, Glovers moved again in 1951 to Plantation House in Mincing Lane and in January 1953 Jocelyn Glover, son of Cedric and great-grandson of John, became a director. With his retirement in 1974 the last

Shakespear (3) was one of the last two ships owned by Glovers. *[Roy Fenton collection]*

link with the founding family was broken, though Jocelyn Glover did not die until 1987.

The firm's ship chartering work received two boosts in the immediate post-war years, first for Swedish companies through Eric Roessler who became a director in 1949 but regrettably died at the end of that year, and then with an extension into work for liner companies. The long established business of A. Temperley and Co., which brought valuable connections with the West Australian trade, was acquired in 1952 and eventually absorbed into Glovers which dropped the (London) from its title. Further expansion came in 1958 with the purchase of a half interest in the British Italian Shipping and Coal Co. Ltd. which was renamed Glover Brothers (Coal and Shipping) Ltd. The other half was held by Mario Alberti S.p.a. until 1970 when the enterprise became wholly owned by Glovers following the virtual disappearance of its coal business. This company's guiding spirit was Andy Andrews who became a Glover director in 1964, taking charge of the agency side of the business.

Brian Turner succeeded Charles Bird as managing director in 1965 and followed tradition in becoming Chairman of the Baltic Exchange from 1969 to 1971. On his retirement in 1971, Jimmy Blott took over and was instrumental in Glovers moving strongly into freight forwarding. In 1972 EDB Marketing Ltd, a company involved in shipping and groupage services to Ireland and near Continental ports, was acquired and renamed EDB (Shipping) Ltd., operating from a base in Leicester. In its turn it purchased in 1980 a haulage company called Transwind Transport and the two businesses were then combined at Transwind House from 1981. Glovers' chartering business continued to be based in the Baltic Exchange Buildings, while an office in Felixstowe handled agency traffic at that port. B.W. Hadida (Shipping) Ltd., a freight forwarding company dating from 1965, was acquired in 1980 with more far reaching changes soon to follow.

Michael Deakin became managing director of Glovers from 1981 with Peter Davis, who had been a director since 1963, taking over the chair from Sir Frederic Bolton who remained on the board. In the same year the businesses were re-allocated to two separate subsidiaries, Glover Brothers (Chartering) Ltd. and Glover Brothers (Agencies) Ltd.

This series of changes was to prove disastrous for the agency company which ran into obligations beyond its capacity and was obliged to cease trading in January 1983. The parent Bolton company could have left the creditors to sort matters out with its subsidiary, but the Bolton board took the honorable course by agreeing to meet the obligations at the cost of having to sell the group's Lloyd's broking business to Frizzells. That concern was later taken over by Bowrings which in turn was absorbed into the U.S. company, Marsh McLennan.

Glover Brothers (Chartering) Ltd., as a separate legal entity, was only indirectly affected by the demise of its sister company, but the liquidator chose to sell it against the wishes of those directly involved. Their only way out of the dilemma was to resign *en bloc* and set up again with the backing of Boltons and the Arison Group which had bought the Bolton shipping interests. The Glover name had regrettably lost much of its shine and reputation as a result of the agency company collapse, so the new enterprise emerged as BMM and London Shipbrokers Ltd., operating from 4c Lanterns Court, London, E14, the B standing for Bolton and the two Ms for Marine Management.

When the Bolton family decided to wind up their connection in 1988, a management buy-out was negotiated and BMM and London Shipbrokers continued as an independent concern until the business was acquired in October 1996 with nine staff members by Anderson Hughes, a P&O Group subsidiary. The company itself was not part of the transaction and remained in existence until 1999 to wind up remaining commitments. So, though somewhat heavily disguised, the Glover inheritance continued indirectly as a small component of one of the major British shipping groups.

FLEET LIST

1. W.E. GLADSTONE 1865-1880
Composite barque
O.N. 54581 534g 534n
148.5 x 29.9 x 17.3 feet
2.12.1865: Completed by George Peverill, Sunderland.
12.12.1865: Registered in the ownership of Robert R. Glover, London as W.E. GLADSTONE.
29.1.1880: Sold to George B. Meager, Swansea.
5.9.1881: Foundered in the Pacific 400 miles west of Huanco, Chile in position 28.30 south by 87.45 west whilst on a voyage from Pisagua to Queenstown/ Falmouth for orders.
231.12.1881: Register closed.

2. DIONE 1867-1879 **Wooden barque**
O.N. 18725 289g 289n
122.8 x 25.0 x 15.5 feet
1.6.1857: Completed at Bristol for George and William Gordon, London as DIONE.
24.1.1867: Acquired by Robert R. Glover, London.
12.3.1867: Owners became John Wilson (29/64), Lancelot Wilson (16/64), Catherine S. Thompson, Sunderland (11/64), and Robert R. Glover, London (8/64).
1879: Sold at Batavia to Said Hassan bin Amin Hailla, Sourabaya, Java and renamed DJOEDOEL KARIM.
After 1886: Transferred to Said Achmah bin Hassan Mola Heila, Sourabaya.
1893: Abandoned.

3. JUNGFRAU 1867-1880 **Composite barque**
O.N. 56891 585g 585n
158.3 x 30.0 x 18.6 feet
18.11.1867: Completed by William Doxford and Sons, Sunderland (Yard No. 22).
2.12.1867: Registered in the ownership of Glover Brothers, London as JUNGFRAU.
12.1879: Sold to Joseph A. Nicholson, Swansea.
18.10.1886: Sold to L. Glycas, Syra, Greece.
1892: Sold to G. Nicolaiki, Syra, later Zante, and renamed LEONIDAS.
6.1901: Broken up.

4. INARIME 1869 **Composite barque**
O.N. 60913 665g 665n
173.0 x 31.1 x 18.6 feet.
31.1.1869: Launched by William Doxford and Sons, Sunderland (Yard No. 28) for Glover Brothers, London as INARIME.
4.10.1869: Wrecked in the China Sea.

5. TITIAN 1870-1881 **Iron**
O.N. 63581 1,101g 821n
231.0 x 31.1 x 16.6 feet
2-cyl. simple engines by George Clark, Sunderland; 98 NHP.
1877: Compounded by the Wallsend Slipway Co. Ltd., Wallsend-on-Tyne.
2.1870: Launched by Iliff, Mounsey and Co., Sunderland (Yard No. 41).
31.3.1870: Completed.
2.4.1870: Registered in the ownership of Glover Brothers, London as TITIAN.
6.12.1871: Collided with and sank the US schooner DANIEL WILLIAMS off Little Gull Island whilst on a voyage from Sydney, Cape Breton, to New York. She was badly damaged and flooded forward, but reached New York for major repairs.
9.1881: Sold to the Société Rouennais de Transportes Maritimes à Vapeur, Rouen, France and renamed COLBERT.
4.4.1883: Registered in the ownership of Robert Thomson, London as TITIAN.
1883: Sold to Thomas E. Angel, London.
1884: Sold to Alfred Suart, London.

1886: Converted to a tanker.
24.3.1891: Owners became the Petroleum Transport and Storage Co. Ltd. (Alfred Suart, manager), London.
6.11.1896: Owners became the European Petroleum Co. Ltd. (Alfred Suart, manager), London.
1898: Sold to E. Basso, Genoa, Italy and renamed EZIO.
1899: Sold to F.G. Piaggio, Genoa.
1906: Transferred to Peruvian registry.
13.6.1911: Destroyed by fire at Callao.

6. DANTE 1874-1875 Iron
O.N. 70583 1,743g 1,133 n
275.8 x 33.6 x 24.4 feet
C.2-cyl. by John Dickinson, Sunderland; 160 NHP.
18.5.1874: Launched by John Softley and Co., South Shields (Yard No. 110).
11.7.1874: Registered in the ownership of Glover Brothers, London as DANTE.
29.12.1875: Run down and sunk in fog by the Norwegian barque GROSVENOR in St. George's Channel with the loss of 22 lives.
11.7.1876: Register closed.

7. MILTON (1) 1874-1898 Iron
O.N. 70602 1,357g 861n
245.0 x 31.6 x 22.6 feet
C.2-cyl. by Thomas Richardson and Sons, Hartlepool.
7.1874: Launched by Edward Withy and Co., West Hartlepool (Yard No. 45).
12.8.1874: Registered in the ownership of Glover Brothers, London as MILTON.
12.1898: Sold to Compania Maritima Comercial (J. Roca, manager), Barcelona, Spain and renamed JOSE ROCA.
1913: Sold to D. Mumbru, Barcelona and renamed DOMINGO MUMBRU.
1922: Sold to Sociedad Anonima Cros, Barcelona and renamed S.A.C.
17.4.1925: Sunk in collision off Carthagena whilst on a voyage from Alicante to Huelva.

8. AMAZON 1874-1875 Iron
O.N. 63040 633g 402n
181.5 x 28.6 x 15.3 feet
2-cyl. by Thomas Richardson and Sons, Hartlepool; 86 NHP.
4.1870: Launched by Withy, Alexander and Co., West Hartlepool (Yard No. 9).
24.5.1870: Registered in the ownership of Septimus Glover, West Hartlepool as AMAZON.
1874: Owners became Glover Brothers, London.
9.1875: Sold to E. Oxeda, Bayonne, France and renamed PERSÉVÉRANT.
12.1879: Lost whilst on a voyage from Bayonne to Antwerp.

9. ANNAN 1874-1882 Iron
O.N. 67534 1,025g 662n
230.3 x 30.8 x 17.0 feet
C. 2-cyl. by Hawks Crawshay and Co., Gateshead; 98 NHP.
1872: Launched by Davidson and Stokoe, Sunderland.

12.12.1872: Registered in the ownership of Septimus Glover, West Hartlepool as ANNAN.
1874: Owners became Glover Brothers, London.
1882: Sold to J. Lohden and Co., West Hartlepool.
10.1.1884: Stranded on Klockfoten Reef, off the island of Nidingen, Sweden whilst on a voyage from Danzig to Tunis.
2.2.1884: Register closed.

10. BURLINGTON 1874-1882 Iron
O.N. 67526 837g 540n
202.7 x 29.1 x 16.3 feet
C.2-cyl. by Thomas Richardson and Sons, Hartlepool.
4.1872: Launched by William Doxford and Sons, Sunderland (Yard No. 50).
21.6.1872: Registered in the ownership of Septimus Glover, West Hartlepool as BURLINGTON.
1874: Owners became Glover Brothers, London.
12.1881: Sold to Jacob Lohden and Co., West Hartlepool.
20.12.1892: Sold to John W. Thompson and John R. Elliott, South Shields.
15.7.1896: Sold to the Burlington Steamship Co. Ltd. (Cuthbert Wilkinson, manager), Sunderland.
8.5.1898: Wrecked near Penzance whilst on a voyage from Swansea to Rouen with a cargo of coal.
13.5.1898: Register closed.

11. HIMALAYA 1874-1876 Iron
O.N. 65039 773g 499n
200.8 x 28.5 x 15.9 feet
C. 2-cyl. by Thomas Richardson and Sons, Hartlepool; 96 NHP.
1.1871: Launched by Withy, Alexander and Co., West Hartlepool (Yard No. 15).
4.2.1871: Registered in the ownership of Septimus Glover, (32/64) and George Steel (32/64), West Hartlepool as HIMALAYA.
1874: Transferred to Glover Brothers, London.
8.1876: Sold to Steel, Young and Co., London.
8.1886: Sold to A. Caramanian Chahinoglou and Co., Constantinople, Turkey and renamed HERACLEE.
1890: Sold to Idarei Massousieh, Constantinople and renamed PARS.
1912: Deleted from Lloyd's Register; possibly sunk as a blockship.

12. OCEAN ROVER 1875-1879 Composite barque
O.N. 58076 548g 548n
153.0 x 28.7 x 18.0 feet
17.7.1867: Completed by Thompson and Co., Sunderland.
20.7.1867: Registered in the ownership of Thomas Thompson (22/64), John Thompson (21/64) and Joseph Thompson (21/64), Sunderland as OCEAN ROVER.
25.10.1875: Acquired by Glover Brothers, London.

12.1879: Sold to Jeremiah and George Richardson, Swansea.
20.3.1891: Destroyed by fire at Larequeta.
25.5.1891: Register closed.

13. BENGAL 1875-1888 Iron
O.N. 70578 1,673g 1,095n
270.0 x 33.3 x 24.4 feet
C.2-cyl. by Blair and Co. Ltd., Stockton.
16.5.1874: Launched by Raylton Dixon and Co., Middlesbrough (Yard No. 105).
1.7.1874: Registered in the ownership of George N. Wilkinson and James B. Watt, London as BENGAL.
17.8.1875: 58/64 shares sold to Raylton Dixon, Middlesbrough.
11.12.1875: Acquired by Robert R. Glover, London.
1.1.1876: Owners became Glover Brothers, London.
1.1.1888: Foundered off Cape Finisterre whilst on a voyage from Cardiff to Port Said.
21.1.1888: Register closed.

14. OSSIAN 1876-1893 Iron
O.N. 73720 1,869g 1,211n
284.4 x 34.2 x 24.5 feet
C. 2-cyl. by Black, Hawthorn and Co., Gateshead; 180 NHP.
9.1876: Launched by C.S. Swan and Co., Newcastle-upon-Tyne (Yard No. 24).
10.10.1876: Registered in the ownership of Glover Brothers, London as OSSIAN.
8.11.1893: Sailed from Malta for Copenhagen with a cargo of cereals and went missing with all hands.
29.3.1894: Register closed.

15. HOMER 1877-1878 Iron
O.N. 77016 1,916g 1,238n
285.0 x 34.2 x 24.4 feet
C.2-cyl. by Black Hawthorn and Co., Gateshead-on-Tyne; 180 NHP.
8.9.1877: Launched by Charles Mitchell and Co., Low Walker, Newcastle-upon-Tyne (Yard No. 346).
10.10.1877: Registered in the ownership of Glover Brothers, London as HOMER.
17.12.1878: Sailed from Boston for Liverpool and went missing in the North Atlantic.
8.3.1879: Register closed.

16. SHELLEY (1) 1881-1906 Iron
O.N. 85038 1,998g 1,303n
285.0 x 35.4 x 24.5 feet
C.2-cyl. by Black, Hawthorn and Co., Gateshead-on-Tyne; 200 NHP.
28.5.1881: Launched by William Gray and Co., West Hartlepool (Yard No. 232).
25.7.1881: Registered in the ownership of Glover Brothers, London as SHELLEY.
4.4.1898: Transferred to the Shakespear Shipping Co. Ltd. (Glover Brothers, managers), London.
5.1906: Register closed following sale to Compañia Chilena de Nav. A Vapores, Valparaiso, Chile and renamed PRESIDENTE SANTA MARIA.
1912: Stranded and condemned.

Shelley (1) in the Avon. *[Roy Fenton collection]*

17. BURNS 1882-1883 Iron

O.N. 85197 2193 g 1425 n
285.0 x 36.0 x 24.1 feet
C. 2-cyl. by Thomas Richardson and Sons,
Hartlepool.
1.7.1882: Launched by Edward Withy and
Co., West Hartlepool (Yard No. 109).
1.9.1882: Registered in the ownership of
Glover Brothers, London as BURNS.
7.10.1883: Wrecked near Suakim whilst on
a voyage from Bussorah to London.
3.11.1883: Register closed.

18. WORDSWORTH (1) 1882-1906 Iron

O.N. 87010   1,990g 1,335n
285.7 x 36.0 x 24.2 feet
C.2-cyl. by Thomas Richardson and Sons,
West Hartlepool; 240 NHP.
14.10.1882: Launched by William Gray and
Co., West Hartlepool (Yard No. 262).
18.11.1882: Registered in the ownership
of Glover Brothers, London as
WORDSWORTH.
1898: Transferred to the Shakespear
Shipping Co. Ltd. (Glover Brothers,
managers), London.
1906: Register closed following sale
to Sociedad Anonima Balbenera de
Magallanes, Punta Arenas, Chile and

Wordsworth (1). [Roy Fenton collection]

renamed GOBERNADOR BORIES.

1914: Sold for demolition, but resold to the British Admiralty.

12.10.1914: Sunk as a block ship at Burra Sound, Scapa Flow.

19. SHAKESPEAR (1) 1885-1911
Iron

O.N. 91869   1,851g   1,163n

271.3 x 36.1 x 20.5 feet

T.3-cyl. by Thomas Richardson and Sons, Hartlepool; 160 NHP.

15.8.1885: Launched by J.L. Thompson and Sons, Sunderland (Yard No. 210).

16.9.1885: Registered in the ownership of Glover Brothers, London as SHAKESPEAR.

29.3.1898: Transferred to the Shakespear Shipping Co. Ltd. (Glover Brothers, managers), London.

24.11.1911: Sold to John Gaff and Co., Glasgow.

29.11.1911: Renamed PROTEAN.

21.1.1915: Register closed following sale to Damps. Akt. Faedreland (T. Halvorsen, manager), Bergen, Norway and renamed FAEDRELAND.

1916: Sold to Akties. Vestland (Johs. Leborg, manager), Aalesund, Norway and renamed LANGTIND.

1919: Sold to Akties. Furuland (S. Ugelstad and Co., managers), Brevik, Norway.

1920: Renamed BOGELUND.

1921: Renamed BOKLUND.

1925: Sold to Hans Sergo and Co., Reval, Estonia and renamed VENDLUS.

22.2.1927: Wrecked on Hermano Island, west coast of Sweden, whilst on a voyage from Immingham to Odense with a cargo of coal.

20. BYRON 1889-1912

O.N. 95519   2,095g   1,321n

275.0 x 38.2 x 20.6 feet

T.3-cyl. by John Dickinson, Sunderland; 250 NHP.

10.12.1888: Launched by J.L. Thompson and Sons, Sunderland (Yard No. 245).

1.1889: Completed.

11.1.1889: Registered in the ownership of Glover Brothers, London as BYRON.

29.3.1898: Transferred to the Shakespear Shipping Co. Ltd. (Glover Brothers, managers), London.

16.11.1912: Register closed on sale to Hijos de M. Barcena y Franco, Montevideo, Uruguay and renamed BARCENA.

1.6.1913: Foundered in the Atlantic whilst on a voyage from Bilbao to Cardiff with a cargo of iron ore.

21. TENNYSON 1894-1915

O.N. 104809   2,084g   1,315n

280.0 x 39.0 x 17.3 feet

T.3-cyl. by John Dickinson, Sunderland; 200 NHP, 900 IHP.

27.9.1894: Launched by J.L. Thompson and Sons Ltd., Sunderland (Yard No. 319).

11.1894: Completed.

3.11.1894: Registered in the ownership of Glover Brothers, London as TENNYSON.

29.3.1898: Transferred to the Shakespear Shipping Co. Ltd. (Glover Brothers, managers), London.

15.9.1915: Sold to the Colonial Coal and Shipping Co. Ltd. (John G. Scaramanga, manager), London.

27.10.1915: Renamed BRIGITTA.

4.12.1917: Mined and sunk six miles south west of the Nab Light Vessel whilst on a

Shakespear (1). *[Nigel Farrell collection]*

Byron. [J. and M. Clarkson collection]

Tennyson. [J. and M. Clarkson collection]

voyage from Barry to Dieppe with a cargo
of coal. The mine was laid by the German
submarine UC 63.
10.12.1917: Register closed.

22. MILTON (2) 1899-1924
O.N. 110120 3,267g 2,094n
325.0 x 44.5 x 26.5 feet
T.3-cyl. by Thomas Richardson and Sons,
Hartlepool; 265 NHP, 1,400 IHP, 10½ knots.
29.3.1899: Launched by J.L. Thompson and
Sons Ltd., Sunderland (Yard No. 371).

5.1899: Completed.
11.5.1899: Registered in the ownership of
the Shakespear Shipping Co. Ltd. (Glover
Brothers, managers), London as MILTON.
4.1924: Sold to A. Danielli, Greece and
renamed ARGONAFTIS.
1925: Sold to Madame H.I. Iossifoglu (A.
Frangopulo and Co., managers), Piraeus and
renamed ELENI S. IOSSIFOGLU.
1930: Broken up during the fourth quarter at
Genoa, where she had been laid up.

23. OVID (1) 1902-1917
O.N. 115901 4,159g 2,686n
345.0 x 48.5 x 25.9 feet
T.3-cyl. by Richardsons, Westgarth and Co.
Ltd., Hartlepool; 330 NHP, 1,700 IHP, 10½
knots.
16.8.1902: Launched by J.L. Thompson and
Sons Ltd., Sunderland (Yard No. 402).
2.10.1902: Registered in the ownership of
the Shakespear Shipping Co. Ltd. (Glover
Brothers, managers), London as OVID.
25.11.1917: Torpedoed and sunk by the

Milton (2). [J. and M. Clarkson collection]

German submarine UC 74 65 miles north east by half east of Suda Bay whilst on a voyage from Bombay to the Mediterranean with a cargo for the Admiralty.
15.2.1918: Register closed.

24. SHAKESPEAR (2) 1912-1926

O.N. 132692   3,466g   2,179n
342.0 x 49.1 x 22.9 feet
T.3-cyl. by Blair and Co. Ltd., Stockton-on-Tees; 294 NHP, 1,300 IHP, 9 knots.
3.2.1912: Launched by J.L. Thompson and Sons Ltd., Sunderland (Yard No. 490).
3.1912: Completed.
22.3.1912: Registered in the ownership of the Shakespear Shipping Co. Ltd. (Glover Brothers, managers), London.
7.1926: Sold to the Muko Kisen K.K., Mikage, Japan and renamed MIKAGE MARU No. 8.
29.6.1943: Sunk in collision in fog with the Japanese steamer NIKKO MARU (3,098/1919) 33 miles from Kamoisaki, Hokkaido in position 45.04 north by 142.03 east whilst on a voyage from Kamaishi to Toro, Sakhalin Island.

25. WORDSWORTH (2) 1915-1917

O.N. 136807   3,509g   2,203n
343.0 x 49.1 x 23.0 feet
T.3-cyl. by the Central Marine Engine Works, West Hartlepool, 299 NHP, 1,236 IHP, 9 knots.
3.2.1915: Launched by William Gray and Co. Ltd., West Hartlepool (Yard No. 854).
11.3.1915: Registered in the ownership of for the Shakespear Shipping Co. Ltd. (Glover Brothers, managers), London as WORDSWORTH.
11.3.1917: Captured by the German auxiliary cruiser WOLF west of the Chagos

The short-lived *Wordsworth* photographed from *Wolf*. Part of the crew can been seen pulling away from the *Wordsworth* in one of the ship's lifeboats. *[Nigel Farrell collection]*

Archipelago 680 miles east of Male in the Seychelles whilst on a voyage from Bassein to Delagoa Bay and London with a cargo of rice.
16.3.1917: Sunk by bombs.
2.11.1917: Register closed.

26. KEATS 1921-1933

O.N. 118743   4,336g   2,740n
380.5 x 47.5 x 19.0 feet
T. 3-cyl. by Gourlay Brothers and Co., Dundee; 415 NHP, 2,200 IHP, 12 knots.
3.2.1905: Launched by Gourlay Brothers and Co., Dundee (Yard No. 214).
2.3.1905: Registered in the ownership of the Den of Seaton Steamship Co. Ltd. (Charles Barrie and Co., managers), Dundee as DEN OF KELLY.
31.12.1905: Sold to the Hamburg Amerika Packetfahrt A.G., Hamburg, Germany and

renamed ILLYRIA.
8.1914: Interned at Las Palmas.
31.5.1919: Provisionally allocated to the French Government.
14.2.1920: Reallocated to Great Britain.
27.4.1921: Registered in the ownership of the Shakespear Shipping Co. Ltd. (Glover Brothers, managers), London.
17.5.1921: Renamed KEATS.
13.12.1930: Laid up at Sunderland.
27.12.1933: Arrived at Rosyth in tow from Sunderland for breaking up by Metal Industries Ltd.
16.5.1934: Work began.
14.9.1934: Register closed.

27. OVID (2) 1920-1933

O.N. 115865   3,928g 2,463 n
365.8 x 57.0 x 28.2 feet
T.3-cyl. by George Clark Ltd, Sunderland.

Keats. [Solomon/Roy Fenton collection]

Ovid (2) docking at Avonmouth. *[J. and M. Clarkson collection]*

14.5.1902: Launched by Sir James Laing and Sons, Sunderland (Yard No. 593).
30.7.1902: Registered in the ownership of Bucknall Nephews, London as CASILDA.
11.1908: Sold to the Société Les Affréteurs Réunis, Rouen, France and renamed CERES.
11.10.1913: Sold to the Deutsche Levante Linie, Hamburg, Germany and renamed LIPSOS.
8.1914: Seized at Antwerp.
9.10.1914: Recovered by Germany.
28.6.1919: Surrendered to the United Kingdom.

10.9.1919: Registered in the ownership of the Shipping Controller, London (Lyle Shipping Co. Ltd., Glasgow, managers).
24.12.1920: Acquired by the Shakespear Shipping Co. Ltd. (Glover Brothers, managers), London.
9.2.1921: Renamed OVID.
9.8.1931: Laid up at Swansea.
7.1933: Sold to O. Turito, Venice and renamed OVIDIO for delivery voyage to the breakers.
12.9.1933: Arrived at Genoa to be broken up by Alberto Trivero.

28. WORDSWORTH (3) 1920-1934
O.N. 143114 3,632g 2,305n
354.8 x 48.1 x 26.0 feet
T. 3-cyl. by the North Eastern Marine Engineering Co. Ltd., Newcastle-upon-Tyne; 1,950 IHP.
15.9.1905: Launched by William Dobson and Co., Newcastle-upon-Tyne (Yard No. 140).
3.11.1905: Completed for the Rhederei A.G. von 1896, Hamburg, Germany as ORISSA.
12.2.1906: Sold to the Syndikats Rhederei G.m.b.H., Hamburg, and renamed ELBE.

Ovid (2) at Cape Town, South Africa. *[Solomon/Roy Fenton collection]*

Wordsworth (2). [Roy Fenton collection]

30.3.1919: Surrendered to the United Kingdom.
11.4.1919: Registered in the ownership of the Shipping Controller (R. Gordon and Co., managers), London.
25.1.1921: Acquired by the Shakespear Shipping Co. Ltd. (Glover Brothers, managers), London.
7.3.1921: Renamed WORDSWORTH.
8.8.1931: Laid up on the Tyne.
3.4.1934: Arrived at Rosyth to be broken up by Metal Industries Ltd.
25.4.1934: Breaking up began at Charlestown, Fife.
21.6.1934: Register closed.

29. SHELLEY (2) 1921-1934
O.N. 145191 4,476g 2,733n
399.7 x 52.8 x 23.3 feet
Q.4-cyl. by J.C. Tecklenborg A.G., Wesermunde; 2,500 IHP, 10 knots.
27.7.1911: Launched by J.C. Tecklenborg

A.G., Wesermunde (Yard No. 241).
20.9.1911: Completed for the Hamburg Amerika Packetfahrt A.G., Hamburg, Germany as ALTMARK.
28.3.1919: Left Stettin for Brest.
17.4.1919: Surrendered to the French Government but transferred to the United Kingdon.
27.4.1921: Registered in the ownership of the Board of Trade, London.
27.4.1921: Acquired by the Shakespear Shipping Co. Ltd. (Glover Brothers, managers), London.
28.4.1921: Renamed SHELLEY.
5.7.1934: Arrived at Blyth to be broken up by Hughes Bolckow Shipbreaking Co. Ltd.
19.7.1934: Register closed.

30. NOVGOROD 1923
O.N. 142364 4,866g 3,368n
390.0 x 50.7 x 28.0 feet
T.3-cyl. by Swan, Hunter and Wigham

Richardson, Newcastle-upon-Tyne; 427 NHP, 11.5 knots.
15.3.1913: Launched by Sir James Laing and Sons Ltd, Sunderland (Yard No. 641) for the Russian Volunteer Fleet Association, Odessa, Russia as NOVGOROD.
1918: Taken over by the Shipping Controller (Royal Mail Steam Packet Company, managers), London.
3.1923: Returned to the Russian Volunteer Fleet Association, after being laid up at Milford Haven since 9.1921.
4.1923: Acquired at auction by Glover Brothers, London.
5.1923: Resold to the William Thomas Shipping Co. Ltd. (Robert J. Thomas and Co., managers), Liverpool and renamed CAMBRIAN DUCHESS.
1931: Sold to A/S Skjold (V. Skogland, manager), Haugesund, Norway and renamed VALHALL.
11.1932: Sold to the Moller Line Ltd.

The German-built *Shelley* (2) off Greenhithe on the Thames on 3rd June 1933. *[R.A. Snook/Roy Fenton collection]*

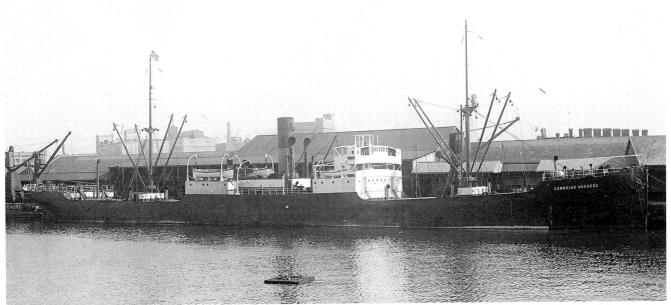

The *Novgorod* was bought at auction in April 1923. Resold the following month her new owners renamed her *Cambrian Duchess* (above). *[J. and M. Clarkon collection]*

(Moller and Co., managers), Shanghai (British flag).
1933: Renamed LILIAN MOLLER.
18.11.1940: Torpedoed and sunk with all hands by the Italian submarine MAGGIONE FRANCESCO BARACCA 300 miles west of Ireland in position 52.57 north by 18.05 west whilst on a voyage from Calcutta to London via Cape Town.

31. MILTON (3) 1924-1932
O.N. 118700   3,760g 2,322n
365.0 x 47.3 x 17.9 feet
T.3-cyl. by Dunsmuir and Jackson, Glasgow; 390 NHP, 2,000 IHP, 11½ knots.
24.11.1904: Launched by Charles Connell and Co., Scotstoun, Glasgow (Yard No. 290).
28.12.1904: Registered in the ownership of James Warrack and Co., Leith as MONTROSE.
15.7.1919: Sold to the Australind Steam Shipping Co. Ltd. (Trinder, Anderson and Co., managers), London.
10.4.1924: Acquired by the Shakespear Shipping Co. Ltd. (Glover Brothers, managers), London.
2.5.1924: Renamed MILTON.
2.11.1932: Register closed following sale to Italian shipbreakers.
24.11.1932: Arrived Genoa having been renamed MILTONIA for the delivery voyage.

32. SPENSER 1924-1934
O.N. 118701   3,779g 2,342n
365.0 x 47.4 x 17.9 feet
T.3-cyl. by Dunsmuir and Jackson, Glasgow.
23.12.1904: Launched by Charles Connell and Co., Scotstoun, Glasgow (Yard No. 291).
8.2.1905: Registered in the ownership of

Milton (3). *[William Schell]*

Milton (3) at Cape Town. *[Solomon/Roy Fenton collection]*

John Warrack and Co., Leith as ERROLL.
25.7.1919: Sold to the Australind Steam
Shipping Co. Ltd. (Trinder, Anderson and
Co., managers), London.
31.3.1924: Acquired by the Shakespear
Shipping Co. Ltd. (Glover Brothers,
managers), London.
3.4.1924: Renamed SPENSER.
31.3.1934: Arrived at Rosyth to be broken
up by Metal Industries Ltd.
25.4.1934: Work began.
21.6.1934: Register closed.

33. SHAKESPEAR (3) 1926-1940
O.N. 149747 5,029g 3,154n
407.0 x 53.5 x 26.7 feet.
T.3-cyl. by David Rowan and Co. Ltd.,
Govan; 531 NHP, 2,450 IHP, 11 knots.
1926: Launched by R. Duncan and Co. Ltd.,
Port Glasgow (Yard No. 374).
5.11.1926: Registered in the ownership
of the Shakespear Shipping Co. Ltd.

Two views of *Spenser.* [Above: Solomon/George Scott collection, below: Newall Dunn collection]

Shakespear (3). *[Collection of the late W.A. Laxon]*

(Glover Brothers, managers), London as SHAKESPEAR.

12.1940: Sold to the South American Saint Line Ltd., Cardiff, but was sunk before she could be handed over to the management of B. and S. Shipping Co. Ltd.

5.1.1941: Sunk by gunfire from the Italian submarine COMMANDANTE ALFREDO CAPPELLINI east of the Cape Verde Islands in position 18.05 north by 21.10 west whilst on a voyage from Barry to Suez and Alexandria with coal and military stores..

15.7.1941: Register closed.

34. CHAUCER 1929-1940
O.N. 161227   5,792g 3,629n
420.0 x 57.0 x 28.2 feet
T.3-cyl. by David Rowan and Co. Ltd., Govan; 557 NHP, 2,600 IHP, 11 knots.

1929: Launched by R. Duncan and Co. Ltd., Port Glasgow (Yard No. 389).

16.4.1929: Registered in the ownership of the Shakespear Shipping Co. Ltd. (Glover Brothers, managers), London as CHAUCER.

14.4.1941: Manager became Richard G.M. Street, Cardiff.

12.1940: Managers became the South American Saint Line Ltd., Cardiff following their acquisition of the owning company.

29.7.1941: Sunk by gunfire from the German auxiliary cruiser ORION in the South Atlantic in position 16.46 north by 38.01 west whilst on a voyage from Middlesbrough to Buenos Aires in ballast.

22.10.1941: Register closed.

Chaucer. [J. and M. Clarkson collection]

Managed ships

Sir Ernest Glover's work with the Shipping Controller led to him being named as manager of a large number of ships either built for or taken over by the Shipping Controller during and after the First World War, whilst his brother John H. Glover also managed his share of vessels. The ships managed by both brothers are listed below, in chronological order of the date management commenced, where this is known. In many cases, Sir Ernest's involvement was probably minimal. Formal registration of a ship usually required an individual to be named as manager. However, as many ships were managed only for the short period between completion or repair and sale to a commercial owner, during which time they are unlikely to have traded, their management was not onerous.

There is considerable disagreement between sources as to which ships were managed by Sir Ernest Glover. For a number of vessels listed under his name in contemporary editions of 'Lloyd's Confidential Index' and under Glover Brothers in 'Lloyd's Register', management cannot be confirmed from official registration documents (filed in Class BT110 in the National Archives). This includes all those owned by the Admiralty, for whom the Secretary to the Board is usually listed as manager, and several ships managed for the Shipping Controller or its successor the Board of Trade which ships – contrary to convention – have no manager assigned in registration papers. It has been decided to include all vessels for which there is some evidence of

management by a Glover brother, but it should be noted that management cannot be confirmed from registration papers in the case of all the Admiralty ships and of the *Mellon, Sylvia Victoria, Willdomino,* and *Trialos.* The former German steamer *Pangani* (5,735/1915) is also listed under Glovers in 'Lloyd's Confidential Index' for June 1919, but her registration documents show her to be managed by Glen Line, and a clerical error has probably assigned her to Glover who appears on the same page as Glen Line.

In several cases ships built for the Shipping Controller appear to have been registered before completion, and even in some cases before launch. The *War Glory,* for instance, was registered on 1st April 1920, and was launched at Chepstow on 21st April with her machinery installed and ran trials the same day.

The managed vessels are a fascinating bunch, ranging from wooden cargo ships built in Canada through paddle steamers and hopper barges to the substantial passenger ship *Asturias* and many conventional cargo ships, and outnumber the ships which Glover Brothers actually owned. If this was not enough, at least 58 of the 64 ferro-concrete tugs and barges built during and just after the First World war were also put under Glover management. These are not listed here.

The managed fleets listed also include ships under commercial management and those managed for the British government during the Second World War.

Managed for the Admiralty

M1. EMIL 1914-1915
O.N. 118424 2,991g 1,954n
325.5 x 47.0 x 22.0 feet
T.3-cyl. by Richardsons, Westgarth and Co. Ltd., Sunderland; 281 NHP.
20.2.1904: Launched by the Northumberland Shipbuilding Co. Ltd., Howdon-on-Tyne (Yard No. 113).
30.4.1904: Registered in the ownership of Richard H. Holman, London as FURTOR. She had been laid down as CRANFORD.
28.7.1908: Sold to the Woodgrove Steam Shipping Co. Ltd. and F.A. Woodruff and Co. Ltd., Cardiff.
20.4.1909: Sold by mortgagee in possession, Richard H. Holman, to Cyril H. Walton (Richard H. Holman, manager), London.
13.3.1912: 38/64 shares sold to Richard H. Holman, London.
18.10.1913: Sold to E.R. Retzlaff, Stettin, Germany and renamed EMIL.
16.6.1914: Sold to Dampfschiffs Rhederie Union, Hamburg, Germany and renamed BRAILA.
1.8.1914: Seized on arrival at Alexandria by the Admiralty, London.
23.2.1915: Registered in the ownership of the Admiralty (Glover Brothers, managers), London as EMIL.
21.9.1915: Sold to the Aquarius Steamship Co. Ltd. (Moller and Co., managers), London.
3.11.1915: Renamed AQUARIUS.
2.7.1917: Transferred to the Zodiac Shipping Co. Ltd. (Moller and Co., managers), London.
6.9.1918: Sold to Watkin J. Williams, Cardiff.
10.11.1918: Sunk in collision with an unknown steamer 45 miles off Corfu in position 39.11 north by 19.21 east whilst on a voyage from Penarth to Corfu with a cargo of coal.
17.12.1918: Register closed.

M2. ROSTOCK 1914-1916
O.N. 139173 4,972g 2,884n
391.0 x 47.8 x 21.6 feet
Q.4 cyl. by Flensburger Schiffsbau Gesellschaft, Flensburg; 810 NHP.
16.10.1901: Launched by the Flensburger Schiffsbau Gesellschaft, Flensburg (Yard No. 208) for the Deutsche Australische Dampfschiffs Gesellschaft Hamburg, Germany as ROSTOCK.
5.8.1914: Seized at Port Said by the Admiralty, London.
2.1915: Condemned in prize (Glover Brothers, managers).
7.1916: Management transferred to G. Heyn and Sons, Belfast.
28.11.1916: Registered in ownership of the Admiralty, London as HUNTSMOOR.
1918: Management transferred to Jenkins Brothers, Cardiff.
20.2.1918: Torpedoed and sunk by the German submarine UB 40, 23 miles south

Rostock in the Suez Canal. *[Newall Dunn collection]*

by half west from the Owers Light Vessel whilst on a voyage from Le Havre to Southampton in ballast.
28.11.1916: Register closed.

M3. ACHAIA 1915-1916
O.N. 136813 2,733g 1,729n
291.6 x 43.9 x 16.6 feet
T.3-cyl. by A.G. 'Neptun', Rostock, Germany; 192 NHP.
30.1.1907: Launched by A.G. 'Neptun', Rostock (Yard No. 260).
24.3.1907: Completed for the Bremer Dampferlinie 'Atlas' m.b.H., Bremen, Germany as ACHAIA.
31.12.1910: Transferred to the Deutsche Levante Linie, Hamburg, Germany.
3.8.1914: Seized at Alexandria by the Admiralty.
6.2.1915: Condemned in prize
13.3.1915: Registered in the ownership of the Admiralty (Glover Brothers, managers), London.
It was announced that she was to be renamed ALEXANDRIA, but this was never carried out.
7.9.1916: Mined and sunk 300 yards east north east of the entrance to Oran whilst on a voyage from Karachi to Cardiff with a cargo of wheat. The mine had been laid that day by the German submarine U 72.
20.12.1916: Register closed.

M4. RAVENROCK 1919-1922
O.N. 139031 4,678g 2,893n
390.4 x 51.5 x 27.5 feet
T. 3-cyl. by Swan, Hunter and Wigham Richardson Ltd., Newcastle-upon-Tyne; 492 NHP, 11 knots.
12.1903: Completed by Swan, Hunter and Wigham Richardson Ltd., Newcastle-upon-Tyne (Yard No. 407) for Deutsche Dampfschiffs Gesellschaft 'Hansa', Bremen, Germany as RABENFELS.
8.1914: Seized at Port Said by the Admiralty.

26.5.1915: Registered in the ownership of the Admiralty (Grahams and Co., managers), London as RABENFELS.
12.6.1915: Commissioned in the Royal Navy as a seaplane carrier, armed with one 12-pounder gun.
8.1915: Renamed RAVEN II. Subsequently served in the eastern Mediterranean.
5.4.1918: Renamed RAVENROCK and subsequently used under the Red Ensign as a store carrier, collier and troop transport.
1919: Glover Brothers became managers.
2.1.1922: Registered in the ownership of the Board of Trade, London.
12.3.1923: Sold to British Dominions Steamship Co. Ltd. (Smith, Pritchard and Co., managers), London.
13.6.1924: Register closed on sale to Kabafuto Kisen K.K., Tokyo, Japan and renamed HEIYEI MARU No. 7.
1934: Sold to Inui Kisen K.K., Tokyo.
1938: Name rendered as HEIEI MARU No. 7.
1940: Renamed KENEI MARU.
12.1.1945: Sunk by United States Navy air attack in the Saigon River in position 10.46 north by 106.42 east.

Managed for the Shipping Controller/Board of Trade

M5. DAGHILD 1916-1917
O.N. 139168 8,000g, 4,862n
455.0 x 58.1 x 33.2 feet
T.3 cyl by William Doxford and Sons Ltd., Sunderland; 570 NHP, 3,000 IHP, 11 knots.
26.8.1916: Launched by William Doxford and Sons Ltd., Sunderland (Yard No. 475) for A/S Daghild (John P. Pedersen and Søn, managers), Christiania, Norway.
15.11.1916: Registered in the ownership of John H. Glover, London as DAGHILD. This may have been on behalf of the Shipping Controller, London.
20.6.1917: Sold to G. Heyn and Sons, Belfast.

The Turret steamer *Clan Graham* came into the ownership of the Shipping Controller and under Glover management after she had been damaged by a torpedo in the Mediterranean and war risk insurance paid out to her owners. *[J. and M. Clarkson collection]*

2.11.1917: Registered in the ownership of the Shipping Controller, London (Jenkins Brothers, Cardiff, managers).

20.11.1922: Register closed following return to A/S Daghild (John P. Pederson & Søn), Christiania.

25.6.1923: Registered in the ownership of the Daghild Canadian Steamship Co. Ltd., Halifax, Nova Scotia (Francis J. Bassett, London, manager).

1926: Managers became The Dominion Shipping Co. Ltd. and registry transferred to London.

17.2.1934: Sold to the Tenax Steamship Co. Ltd. (Muir, Young Ltd., managers), London.

1.1937: Sold to Wilhelm Kunstmann, Stettin, Germany and renamed KATHARINA DOROTHEA FRITZEN.

1938: Sold to John Fritzen and Sohn vormals W. Kunstmann O.H.G., Hamburg, Germany.

4.6.1942: Mined and sunk off Borkum.

M6. GUDRUN 1917-1920

O.N. 143106 4,183g 2,667n
346.9 x 49.5 x 29.3 feet
T.3-cyl. by John Dickinson and Sons Ltd., Sunderland; 350 NHP, 1,800 IHP, 10.5 knots.

14.3.1907: Launched by J.L. Thompson and Sons Ltd., Sunderland (Yard No. 451) for Jacob R. Olsen, Bergen, Norway as EIR.

1915: Sold to A/S Eir (I.A. Christensen, manager), Christiania, Norway and renamed GUDRUN.

About 1917: To Dampfschiffs Gesellschaft 'Stettin', Stettin, Germany and renamed GUDRUN

10.4.1917: Registered in the ownership of the Shipping Controller (John H. Glover, manager), London.

10.12.1920: Sold to the Eirene Steamship Co. Ltd. (George P. Sechiari, manager), London.

28.1.1921: Renamed EIRENE.

5.11.1925: Sold to the Wyn Shipping Co. Ltd. (William A. Young and Co., managers), London.

18.1.1926: Renamed WYNCOTE.

14.9.1931: Register closed on sale to M. Querci, Genoa, Italy and renamed COLLAZZI.

21.11.1935: Stranded in Novorossisk Roads after dragging her anchor and abandoned to the Soviet authorities.

1939: Following repair, recommissioned for Chermorskoye g.m.p., Odessa as VOLOCHAYEVKA

18.8.1941: Scuttled at Kherson.

1942: Raised by the Germans and recommissioned for the Schwarzmeer Schiffart G.m.b.H., Hamburg as THEODERICH.

12.11.1943: Torpedoed by the Soviet submarine M 111 in position 45.52 north by 30.20 east and beached.

22.11.1943: After refloating, mined and sunk again 10 miles west of Ochkov while under tow to Odessa.

M7. CLAN GRAHAM 1918-1919

Turret
O.N. 124211 5,213g 3,289n
400.2 x 52.1 x 27.5 feet
T. 3-cyl. by William Doxford and Sons Ltd., Sunderland; 504 NHP, 2,800 IHP, 11 knots.
1919: T.3-cyl. made by Mackie and Baxter Ltd., Glasgow in 1917; 557 NHP.

24.7.1907: Launched by William Doxford and Sons Ltd., Sunderland (Yard No. 331).

20.8.1907: Registered in the ownership of The Clan Line Steamers Ltd. (Cayzer, Irvine and Co. Ltd.), Glasgow as CLAN GRAHAM.

10.1907: Completed.

17.2.1909: Transferred to Sir Charles W. Cayzer.

23.3.1915: Transferred to The Clan Line Steamers Ltd. (Cayzer, Irvine and Co. Ltd.), Glasgow.

4.3.1918: Torpedoed by the German submarine UC 74 in Kassos Strait, 15 miles south south east of Cape Sidero, whilst on a voyage from Avonmouth to Port Said in ballast, but although abandoned was reboarded and towed into Mudros.

2.10.1918: Registered in the ownership of the Shipping Controller (Sir Ernest W. Glover, manager), London.

6.8.1919: Resold to The Clan Line Steamers Ltd. (Cayzer, Irvine and Co. Ltd.), London and towed to Rotterdam for repair and fitting a new engine.

11.11.1920: Collided with the steamer CHOLMLEY (1,368/1880) in the Wielingen and beached on Rommelan Bank whilst on a voyage from Chittagong and London to Antwerp with general cargo.

13.11.1920: Caught fire and heavily damaged.

25.11.1920: Refloated and later declared a constructive total loss.

21.12.1922: Register closed on sale to shipbreakers.

1923: Broken up by Produits Métallurgiques S.A. at Antwerp during the first quarter.

M8. ASTURIAS 1918-1919
O.N. 124669 12,002g 7,509n
520.3 x 62.3 x 31.85 feet
Q. 4-cyl. by Harland and Wolff Ltd.,
Belfast; 1,385 NHP, 7,000 IHP, 16½ knots.
1.1908: Completed by Harland and Wolff
Ltd., Belfast (Yard No. 388).
6.1.1908: Registered in the ownership of
the Royal Mail Steam Packet Company,
London as ASTURIAS.
21.3.1917: Torpedoed by the German
submarine UC 66 five miles south of Start
Point, while serving as a hospital ship.
Beached and subsequently salved.
2.11.1918: Registered in the ownership
of the Shipping Controller (Sir Ernest W.
Glover, manager), London.
15.12.1919: Sold to the Royal Mail Steam
Packet Company, London.
7.5.1923: Renamed ARCADIAN.
12.10.1932: Transferred to Royal Mail
Lines Ltd., London.
11.2.1933: Sold to Galbraith Pembroke and
Co. Ltd., London.
18.4.1933: Arrived at Osaka to be broken up
16.5.1933: Register closed.

M9. WAR FAITH 1918-1919
O.N. 142734 4,342g 2,598n
380.0 x 49.2 x 26.7 feet
T.3-cyl. by Canadian Vickers Ltd., Montreal,
Quebec, Canada; 266 NHP, 2,400 IHP, 11.25
knots.
10.1918: Launched by Canadian Vickers
Ltd., Montreal, Quebec (Yard No. 64).
5.12.1918: Registered in the ownership of
the Shipping Controller (John H. Glover,
manager), London as WAR FAITH.
14.10.1919: Sold to the British Africa
Shipping and Coaling Co. Ltd., Cape Town
(Mitchell, Cotts and Co., London, managers).
29.10.1919: Renamed CAPE PREMIER.
17.3.1921: Sold to the Adelaide Steam Ship
Co. Ltd., Adelaide.
23.6.1921: Renamed BARUNGA.
2.1935: Sold to V.K. Song, Tsingtao, China
and renamed SHING HO.
1938: Sold to the Miyachi Kisen K.K., Kobe,
Japan and renamed SEIZAN MARU.
23.2.1944: Bombed and sunk by United
States carrier-based aircraft off Saipan in
position 15.00 north by 145.30 east.

M10. WAR JOY 1919
O.N. 142779 4,331g 2,637n
381.0 x 49.3 x 26.9 feet
T.3-cyl. by Canadian Vickers Ltd.,
Montreal, Quebec, Canada; 266 NHP, 2,450
IHP, 11.25 knots.
10.1918: Launched by Canadian Vickers
Ltd., Montreal, Quebec (Yard No. 65).
7.2.1919: Registered in the ownership of
the Shipping Controller (Ernest W. Glover,
managers), London as WAR JOY.
24.7.1919: Register closed on sale to La
Veloce Navigazione Italiana à Vapeur,
Genoa, Italy and renamed VITTORIO
VENETO.
1925: Sold to Navigazione Generale
Italiana, Genoa

The hospital ship *Asturias*, managed after being damaged by a torpedo. *[J. and M. Clarkson collection]*

1929: Sold to the Società Anonima di
Navigazione 'La Camogliese', Genoa.
1941: Seized by Argentina, owners became
Flota Mercante del Estado, Buenos Aires,
and renamed RIO GUALEGUAY.
1946: Returned to the Società Anonima di
Navigazione 'La Camogliese', Genoa and
renamed VITTORIO VENETO.
10.3.1959: Arrived at Spezia to be broken
up by Cantiere Navale Santa Maria.
4.1959: Work began.

M11. WAR ERIE 1919 Wood
O.N. 143052 2,291g 1,389n
250.0 x 43.3 x 22.6 feet
T.3-cyl. by the Dominion Bridge Co.,
Lachine, Quebec, Canada; 147 NHP, 1,000
IHP, 9 knots.
7.1918: Launched by Fraser, Brace and Co.
Ltd., Montreal, Quebec (Yard No. 9).
15.3.1919: Registered in the ownership
of the Shipping Controller (Sir Ernest W.
Glover, manager), London as WAR ERIE.
19.8.1919: Register closed on sale to Lloyd
Royal Belge S.A., Antwerp, Belgium and
renamed SICILIER.
5.1920: Sold to G.D. Caravagno, Savona,
Italy and renamed BACICIN SERRA.
29.9.1925: Sprang a leak and foundered
25 miles off Gozo Lighthouse whilst on a
voyage from Sfax to Venice.

M12. QUITO 1919
O.N. 111250 3,358g 2,152n
330.7 x 45.7 x 23.9 feet
T. 3-cyl. by Dunsmuir and Jackson, Govan;
300 NHP, 1,600 IHP, 9.5 knots.
4.1900: Completed by William Hamilton
and Co., Port Glasgow (Yard No. 152).
2.4.1900: Registered in the ownership of
Ocean Navigation Co. Ltd. (Andrew Weir
and Co., managers), Glasgow as QUITO.
20.6.1913: Transferred to Bank Line
Ltd. (Andrew Weir and Co., managers),
Glasgow.
15.9.1915: Sold to the Hopeside Steam
Shipping Co. Ltd. (Charlton, McAllum and
Co., managers), Newcastle-upon-Tyne.
26.11.1915: Sold to Tom Lewis, Cardiff.
4.1.1916: Transferred to the Lewis Steam

Ship Co. Ltd. (Tom Lewis, manager),
Cardiff.
19.3.1919: Registered in the ownership
of the Shipping Controller (Sir Ernest W.
Glover, manager), London.
14.5.1919: Sold to the Dean Shipping
Co. Ltd. (E.I. Harris and Co., managers),
Cardiff.
8.8.1922: Struck submerged wreckage and
sank, 150 miles east of Culvercoats, whilst
on a voyage from Luleå to Middlesbrough
with a cargo of iron ore.
19.9.1922: Register closed.

M13. TENERIFFE 1919-1920
O.N. 90019 1,800g 1,148n
301.0 x 36.0 x 19.8 feet
C. 2-cyl. by Harland and Wolff, Belfast; 200
NHP.
2.1885: Launched by Harland and Wolff,
Belfast (Yard No. 178).
4.4.1885: Registered in the ownership of
British and African Steam Navigation Co.
Ltd. (Elder, Dempster and Co., managers),
Glasgow as TENERIFFE.
13.12.1900: Transferred to British and
African Steam Navigation Co. (1900) Ltd.
(Elder, Dempster and Co., managers),
Liverpool.
17.2.1909: Transferred to the British and
African Steam Navigation Co. Ltd. (Elder,
Dempster and Co., managers), Liverpool.
6.1918: Purchased by The Admiralty for
possible use as a blockship.
27.3.1919: Registered in the ownership
of the Shipping Controller (Sir Ernest W.
Glover, manager), London.
23.1.1920: Sold to George M. Wheater,
Newcastle-upon-Tyne.
7.5.1920: Register closed on sale to
Compania Maritima Arenas, Bilbao, Spain
and renamed ZUGATZARTE.
17.3.1921: Wrecked at Punta Galea, near
Bilbao, whilst on a voyage from Bilbao to
Glasgow with a cargo of iron ore.

M14. EICHSFELD 1919-1920
O.N. 143113 4,552g 2,938n
370.5 x 46.6 x 27.2 feet
Q.4 cyl. by David Rowan and Sons,

Glasgow; 1,650 IHP.

22.8.1896: Launched by Charles Connell and Co., Glasgow (Yard No. 228).

30.10.1896: Completed for A.G. Deutsche Dampfschiffs Gesellschaft, Hamburg, Germany as AMASIS.

17.5.1913: Sold to Continentale Rhederei A.G., Hamburg.

10.6.1913: Renamed EICHSFELD.

4.4.1919: Surrendered to the British Government.

11.4.1919: Registered in the ownership of the Shipping Controller (John H. Glover, manager), London.

5.10.1920: Sold to the Service of Maritime Transport, Greek Government, Piraeus, Greece.

23.10.1920: Register closed.

1922: Renamed ARCHIPELAGOS.

12.1931: Broken up at Fiume.

M15. WAR HURON 1919-1920 Wood

O.N. 143124 2,284g 1,384n

250.1 x 43.6 x 22.6 feet

T.3-cyl. by the Canadian Ingersoll Rand Company, Sherbrooke, Quebec, Canada; 147 NHP, 1,000 IHP, 9 knots.

7.1918: Launched by Fraser, Brace and Company, Montreal, Quebec (Yard No. 8).

14.4.1919: Registered in the ownership of the Shipping Controller (John H. Glover, manager), London as WAR HURON.

5.2.1920: Register closed on sale to Fratelli Accame, Genoa, Italy and renamed DINA ACCAME.

2.8.1923: Caught fire at Genoa.

3.8.1923: Fire extinguished, but broke out again and the ship foundered. Raised, sold and broken up at Genoa.

M16. WAR GASPE 1919-1920 Wood

O.N. 143143 2,269g 1,368n

250.6 x 43.5 x 22.5 feet

T.3-cyl. by the Robb Engineering Co. Ltd., Amherst, Nova Scotia, Canada; 147 NHP, 1,000 IHP, 9 knots.

7.1918: Launched by Quinlan and Robertson, Montreal, Quebec (Yard No. 3).

19.4.1919: Registered in the ownership of the Shipping Controller (John H. Glover, manager), London as WAR GASPE.

4.2.1920: Register closed on sale to Credito Industriale de Venezia (Società Esercizi, manager), Venice, Italy and renamed ISSORIA.

16.8.1922: Caught fire at Venice and scuttled to extinguish the flames.

11.10.1922: Refloated, condemned and broken up at Venice.

M17. WAR MOHAWK 1919-1920

Wood

O.N. 143191 2,267g 1,329n

249.7 x 43.5 x 22.7 feet

T.3-cyl. by International Engineering Company, Amherst, Nova Scotia, Canada; 147 NHP, 1,000 knots, 9 knots.

5.1918: Launched by Quinlan and Robertson Ltd., Montreal, Quebec (Yard No. 1).

Eichsfeld. {Kevin J. O'Donoghue collection]

5.5.1919: Registered in the ownership of the Shipping Controller (John H. Glover, manager), London as WAR MOHAWK.

15.1.1920: Sold to the Società Italiana di Armamento e di Navigazione, Rome, Italy and renamed IDRA.

21.1.1920: Register closed.

1923: Broken up in Italy during the fourth quarter.

M18. SCARLET TOWER 1919

O.N. 127078 3,187g 2,044n

334.0 x 48.0 x 22.3 feet

T. 3-cyl. by A. Rodger and Co., Govan; 300 NHP, 1,500 IHP, 9 knots.

4.1910: Completed by A. Rodger and Co., Port Glasgow (Yard No. 412).

19.4.1910: Registered in the ownership of the Beaver Shipping Co. Ltd. (Palin, Evans and Co., managers), Bristol as NIGRETIA.

7.12.1916: Sold to the Limerick Steam Ship Co. Ltd., Limerick.

18.12.1916: Renamed SCARLET TOWER.

22.5.1919: Register closed on sale to T. H. Skogland & Søn A/S, Haugesund, Norway and renamed TORLAK SKOGLAND.

30.5.1919: Registered in the ownership

of the Shipping Controller (Sir Ernest W. Glover, manager), London as SCARLET TOWER.

9.8.1919: Register closed on return to T. H. Skogland & Søn A/S, Haugesund, Norway and renamed TORLAK SKOGLAND.

1924: Transferred to A/S Skoglands Linje (T. H. Skogland & Søn A/S, managers), Haugesund.

1925: Transferred to A/S Skoglands Rederi (T. H. Skogland & Søn A/S, managers), Haugesund.

1930: Transferred to A/S Tjømø (A. H. Torbjornsen), Tønsberg, Norway and renamed TJØMØ.

1933: Sold to Kalkavan Zade Riza ve Mahdumu Ismail (Vapur Sirketi), Istanbul, Turkey and renamed METE.

1939: Owners became Kalkavanoglu Mehmet Riza ve Madhumu Ismail Vapur Sirketi, Istanbul.

1941: Owners became Kalkavan Riza ve Oglu Ismail Vapurculuk Sirketi, Istanbul.

1952: Owners became Ismail ve Orhan Kalkavan Vapurculuk Ltd. Sirketi, Istanbul.

15.5.1961: Demolition began by Ismail ve Orhan Kalkavan at Halic, Istanbul.

Nigretia in Bristol ownership at Avonmouth. She later became Scarlet Tower, as which she was managed by Glovers for the Shipping Controller. [Roy Fenton collection]

M19. AMMON 1919-1920

O.N. 143291 7,233g 4,448n
472.0 x 60.8 x 28.6 feet
T.3-cyl. by the Flensburger Schiffbau
Gesellschaft, Flensburg, Germany; 686
NHP, 3,600 IHP, 12 knots
16.5.1914: Launched by the Flensburger
Schiffbau Gesellschaft, Flensburg (Yard No.
339).
6.7.1914: Completed for the Deutsche
Dampschiffs Gesellschaft Kosmos,
Hamburg, Germany as AMMON.
7.10.1915: Requisitioned by the German
navy as a mine sweeper.
29.2.1919: Returned to owner.
1919: Surrendered to the Allied Control
Commission.
14.6.1919: Registered in the ownership of
the Shipping Controller (John H. Glover,
manager), London.
20.9.1920: Delivered to the United
Kingdom.
9.12.1920: Sold to the Hain Steamship Co.
Ltd. (Edward Hain and Son, managers), St
Ives.
28.1.1921: Renamed TREWINNARD.
27.8.1924: Sold to the Federal Steam
Navigation Co. Ltd. (New Zealand Shipping
Co. Ltd., managers), London.
2.9.1924: Renamed PAKIPAKI.
10.1933: Sold to Ditta Luigi Pittaluga
Vapori, Genoa, Italy for breaking up.
3.11.1933: Register closed.
15.12.1933: Arrived at Genoa and broken
up during 1934.

M20. DUCHESS OF YORK 1919-1921 Paddle

O.N. 106903 302g 127n
185.5 x 22.1 x 8.65 feet
C. 2-cyl. by Barclay, Curle and Co. Ltd.,
Whiteinch, Glasgow; 140 NHP, 800 IHP, 14
knots.
6.1896: Completed by Barclay, Curle and
Co. Ltd., Whiteinch, Glasgow (Yard No.
406).
4.7.1896: Registered in the ownership of the
Southampton, Isle of Wight and South of
England Royal Mail Steam Packet Co. Ltd.,
Southampton as DUCHESS OF YORK.
5.1916: Requisitioned by the Admiralty as
an auxiliary patrol vessel.
24.6.1919: Acquired by the Admiralty.
30.6.1919: Registered in the ownership
of the Shipping Controller (Sir Ernest W.
Glover, manager), London.
6.12.1921: Resold to the Southampton, Isle
of Wight and South of England Royal Mail
Steam Packet Co. Ltd., Southampton.
3.7.1928: Renamed DUCHESS OF
CORNWALL.
1950: Broken up at Northam by Pollock
Brown and Co.
14.6.1950: Register closed.

M21. WAR SENECA 1919-1920 Wood

O.N. 143319 2,172g 1,274n
250.3 x 43.4 x 22.6 feet
T. 3-cyl. by Canadian Allis Chalmers
Company, Toronto, Canada; 147 NHP,

Pakipaki in New Zealand ownership. As *Ammon* she had been managed by Glovers.*[Roy Fenton collection]*

1,000 IHP, 9 knots.
6.1918: Launched by Quinlan and
Robertson Ltd., Montreal, Quebec, Canada
(Yard No. 2).
8.7.1919: Registered in the ownership of
the Shipping Controller (John H. Glover,
manager), London as WAR SENECA.
3.1.1920: Register closed on sale to Lloyd
Adriatico, Venice, Italy and renamed
ASIAGO.
1922: Sold to 'Carnaro' Società di
Navigazione, Venice, Italy.
12.1923: Broken up at Trieste during the
first quarter by Ernesto Breda.

M22. WAR OTTAWA 1919-1920 Wood

O.N. 143362 2,305g 1,390n
250.6 x 43.8 x 22.7 feet
T.3-cyl. by J. McDougall Ironworks Ltd.,
Montreal, Quebec, Canada; 147 NHP, 1,000
IHP, 9 knots.
7.1918: Launched by Fraser, Brace and Co.
Ltd., Montreal, Quebec (Yard No. 10).
28.7.1919: Registered in the ownership of
the Shipping Controller (John H. Glover,
manager), London as WAR OTTAWA.
17.3.1920: Register closed on sale to

Credito Industriale di Venezia (Società
Esercizi Marittimi), Venice, Italy and
renamed VIBILIA
1921: Sold to Giulia Società Anonima di
Armamento, Trieste, Italy.
1923: Sold to Dott. G. Calzavara, Venice,
Italy.
1924: Broken up in Italy during first quarter.

M23. WAR NIAGARA 1919 Wood

O.N. 143363 2,261g 1,394n
250.3 x 43.0 x 22.9 feet
T.3-cyl. by Robb Engineering Co. Ltd.,
Amherst, Nova Scotia, Canada; 322 NHP.
9.1918: Launched by Fraser, Brace and Co.,
Montreal, Quebec, Canada (Yard No. 11).
28.7.1919: Registered in the ownership of
the Shipping Controller (John H. Glover,
manager), London as WAR NIAGARA.
13.12.1919: Register closed on sale to
the S.A. de Navigation 'Les Armateurs
Francais', Paris, France and renamed
HAUSSMANN.
1923: Sold to Aquila A.G. fur Handels-u
Industrieunternehmungen and broken up at
Hamburg during the fourth quarter.

The wooden steamer *War Ottawa.* *[J. and M. Clarkson collection]*

M24. WAR MATANE 1919-1920
Wood
O.N. 143387 2,259g, 1,364n
249.6 x 43.6 x 22.6 feet
T.3-cyl. by the Canadian Ingersoll Rand
Company, Sherbrooke, Quebec, Canada;
147 NHP, 1,000 NHP, 9 knots.
9.1918: Launched by Quinlan and
Robertson Ltd., Montreal, Quebec (Yard
No. 4).
18.8.1919: Registered in the ownership of
the Shipping Controller (John H. Glover,
manager), London as WAR MATANE.
24.2.1920: Register closed on sale to
Credito Industriale di Venezia (Società
Esercizi Marittimi), Venice, Italy and
renamed ITONIA.
1921: Sold to Giulia Società Anonima di
Armamento, Trieste, Italy.
1923: Sold to V. Quargnali, Trieste and
broken up during first quarter of 1924.

M25. ARIADNE CHRISTINE 1919
O.N. 129095 3,550g 2,163n
356.0 x 50.5 x 21.9 feet
T. 3-cyl. by Blair and Co. Ltd., Stockton-on-
Tees; 337 NHP, 1,350-1,400 IHP, 9 knots.
5.1910: Completed by Joseph L. Thompson
and Sons Ltd., Sunderland (Yard No. 474).
19.5.1910: Registered in the ownership of
the Ariadne Steamship Co. Ltd. (George P.
Sechiari, manager), London as ARIADNE
CHRISTINE.
8.1.1917: Managers became P. Samuel and
Co. Ltd., London.
1.9.1919: Registered in the ownership of the
Shipping Controller (Sir Ernest W. Glover,
manager), London.
3.10.1919: Register closed on sale to
A/S Skjelbreds Rederi (O.A.T. Skjelbred,

manager), Kristiansand, Norway and
renamed TRUTH
1939: Sold to J. Teng, G.W. Grace and A.B.
Grace (J. Teng, manager), Tallinn, Estonia
and renamed VAHVA.
1940: Sold to Compania de Vapores Ltda.,
Panama (Thrasyvoulos L. Boyazides
and Co., Athens, Greece) and renamed
SUERTE.
1951: Sold to Trinity Compania de
Navegacion S.A., Panama (A. Lusi Ltd.,
London, managers) and renamed TRINITY.
16.11.1953: Arrived at Savona to be broken
up by Ditta Giuseppe Riccardi.
16.1.1954: Work began at Savona.
3.1954: Work completed at Vado Ligure.

M26. AUGUST BELMONT 1919-1920
O.N. 115832 4,679g 2,993n
372.6 x 50.0 x 27.6 feet
T. 3-cyl. by the Wallsend Slipway and
Engineering Co. Ltd., Wallsend-on-Tyne;
350 NHP, 2,000 IHP, 11 knots.
5.1902: Completed by C.S. Swan and
Hunter Ltd., Newcastle-upon-Tyne (Yard
No. 275). She had been ordered by the
Louisville and Nashville Railroad Company.
31.5.1902: Registered in the ownership
of the Pensacola Trading Co. Ltd. (Watts,
Watts and Co., managers), London as
AUGUST BELMONT.
1916: Requisitioned by the Admiralty and
converted to a tanker.
1.7.1918: Manager became Stanley M.
Thompson.
3.9.1919: Sold to the Shipping Controller
(Sir Ernest W. Glover, manager), London.
18.5.1920: Sold to the Anglo-Saxon
Petroleum Co. Ltd., London.
26.5.1920: Renamed ANCULA.

8.12.1920: Sold to the Velefa Steamship
Co. Ltd. (Sir Walter and Philip Runciman,
managers), London.
20.6.1923: Sold to Louis A. Millis, London.
30.1.24: Arrived on the Tyne.
About 26.4.24: Reported under demolition.
26.5.1924: Register closed.

M27. WAR KOCHIA 1919-1921
O.N. 143439 5,216g 3,171n
400.8 x 52.3 x 28.5 feet
T. 3-cyl. by D. and W. Henderson and Co.
Ltd., Glasgow; 517 NHP, 3,000 IHP, 11.5
knots.
29.9.1919: Registered in the ownership
of the Shipping Controller (Sir Ernest
W. Glover, manager), London as WAR
KOCHIA.
18.10.1919: Launched by Lloyd Royal
Belge (Great Britain) Ltd., Glasgow (Yard
No. 10).
18.2.1921: Register closed on sale to Lloyd
Royal Belge S.A., Antwerp, Belgium and
renamed LONDONIER.
1930: Sold to Compagnie Maritime Belge
(Lloyd Royal) S.A., Antwerp.
1939: Sold to Agencia Maritima Colon
Ltda., Panama and renamed ILLENAO.
1940: Sold to Matsuoka Kisen K.K.,
Ashiya, Japan and renamed SHOTO
MARU.
31.8.1943: Torpedoed and sunk by US
submarine SEAWOLF 150 miles north east
of Wenchow in position 28.27 north by
123.03 east.

M28. WAR CRAFT 1920
O.N. 144358 6,521g 4,069n
412.4 x 55.6 x 34.4 feet
Steam turbine by Richardsons, Westgarth

An early bulk carrier, the *August Belmont* is seen in original condition. She was converted into a tanker by the Admiralty, before
passing to the Shipping Controller. *[Roy Fenton collection]*

and Co. Ltd., Hartlepool double reduction geared to a single screw; 2,300-2,900 SHP, 10.5 knots.
23.10.1919: Launched by Furness Shipbuilding Co. Ltd., Middlesbrough (Yard No. 13).
30.1.1920: Registered in the ownership of the Shipping Controller (Sir Ernest W. Glover, manager), London.
3.1920: Completed.
2.3.1920: Register closed on sale to Società di Navigazione Roma, Genoa, Italy and renamed ROANA.
1928: Sold to La Meridionale di Navigazione S.A., Naples, Italy and renamed GAETA.
1936: Broken up at Genoa during the first quarter after being laid up there. Reported renamed ORATA before scrapping.

M29. WAR RELIEF 1920
O.N. 144424 6,521g 4,069n
412.4 x 55.6 x 34.4 feet
Steam turbine by Richardsons, Westgarth and Co. Ltd., Hartlepool double-reduction geared to a single screw; 2,300 SHP, 10.5 knots.
20.12.1919: Launched by Furness Shipbuilding Co. Ltd., Middlesbrough (Yard No. 12).
2.3.1920: Registered in the ownership of the Shipping Controller (Sir Ernest W. Glover, manager), London as WAR RELIEF.
4.1920: Completed.
24.4.1920: Register closed on sale to Lloyd Sabuado Società Anonima per Azioni, Genoa, Italy and renamed POLLENZO.
1927: Sold to Società Anonima Parodi e Corrado, Genoa.
1929: Sold to Corrado Società Anonima di Navigazione, Genoa.
10.6.1940: Beached by crew at Algeciras.
1946: Sold, refloated and repaired.
1946: Owners Sociedad de Navegacion Oceanica Ltda., Panama (Nobre and Garcia Joaguim Ltda., Lisbon, Portugal) and renamed ALCANTARA.
1950: Sold to F.H. de Oliveira and Co. Ltd., Lisbon, Portugal, remaining under the Panama flag.
24.10.1950: Ashore at Keteplaat, off Kruisschans Sluis, River Scheldt, whilst on a voyage from Antwerp to Thessaloniki and Beirut with steel, cement and general cargo.
27.10.1950: Refloated but subsequently declared a constructive total loss and sold to British Iron and Steel Corporation.
24.6.1951: Arrived at Briton Ferry to be broken up by T. W. Ward Ltd.

M30. WAR SUCCOUR 1920
O.N. 144465 6,546g 4,057n
412.4 x 55.6 x 34.5 feet
Steam turbines by Parsons Marine Steam Turbine Co. Ltd., Wallsend-on-Tyne geared to a single screw; 2,300-2,900 SHP, 10.5 knots.
14.8.1919: Launched by Furness Shipbuilding Co. Ltd., Haverton Hill-on-Tees (Yard No. 11).

2.1920: Completed.
30.3.1920: Registered in the ownership of the Shipping Controller (Sir Ernest W. Glover, manager), London.
16.4.1920: Register closed on sale to Edoardo Mazza, Savona, Italy and renamed ASTER.
8.1932: Broken up at Savona, having been sold to shipbreakers while laid up at Savona.

M31. WAR GLORY 1920
O.N. 14469 6,543g 4,072n
412.5 x 55.8 x 34.5 feet
Steam turbines by Parsons Marine Steam Turbine Co. Ltd., Wallsend-on-Tyne geared to a single screw; 2,300-2,900 SHP, 12 knots.
1.4.1920: Registered in the ownership of the Shipping Controller (Sir Ernest W. Glover, manager), London as WAR GLORY.
21.4.1920: Launched by the Monmouth Shipbuilding Co. Ltd., Chepstow, Monmouth (Yard No. 370) and ran trials.
20.5.1920: Register closed on sale to Armatori Riuniti Società di Navigazione, Genoa, Italy and renamed MONTE PASUBIO.
1.4.1924: Wrecked near Quequen whilst on a voyage from Genoa to Bahia Blanca in ballast.

M32. WAR GRAPE 1920
O.N. 144548 2,572g 1,423n
303.0 x 43.0 x 20.7 feet
Steam turbine by Metropolitan Vickers Electrical Co. Ltd., Manchester, double-reduction geared to a single screw; 1,000 SHP, 10.5 knots.
1928: T. 3-cyl. by Maatschappij 'Fyenord', Rotterdam, Holland; 217 NHP.
24.3.1920: Launched by the Monmouth Shipbuilding Co. Ltd., Chepstow (Yard No. 373).
10.5.1920: Registered in the ownership of the Shipping Controller (Sir Ernest W. Glover, manager), London as WAR GRAPE.
15.6.1920: Completed.
17.6.1920: Register closed on sale to Société Anonyme de Navigation 'Les Armateurs Français', Rouen, France and renamed GUEBWILLER.
1928: Sold to Société Union Minière et Maritime, Rouen and renamed HENRI MORY.
1928: Re-engined.
6.10.1931: Wrecked on the north side of Peniche whilst on a voyage from Dunkerque to Casablanca with a cargo of patent fuel.

M33. WAR PROJECT 1920
O.N. 144556 6,521g 4,044n
412.4 x 55.6 x 34.4 feet
Steam turbine by Richardsons, Westgarth and Co. Ltd., Hartlepool double-reduction geared to a single shaft; 2,500 SHP, 10.5 knots.
17.2.1920: Launched by Furness Shipbuilding Co. Ltd., Haverton Hill-on-

Tees (Yard No. 14).
15.5.1920: Registered in the ownership of the Shipping Controller (Sir Ernest W. Glover, manager), London.
8.1920: Completed.
4.8.1920: Register closed on sale to Società di Navigazione Latina, Naples, Italy and renamed ROBILANTE.
1924: Sold to Società Anonima Marittima Industriale 'Janua', Genoa.
1925: Sold to Società Esercizio Navi S.A., Genoa and renamed ULISSE
1929: Sold to 'Corrado' Società Anonima di Navigazione, Genoa and renamed CONFIDENZA
10.6.1940: At Jacksonville.
3.1941: Detained.
24.6.1941: Requisitioned by United States Maritime Commission, Washington (South Atlantic Steam Ship Lines Inc., Savannah, managers) and renamed TROUBADOUR under the Panama flag.
12.1942: Managers became Cosmopolitan Shipping Co.
7.1943: Bareboat chartered to the United States Army.
10.1945: Laid up.
6.1948: Resold to 'Corrado' Società Anonima di Navigazione, Genoa and renamed CONFIDENZA.
1957: Sold to Companhia Armadora Victoria S.A., Panama (Sotramar, S.A., Geneva, Switzerland) (Gastaldi & C. S.p.A., Genoa, Italy) and renamed PARIDA.
16.8.1959: Arrived Moji
12.1959: Demolition began by Hanwa Kogyo K.K. at Fukagawa, Tokyo.

M34. LEOPOLD II 1920-1922
Paddle
O.N. 144583 1,461g 798n
340.0 x 38.0 x 15.0 feet
2-cyl by William Denny and Brothers, Dumbarton; 812 NHP, 22 knots.
22.12.1892: Launched by William Denny and Brothers, Dumbarton (Yard No. 473).
20.3.1893: Completed for the Belgian Government, Ostend, Belgium as LEOPOLD II.
1.6.1920: Registered in the ownership of the Shipping Controller (Sir Ernest W. Glover, manager), London.
4.4.1922: Sold to Stelp and Leighton Ltd., London, who resold her to German shipbreakers the same day.
6.4.1922: Register closed.

M35.WAR ILIAD 1920
O.N. 144634 6,551g 4,040n
412.4 x 55.8 x 34.5 feet
Steam turbine by Metropolitan Vickers Ltd., Manchester, double-reduction geared geared to a single screw; 2,900 SHP, 10.5 knots.
7.7.1920: Registered in the ownership of the Shipping Controller (Sir Ernest W. Glover, manager), London as WAR ILIAD.
17.7.1920: Launched and completed by Monmouth Shipbuilding Co. Ltd., Chepstow (Yard No. 369).

The Belgian paddle steamer *Leopold II*. [*J. and M. Clarkson collection*]

23.7.1920: Register closed on sale to Navigazione Generale Italiana, Genoa, Italy and renamed SILE
17.2.1926: Sold to Kauffahrtei A.G., Bremen, Germany and later renamed PASSAT.
24.3.1936: Sold to A.G. für Handel & Verkehr (Lexau, Scharbau & Co., managers), Emden, Germany.
27.2.1937: Transferred to Lexau, Scharbau & Co., Emden.
1.12.1937: Renamed JANTJE FRITZEN
1.1939: Transferred to Johs. Fritzen und Sohn vorm. Lexau, Scharbau und Co., Emden.
5.1945: Captured by the Allies at Frederikstad.
17.11.1945: Scuttled in the Skagerrak with a cargo of poison gas shells.

M36. WAR MEMORY 1920
O.N. 144650 6,521g 4,040n
412.4 x 55.6 x 34.4 feet
Steam turbine by Richardsons, Westgarth and Co. Ltd., Hartlepool double-reduction geared to a single screw; 2,300 SHP, 11 knots.
22.3.1920: Launched by Furness Shipbuilding Co. Ltd., Haverton Hill-on-Tees (Yard No. 15).
7.1920: Completed.
14.7.1920: Registered in the ownership of the Shipping Controller (Sir Ernest W. Glover, manager), London as WAR MEMORY.
15.7.1920: Register closed on sale to Società Armatrice Ing. Carlo Camuzzi e Co., Genoa, Italy and renamed M.T. CICERONE.
1925: Sold to Società Anonima Armatrice Carbone, Genoa.
6.2.1927: Wrecked at the entrance to Ponta Delgada whilst on a voyage from Philadelphia to Savona with a cargo of coal.

M37. WAR PICTURE 1920
O.N. 145010 6,537g 3,980n
412.4 x 55.6 x 34.0 feet

Steam turbine by Richardsons, Westgarth and Co. Ltd., Hartlepool double reduction geared to a single screw; 2,300 SHP, 10.5 knots.
21.4.1920: Launched by Furness Shipbuilding Co. Ltd., Middlesbrough (Yard No. 16).
26.8.1920: Registered in the ownership of the Shipping Controller (Sir Ernest W. Glover, manager), London as WAR PICTURE.
9.1920: Completed.
1.9.1920: Register closed on sale to La Veloce Navigazione Italiana, Genoa, Italy and renamed DALMAZIA.
1924: Sold to Società Anonima Parodi e Corrado, Genoa.
1929: Owners became Società Anonima Em. V. Parodi, Genoa.
23.3.1933: Sailed from Genoa for La Spezia.
4.1934: Broken up.

M38. WAR ODYSSEY 1920
O.N. 145036 6,547g 4,061n
412.5 x 55.8 x 34.5 feet
Steam turbine by Metropolitan Vickers Electrical Co. Ltd., Manchester, double-reduction geared to a single screw; 2,900 SHP, 10.5 knots.
20.9.1920: Registered in the ownership of the Shipping Controller (Sir Ernest W. Glover, manager), London as WAR ODYSSEY.
30.9.1920: Launched by Monmouth Shipbuilding Co. Ltd., Chepstow (Yard No. 371).
1.10.1920: Completed.
3.11.1920: Register closed on sale to Armatori Riuniti Società di Navigazione, Genoa, Italy and renamed MONTE SAN MICHELE.
8.2.1921: Missing since last in wireless contact in position 36.00 north by 49.40 west whilst on a voyage from New York to Genoa with a cargo of grain.

M39. WAR GENIUS 1920
O.N. 145076 6,573g 4,087n
412.4 x 55.8 x 34.5 feet
Steam turbine by Metropolitan Vickers

Electrical Co. Ltd., Manchester, double-reduction geared to a single screw; 2,900 SHP, 10.5 knots.
29.10.1920: Registered in the ownership of the Shipping Controller (Sir Ernest W. Glover, manager), London as WAR GENIUS
30.10.1920: Launched by Monmouth Shipbuilding Co. Ltd., Chepstow (Yard No. 373).
11.1920: Completed.
2.11.1920: Register closed on sale to Navigazione Generale Italiana, Genoa, Italy and renamed FIUME.
17.2.1926: Sold to Kauffahrtei A.G., Bremen, Germany.
5.8.1926: Renamed TAIFUN.
24.3.1936: Sold to A.G. für Handel & Verkehr (Lexau, Scharbau & Co.), Emden, Germany.
7.1937: Transferred to Lexau, Scharbau & Co., Emden.
1.1938: Renamed CARL FRITZEN.
1939: Transferred to Johs. Fritzen & Sohn vorm. Lexau, Scharbau und Co., Emden.
4.9.1939: Scuttled by crew after interception by HMS AJAX off the coast of Brazil in position 34.19 south by 48.29 west whilst on a voyage from Rotterdam to Buenos Aires.

M40. WAR FIG 1920-1921
O.N. 145093 2,568g 1,425n
303.0 x 43.0 x 20.7 feet
Steam turbine by the Metropolitan Vickers Electrical Co. Ltd., Manchester, double-reduction geared to a single screw; 1,000 SHP, 11 knots.
1929: T. 3-cyl. by G. Fletcher and Co. Ltd., Derby; 275 NHP, 8½ knots.
17.8.1920: Launched by the Monmouth Shipbuilding Co. Ltd., Chepstow, Monmouth (Yard No. 368).
11.1920: Completed.
12.11.1920: Registered in the ownership of the Shipping Controller (Sir Ernest W. Glover, manager), London as WAR FIG.
3.1.1921: Sold to Watkin J. Williams, Cardiff.
24.3.1922: Renamed SILVERWAY.
13.7.1925: Sold to Charter Shipping Co. Ltd. (Lewis and Grove Williams, managers), Cardiff.
28.4.1926: Renamed CHARTERHAGUE.
1929: Re-engined.
6.5.1930: Register closed on sale to Ångfartygs A/B 'Alfa' (H. Lundqvist, manager), Mariehamn, Finland.
1937: A. Karlsson became manager.
1939: Sold to Finska Fiskeri A/B (A/B R. Nordström & Co. O/Y, managers), Hangö/Lovisa, Finland and renamed JÄÄMERI.
26.4.1944: Mined and sunk off the German Baltic coast in position 54.39 north by 12.30 east whilst on a voyage from Bremen to Danzig.

M41. HOPPER No. 6 1920-1923
O.N. 119069 830g 331n
199.5 x 35.1 x 14.8 feet

The *War Fig* became *Charterhague* in the fleet of Lewis and Grove Williams, Cardiff. *[J. and M. Clarkson collection]*

Two T. 3-cyl. by Fleming and Ferguson, Paisley driving twin screws; 10½ knots.
11.1903: Completed by Fleming and Ferguson Ltd., Paisley (Yard No. 323) for the Trustees of the Clyde Navigation, Glasgow as HOPPER No. 6.
1920: Owner became the Shipping Controller (Sir Ernest W. Glover, manager), London.
1923: Sold to Frank Bevis Ltd., Portsmouth and renamed BEVASH.
1923: Sold to the Trustees of the Clyde Navigation, Glasgow and renamed HOPPER No. 6.
1962: Broken up at Port Glasgow by Smith and Houston Ltd.

M42. HOPPER No. 20 1920-1921
O.N. 102609 959g 411n
200.0 x 35.0 x 14.8 feet
Two T.3-cyl. by Fleming and Ferguson, Paisley driving twin screws.
1893: Launched by Fleming and Ferguson,

Paisley (Yard No. 188) for the Trustees of the Clyde Navigation, Glasgow as HOPPER No. 20.
1920: Owners became the Shipping Controller (Sir Ernest W. Glover, manager), London.
1921: Sold to the James Dredging, Towage and Transport Co. Ltd., London and renamed FOREMOST V.
1922: Sold to the Trustees of the Clyde Navigation, Glasgow and renamed HOPPER No. 20.
1948: Sold to William Cooper and Sons Ltd., Liverpool.
1949: Renamed ERIC COOPER.
1965: Broken up at Preston.

M43. HURUNUI 1920-1921
O.N. 145100 9,266g 5,876n
479.0 x 62.5 x 37.7 feet
High and low pressure turbines by Richardsons, Westgarth and Co. Ltd., Hartlepool double-reduction geared to a

single shaft; 4,600BHP, 12 knots.
1915: Ordered by the Federal Steam Navigation Co. Ltd., London as NORFOLK.
1918: Order requisitioned by the Shipping Controller, London.
20.4.1920: Launched by Sir Raylton Dixon and Co. Ltd., Middlesbrough (Yard No. 596a).
22.11.1920: Registered in the ownership of the Shipping Controller (Ernest W. Glover, manager), London as HURUNUI.
24.1.1921: Sold to the Federal Steam Navigation Co. Ltd., London.
6.9.1922: Transferred to the New Zealand Shipping Co. Ltd., London.
14.10.1940: Torpedoed by the German submarine U 93 and sank the following morning 150 miles west of Cape Wrath in position 58.58 north by 09.54 west whilst on a voyage from London and Newcastle-upon-Tyne to Auckland in ballast in convoy OB 227. Two members of the crew were lost.
2.11.1940: Register closed.

M44. WAR EPIC 1920
O.N. 145121 6,574g 4,086n
412 x 55.8 x 34.5 feet
Steam turbine by Metropolitan Vickers Ltd., Manchester double-reduction geared to a single screw; 2,900 SHP, 10.5 knots.
11.12.1920: Launched by Monmouth Shipbuilding Co. Ltd., Chepstow (Yard No. 373).
12.1920: Completed.
15.12.1920: Registered in the ownership of the Shipping Controller (Sir Ernest W. Glover, manager), London as WAR EPIC.
17.12.1920: Register closed on sale to Navigazione Generale Italiana, Genoa, Italy and renamed ADIGE.
17.2.1926: Sold to Kauffahrtei A.G., Bremen, Germany.
5.8.1926: Renamed MONSUN.

Eric Cooper, the former *Hopper No. 20*. *[J. and M. Clarkson]*

Hurunui in New Zealand Shipping Company colours. *[Ships in Focus]*

30.11.1937: Transferred to Kauffahrtei Seereederei Adolf Wiards und Co., Bremen.
18.12.1942: Stranded at Rørvik, Norway

M45. WILLDOMINO 1921-1922

O.N. 141302 5,755g 4,173n
410.6 x 54.1 x 27.5 feet
Steam turbine by Hallidie and Co., Spokane, Washington, USA; 2,500 SHP, 10½ knots.
1922: T. 3-cyl. by J.G. Kincaid and Co. Ltd., Greenock; 267 NHP, 2,500 IHP, 11 knots.
12.1918: Launched by J. Coughlan and Sons, Vancouver, British Columbia, Canada (Yard No. 8).
4.1919: Completed.
2.4.1919: Registered in the ownership of the Imperial Munitions Board, Ottawa, Canada as WAR CONVOY.
7.4.1919: Sold to the Convoy Steamship Co. Ltd., Halifax, Nova Scotia, Canada.
5.12.1919: Renamed WILLDOMINO.
23.8.1921: Sold to the Board of Trade (Glover Brothers, managers), London.
3.8.1922: Sold to Ben Line Steamers Ltd. (William Thomson and Co., managers), Leith.
16.10.1922: Renamed BENCLEUCH.
17.10.1922: Registration details amended following re-engining.
11.12.1941: Caught fire, believed due to sabotage, south east of Cape Farewell whilst on a voyage from London to Hong Kong via Panama with general cargo.
12.12.1941: Sank in position 53.10 north by 38.00 west.
31.12.1941: Register closed.

M46. MELLON 1921-1923

O.N. 142192 3,036g 1,867n
331.0 x 46.5 x 23.0 feet
T-3-cyl. by the Shanghai Dock and Engineering Co. Ltd., Shanghai; 2,500 IHP, 13 knots.
7.1920: Completed by the Shanghai Dock

and Engineering Co. Ltd., Shanghai (Yard No. 1507).
She had been laid down as WAR REGALIA for the Shipping Controller.
15.7.1920: Registered in Shanghai in the ownership of the Shipping Controller (Royal Mail Steam Packet Company, managers), London as MELLON.
28.12.1921: Registered in the ownership of the Board of Trade (Glover Brothers, managers), London.
7.6.1923: Sold to the Pencisely Steamship Co. Ltd. (Hopkins, Saunders and Co. Ltd., managers), Cardiff.
13.7.1923: Renamed PENHILL
3.8.1928: Managers became W.H. Hopkins, Son and Co. Ltd., Cardiff.
23.8.1933: Mortgagees appointed Walter S. Hinde as manager.
19.9.1933: Sold by mortgages to the Penhill Shipping Co. Ltd. (Walter S. Hinde, manager), Cardiff.
28.11.1935: Sold to the Braeside Shipping Co. Ltd. (Richard T.S. Hinde, manager), Cardiff.

28.11.1935: Renamed BRAESIDE.
29.6.1936: Register closed on sale to Companhia Commercio e Navegação, Rio de Janeiro, Brazil and renamed BURY.
1957: Sold to Navegação Mercantil S.A., Rio de Janeiro.
11.1965: Broken up in Brazil

M47. SYLVIA VICTORIA 1922

O.N. 141367 5,757g 4,199n
410.7 x 54.1 x 27.5 feet
Steam turbine by Halliday and Co., Spokane, Washington, USA; 2,500 SHP, 10½ knots.
1922: T. 3-cyl. by J.G. Kincaid and Co. Ltd., Greenock; 536 NHP.
5.1919: Completed by J. Coughlan and Sons, Vancouver, British Columbia, Canada (Yard No. 7).
6.5.1919: Registered at Montreal in the ownership of the Shipping Controller, London as WAR CAVALRY.
31.5.1919: Sold to the Forbes Corporation Ltd., Montreal, Canada.

The *Bencleuch* was managed for a short time as the *Willdomino* in 1922 until sold to Ben Line Steamers Ltd. *[J. and M. Clarkson collection]*

19.11.1919: Renamed SYLVIA VICTORIA.
25.4.1922: Sold to the Board of Trade (Glover Brothers, manager), London.
19.8.1922: Register closed on sale to E.J. Culucundis and S.C. Costomeni, Syra, Greece and renamed ATLANTICOS.
1922: Re-engined.
1929: Sold to Atlanticos Steam Navigation Co. Ltd., Syra.
1930: Transferred to Atlanticos Steam Ship Co. Ltd., Syra.
1932: Managers became Rethymnis and Kulukundis Ltd., London and renamed MOUNT PENTELIKON under the Panama flag.
1933: Sold to Dairen Kisen K.K., Dairen, Japan and renamed KINSHU MARU.
1938: Name rendered KINSYU MARU.
17.6.1944: Torpedoed and sunk by USS HAKE off Cape San Agustin, Mindanao in position 06.17 north by 26.17 east.

M48. PATAGONIA 1922-1923

O.N. 146609 3,016g 1,903n
327.3 x 41.6 x 29.2 feet
T. 3-cyl. by Reiherstieg Schiffswerft und Maschinefabriek, Hamburg, Germany; 302 NHP.
6.9.1890: Launched by Reiherstieg Schiffswerft und Maschinefabriek, Hamburg (Yard No. 377) for Hamburg-Südamerika Dampfschiffahrts Gesellschaft, Hamburg as PATAGONIA.
12.1890: Completed.
5.5.1904: Sold to Hamburg-Amerika Linie, Hamburg.
12.1914: Interned at Bahia Blanca, after serving as a naval supply ship since August 1914.
1917: Machinery damaged by crew. Following the end of the First World War towed back to Hamburg for repairs.

13.4.1921: Delivered to the United Kingdom.
2.8.1922: Registered in the ownership of the Board of Trade (Sir Ernest W. Glover, manager), London.
9.2.1923: Register closed on sale to S.A. Comercial Braun y Blanchard, Valparaiso, Chile and renamed VALDIVIA.
4.10.1933: Wrecked at Punta Grande, 20 miles north of Taltal, whilst on a voyage from Antofagasta to Taltal with passengers and cargo including salt and sulphur.

M49. TRIALOS 1922-1923

O.N. 146631 5,163g 3,307n
400.2 x 52.2 x 28.5 feet
T. 3-cyl. by the Hong Kong and Whampoa Dock Co. Ltd., Hong Kong; 517 NHP, 10 knots.
12.1919: Launched by the Hong Kong and Whampoa Dock Co. Ltd., Hong Kong (Yard No. 570).
She had been laid down as WAR SCEPTRE for the Shipping Controller.
3.1920: Completed for N.E. Ambatielos, Argostoli, Greece as TRIALOS.
8.9.1922: Registered in the ownership of the Board of Trade (Glover Brothers, managers), London.
8.6.1923: Sold to King Line Ltd. (Dodd, Thomson and Co. Ltd., managers), London.
19.7.1923: Renamed KING FREDERICK.
19.7.1944: Torpedoed and sunk by the German submarine U 181 in position 09.29 north by 71.45 east whilst on a voyage from Haifa to Calcutta with a cargo of salt and mail.
4.8.1944: Register closed.

M50. STATHIS 1923

O.N. 151412 5,138g 3,293n
400.9 x 52.4 x 28.3 feet

T. 3-cyl. by the Hong Kong and Whampoa Dock Co. Ltd., Hong Kong; 517 NHP.
3.1920: Launched by the Hong Kong and Whampoa Dock Co. Ltd., Hong Kong (Yard No. 565).
7.1920: Completed.
3.8.1920: Registered at Hong Kong in the ownership of the Shipping Controller (Turnbull, Scott and Co., managers), London as WAR PIPER.
1920: Sold to N.E. Ambatielos, Argostoli, Greece as STATHIS.
30.5.1923: Registered in the ownership of the Shipping Controller (Ernest W. Glover, manager), London.
8.6.1923: Sold at auction to King Line Ltd. (Dodd, Thomson and Co. Ltd., managers), London.
20.6.1923: Renamed KING CADWALLON.
7.7.1929: Caught fire.
12.7.1929: Abandoned south east of Durban in position 32.01 south by 40.41 east, whilst on a voyage from Methil via Port Natal to Melbourne with a cargo of coal.
20.8.1929: Towed into East London, but grounded in a storm.
12.9.1929: Broke in two. Later declared a constructive total loss.
1.10.1929: Register closed.

Managed for the Ornis Steamship Co. Ltd.

M51. ZIMORODOCK 1920-1924

O.N. 119224 3,573g 2,326n
347.0 x 47.4 x 25.2 feet
T.3-cyl. by Richardsons, Westgarth and Co. Ltd., Hartlepool; 317 NHP, 1,300 IHP, 9 knots.
1906: Launched by Furness, Withy and Co. Ltd., West Hartlepool (Yard No. 285).

King Frederick. This ship had been laid down for British government account in Hong Kong, and completed as *Trialos* for Greek owners. When they defaulted on payment she reverted to the ownership of the Shipping Controller and Glover management.
[J. and M. Clarkson]

Zimorodock at Manchester. The number *CT2174* on her bridge suggests the picture was taken whilst owned by the Shipping Controller. *[C. Downs/J. and M. Clarkson collection.]*

11.5.1906: Registered in the ownership of the Neptune Steam Navigation Co. Ltd. (Bolam and Swinhoe, managers), Newcastle-upon-Tyne as MALVERN RANGE.
14.4.1910: Furness, Withy and Co. became managers.
4.1914: Sold to the West Russian Steamship Co., St. Petersburg, Russia and renamed ZIMORODOCK.
9.4.1918: Requisitioned by the United Kingdom.
30.4.18: Registered in the ownership of the Shipping Controller, London (Ellerman's Wilson Line Ltd., Hull, managers).
4.1920: Returned to owners
29.4.1920: Registered in the ownership of the Ornis Steamship Co. Ltd. (Glover Brothers, managers), London.
6.6.1924: Management transferred to George E. Mitchell, London.
15.8.1928: Sold to Constants (South Wales) Ltd. (Martin Constant, manager), London.
26.9.1928: Register closed on sale to E.N. Vassilikos, Syra, Greece and renamed ERMOUPOLIS.
21.9.1931: Stranded at Lobeira, Argentina.
2.11.1931: Refloated.
1.1932: Broken up at Ferrol.

M52. DRONT 1920-1924
O.N. 115377 3,064g 1,953n
325.4 x 48.6 x 21.5 feet
T.3-cyl. by the North Eastern Marine Engineering Co. Ltd., Sunderland; 280 NHP, 1,450 IHP, 10 knots.
11.6.1903: Launched by Robert Thompson and Sons, Sunderland (Yard No. 229).

23.7.1903: Registered in the ownership of James Hoggarth, Cardiff.
12.8.1903: Transferred to the Felbridge Steamship Co. Ltd. (J. Hoggarth and Co., managers), Cardiff as FELBRIDGE.
9.1913: Sold to the West Russian Steamship Co., St. Petersburg, Russia and renamed ALBATROSS.
13.5.1918: Registered in the ownership of the Shipping Controller, London (Ellerman's Wilson Line Ltd., Hull, managers).
5.1920: Returned to owners.
18.5.1920: Registered in the ownership of the Ornis Steamship Co. Ltd. (Glover Brothers, managers), London as DRONT.
6.6.1924: Management transferred to George E. Mitchell, London
3.1927: Sold to P.S. Antippas, Braila, Roumania and renamed URANIA.
13.6.1931: Sunk in collision with the Norwegian tanker BEAUFORT (5,053/1929) off the Noord Hinder Light Vessel.

M53. BERKUT 1921-1924
O.N. 143280 4,415g 2,803n
388.4 x 51.9 x 16.8 feet
Q.4 cyl. by Bremer Vulkan, Vegesack, Germany; 445 NHP, 2,000 IHP, 10 knots.
14.10.1905. Launched by Bremer Vulkan, Vegesack (Yard No. 486).
17.11.1905: Completed for D.D.G. Hansa, Bremen, Germany as WARTBURG.
8.1914: Seized at Antwerp by Belgium.
9.1918: Returned to Germany.
10.1918: Surrendered to Belgium.
1.6.1919: Delivered to the United Kingdom.

7.6.1919: Registered in the ownership of the Shipping Controller, London (Lyle Shipping Co. Ltd., Glasgow, managers).
22.2.1921: Acquired by the Ornis Steamship Co. Ltd. (Glover Brothers, managers), London.
7.4.1921: Renamed BERKUT.
6.6.1924: Management transferred to George E. Mitchell, London.
6.5.1926: Register closed on sale to the Compagnie Marseillaise de Navigation à Vapeur (Compagnie Fraissinet, managers), Marseille, France and renamed CAVALLY.
24.12.1932: Arrived at Genoa to be broken up.

M54. WORON 1921-1924
O.N. 143101 5,233g 3,314n
420.8 x 54.5 x 27.7 feet
Q.4 cyl. by Bremer Vulkan, Vegesack, Germany; 386 NHP, 2000 IHP, 10 knots.
10.6.1907: Launched by Bremer Vulkan, Vegesack (Yard No. 500).
6.7.1907: Completed for the Roland Linie A.G., Bremen, Germany as NAIMES.
28.3.1919: Delivered to the United Kingdom following surrender to the British Government.
9.4.1919: Registered in the ownership of the Shipping Controller (Andrew Weir and Co., managers), London.
12.5.1921: Acquired by the Ornis Steamship Co. Ltd. (Glover Brothers, managers), London.
20.7.1921: Renamed WORON.
6.6.1924: Management transferred to George E. Mitchell, London
5.1927: Sold to A/B Naxos Prince

(R. Mattson, manager), Helsingfors, Finland and renamed KASTELHOLM.

1941: Sold to Lovisa Rederi A/B (A/B R. Nordstrom & Company O/Y, managers), Helsigfors, Finland.

2.6.1941: Sunk, probably after striking a British-laid mine, 125 miles west of the Faroe Islands in position 63.07 north by 11.18 west whilst on a voyage from Petsamo to South America with a cargo of wood pulp and paper. The sinking has also been attributed to the German submarine U 559 and dated 6.6.1941 with a position 63.07 north by 34.19 west.

Managed for the Ministry of Shipping and/or the Ministry of War Transport

M55. EMPIRE LYNX 1940-1942

O.N. 168056 5,981g 3,742n
402.5 x 54.2 x 31.2 feet
T.3-cyl. by the H.G. Trout Company, Buffalo, New York, USA; 391 NHP.
1917: Launched by the Texas Steamship Company, Bath, Maine, USA (Yard No.1) for the Texas Company, New York, USA as MAINE.
10.1917: On completion delivered to the United States Shipping Board, New York.
1920: Sold to the Green Star Steam Ship Corporation, New York.
1921: Repossessed by the United States Shipping Board.
1923: Sold to the Fairfield Steam Ship Corporation (Sea Shipping Co. Inc., managers), New York.
10.1.1940: Registered in the ownership of the Ministry of Shipping (Glover Brothers, managers), London and renamed EMPIRE LYNX.

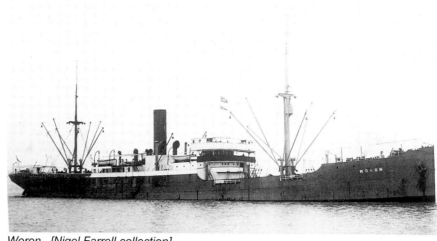

Woron. *[Nigel Farrell collection]*

9.1941: Owners became the Ministry of War Transport.
4.11.1942: Torpedoed and sunk by the German submarine U 132 in the North Atlantic in position 55.20 north by 40.01 west whilst on a voyage from New York to Liverpool with general cargo. The crew of 35 and eight gunners were saved.
16.12.1942: Register closed.

M56. EMPIRE LOTUS 1940-1942

O.N. 140864 3,496g 2,204n
346.7 x 51.0 x 24.1 feet
T. 3-cyl. by Blair and Co. Ltd., Stockton-on-Tees; 301 NHP, 1800 IHP; 10 knots.
13.9.1920: Launched by the Ropner Shipbuilding and Repairing Co. (Stockton) Ltd., Stockton-on-Tees (Yard No. 534).
28.10.1920: Registered in the ownership of the Cornborough Shipping Line Ltd. (William Reardon Smith and Sons (London) Ltd., managers), Cardiff as ALNESS.
5.12.1923: Transferred to the Oakwin Steamship Co. Ltd. (William Reardon Smith

and Sons (London) Ltd., managers), Cardiff.
15.10.1926: Transferred to the St. Just Steamship Co. Ltd. (William Reardon Smith and Sons (London) Ltd., managers), Cardiff.
2.7.1928: Owners renamed the Reardon Smith Line Ltd. (William Reardon Smith and Sons (London) Ltd., managers), Cardiff.
7.1933: Sold to the Alexandria Navigation Co. S.A.E., Alexandria, Egypt (Watts, Watts and Co., London, managers) and renamed STAR OF RAMLEH.
1935: Watts, Watts management ceased.
14.6.1940: Registered in the ownership of the Ministry of Shipping (Glover Brothers, managers), London and renamed EMPIRE LOTUS.
9.1941: Owners became the Ministry of War Transport.
12.4.1942: Foundered in heavy weather 100 miles south east of Halifax in position 44.06 north by 62.70 west whilst on a voyage from New York and Halifax to Belfast.
28.5.1942: Register closed.

The *Star of Ramleh,* later *Empire Lotus,* sailing from Liverpool on 29th June 1935. *[John McRoberts/J. and M. Clarkson].*

Derivations of Glover names

Once they settled down to a distinctive scheme, Glovers named most of their ships after poets, with the exceptions being one Venetian painter and one politician.

Burns Robert Burns (1759-1796) was a Scottish poet and folk song collector, notable (and punished) for his anti-clericalism and anti-establishment views. He used Scottish dialect to great effect in ballads and poems such as 'Tam O'Shanter', which famously gave the name to the tea clipper *Cutty Sark*.

Byron Lord Byron (1788-1824) was a writer of romantic melodramas, acclaimed in his own lifetime for his 'Childe Harold' and 'Don Juan'. After an unhappy marriage and several affairs, he left England in 1816 and became involved with the Greek fight for independence from Turkey, during which he lost his life.

Chaucer Geoffrey Chaucer (1340?-1400) is best known for 'The Canterbury Tales', a set of stories loosely connected by the theme of pilgrimage, and celebrated for their wit, humanity and vivid characterization.

Dante The Italian poet Dante Alighieri (1265-1321) is most famous for his 'Divine Comedy', an allegorical journey through hell, purgatory and paradise, guided by the Roman poet Virgil and his lover Beatrice.

Homer A poet active about 800BC, to whom are attributed the greatest surviving Greek epic poems, the 'Iliad' and the 'Odyssey'. He may have been born, like many shipowners, on the island of Chios.

Keats John Keats (1795-1821) trained in medicine before turning to poetry. His most famous works were 'Ode to a Nightingale' and 'Ode to a Grecian Urn' in which he explores the relationship of art and life.

Milton As well as being a prolific poet, John Milton (1608-1674) was involved in movements to reform politics and organized religion. These interests led him to write his great work about the fall of man, 'Paradise Lost'.

Ossian Ossian was a gaelic bard of the third century AD, most famous because of a literary forgery. In the 1760s the Scottish poet James Macpherson passed off his own work as that of Ossian to considerable critical acclaim. It strongly influenced Sir Walter Scott.

Ovid Publius Ovidius Naso (43BC-17AD) was one of the three major Roman poets. As well as writing on love and women, he composed the 15-book 'Metamorphoses', nothing less than a history of the cosmos. His poetic style had a major influence on European art and literature, including the works of Chaucer, Dante, Milton and Shakespeare.

Shakespear William Shakespeare (1564-1616), undisputedly England's greatest dramatist and poet, was notorious for spelling his name in several different ways. Glovers left off the final letter 'e' to reduce telegraphic costs.

Shelley Percy Byshe Shelley (1792-1822) was a radical, sent down from Oxford because of his atheism, and many of his poems – although vivid and highly articulate – reflect his naïve idealism. He spent the last years of his short life in Italy where he drowned under mysterious circumstances.

Spenser Edmund Spenser (1552?-1599) gained fame for 'The Faerie Queene', a moral allegory based on the early life of King Arthur and his quest for a vision of beauty.

Tennyson Alfred Lord Tennyson (1809-1892) was the favourite poet of the Victorians, and probably of Queen Victoria herself. Although criticized for his moralizing and jingoism, Tennyson was a master of using the rhythmic qualities of language, famously in his poems 'The Lady of Shallott'and 'The Charge of the Light Brigade'.

Titian Tiziano Vecellio (?1490-1576), Titian for short, was the most famous painter of the 16th century Venetian school, specializing in religious and mythological subjects. He is celebrated for his revolutionary alterpiece in the Santa Maria dei Frari, Venice, depicting the Assumption of the Virgin.

W.E. Gladstone William Ewart Gladstone (1809-1898), a Liberal Party politician and statesman, who became British prime minister a record four times during Victoria's reign. He was noted for his rivalry with the Conservative leader Benjamin Disraeli which was both political and bitterly personal.

Wordsworth The most famous of the Lake Poets, William Wordsworth (1770-1850) lived in and was inspired by the scenery of the English Lake District, its daffodils and people. Wordsworth became Poet Laureate in 1843 and, as well as his poems themselves, he also wrote influentially about the nature of poetry.

INDEX

All ships mentioned are listed. Names in capitals are those carried whilst in ownership or management by one of the featured companies. For these ships, the page numbers of fleet list entries are in bold type. A page number in italics indicates a photograph. Names in brackets were proposed but not used.

191

  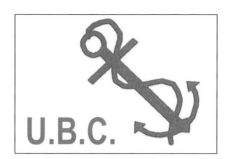

United Baltic Corporation Ltd.
The second funnel was adopted when motor ships were introduced in the 1950s.

 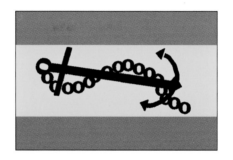

Anglo-Lithuanian Shipping Co. Ltd.

 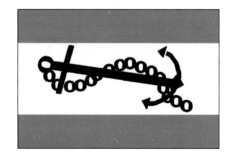

Anglo-Latvian Shipping Co. Ltd.

 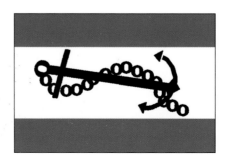

Anglo-Estonian Shipping Co. Ltd.